# JIGGER, BEAKER, & GLASS

## DRINKING AROUND THE WORLD

*Charles H. Baker Jr.*

FOREWORD BY
Susan Waggoner and Robert Markel,
authors of *Vintage Cocktails*

LYONS
PRESS

Essex, Connecticut

An imprint of The Globe Pequot Publishing Group, Inc.
64 South Main Street
Essex, CT 06426
www.globepequot.com

Distributed by NATIONAL BOOK NETWORK

British Library Cataloguing in Publication Information available

The 1992 edition of this book was cataloged by the Library of Congress as
follows:

Baker, Charles Henry, 1895–
    Jigger, beaker, and glass : drinking around the world / Charles H. Baker, Jr.
        p. cm.
    Originally published: Gentleman's companion. Vol. 2. Lyon, Miss. :
Derrydale Press, 1992.
    Includes index.
    ISBN 978-1-4930-7999-5 (paperback)
    1. Beverages. I. Baker, Charles Henry, 1895– Gentleman's companion.
Vol. 2. II Title.

TX815 .B19 2001
641.8'74—dc21                                        00-060138

♾™ The paper used in this publication meets the minimum requirements of
American National Standard for Information Sciences—Permanence of Paper for
Printed Library Materials, ANSI/NISO Z39.48-1992.

*Drink no longer Water but use a little Wine for thy Stomach's sake and thine often Infirmities . . .*

Saint Paul, the Apostle,
*1 Timothy, V. 23*

## DEDICATION

To all that Company of Friends, from Pine to Palm,
with whom we have So Happily Raised the Glass.

# CONTENTS

# FOREWORD TO THE NEW EDITION

NOT LONG AGO we asked a drinking friend of ours, an old and accomplished hand, how it was he came to the art of imbibing.

"When I was a very young boy," he replied, "my father set a fine example." This was in that breathing space between the wars when every man worth his salt, from Bangor, Maine to Barstow, California, took pride in rounding off the day with a tip of the arm or two. This was as true for the working man as it was for the bank presidents and executives of the world, the class to which our friend's father belonged.

"My father drank regularly and with flair, and our family clicked happily along in this manner for some time. Then America joined World War II and true tragedy ensued."

"Your father went overseas?" we asked naively.

Even worse, we were informed. Too old for combat, our friend's father was prepared to sit out the war on the sidelines, keeping home front spirits high with . . . well, his usual flow of spirits.

While much has been made of the wartime shortages of sugar, shortening, and gasoline, far less has been said about the shortage of that other staple, scotch whiskey. And for this crucial shortage there was, alas, no ration card.

Enterprising drinkers fell back on a method perfected during Prohibition: the dubiously legal purchase. A well-to-do and well-connected drinker, like our friend's father, who had over the years favored a particular bar with his business, now had the edge in purchasing directly from the bar's proprietor. There was, however, a catch. Single bottles could not be bought. The private buyer could purchase only by the case. And, for every case of scotch he bought, he had to purchase an equal amount of rum, a liquor that was available in great surplus, though the actual demand was low. Seeing how things stood, enterprising bar owners across the country now seized the opportunity to turn a quick profit. The widespread practice of selling scotch case-for-case with rum gave rise to the saying, "a bottle of rum for a bottle of scotch." In other words, you may buy the wheat, but you must also buy the chaff, and at a pretty penny, too.

"I was about fourteen at this time," our friend went on. "My father had now secured a supply of his much-loved scotch, but this resulted in an overflow of rum. Not one to waste anything, he fell into the habit of offering me an after-school topper. I would come through the door and he would say, 'Well, how about a rum and coke?' I enjoyed those afternoons and my father, very handily, got rid of his rum." Which only goes to show you that behind every drinker, there is a great story. And behind every great drinker, there are a great many stories.

In the realm of great drinkers, there are few whose acquaintance is as worth the trouble of making as Charles Baker Jr. We first encountered him in a used bookstore, in the distinctly out of print section, while researching our book, *Vintage Cocktails*. We had barely gotten him home and properly opened up before we were raving to our friends, "Have you read him?" and calling used book stores in search of copies to pass along to the truly deserving.

Thus we were delighted to hear that Derrydale has undertaken the worthy mission of putting Mr. Baker into print again, for there are almost as many reasons to read *The Gentleman's Companion*, now titled *Jigger, Beaker, and Glass*, as there are beverages to accompany our reading. Unlike works whose relevance evaporates with their times, Charles Baker's work sparkles across the intervening decades, emitting its cheerful invitation to take very seriously the frivolities of life.

The first reason most people turn to *Jigger, Beaker, and Glass* is because they are searching for a particular and authentic recipe. On this score, Mr. Baker will not disappoint. Our present era takes a sadly haphazard approach to the business of mixing drinks. Everything seems to come with a wedge of citrus lopped onto the side, cocktails that should be shaken and strained are neither, and complex drinks are reduced to a few simple components. Were the author of *Jigger, Beaker, and Glass* to return to earth, we can only imagine the extent of his horror.

Charles Baker was, above all, a stickler for getting it right. His first experiment in authenticity was to work his way through a mixology book of his own era, a comprehensive volume published in 1931. "We cut no corners; we didn't cheat," he wrote. "We measured accurately, chilled properly." Yet his efforts ended in dark disappointment. "The bald-faced conclusions were as plain as the nose on our face—much of that welter of mixed things with fancy names were egotistically-titled, ill-advised conceptions of low-brow mixers who either had no access to sound spirits or, if they did have, had so annealed their taste buds with past noxious cups that they were forevermore incapable of judicious authority."

To correct this sorry state of affairs, Mr. Baker set out to create a reliable compendium of drink recipes, a job he undertook with the utmost sincerity. In his quest, Mr. Baker traveled thousands of miles and made himself the friend and confidant of barmen from Saratoga to Singapore. The result is a compendium of recipes that would otherwise, through negligence and modern "improvement," have been lost to the ages.

In creating *Jigger, Beaker, and Glass,* Charles Baker rescued a unique sliver of history. He also gave much of himself. His running commentary, as much as the recipes themselves, provides a good share of the book's charm. When it comes to the business of drinking, he is never without opinions—opinions that are often set forth, in numbered paragraphs or "Words to the Wise," as rules governing one aspect of mixology or another.

The attentive reader would be well to pay attention to these guideposts. Many of the trends Mr. Baker objects to are the same trends that have despoiled the contemporary bar scene. He firmly believes, for example, that too many drinks get by on gimmick and a cute name, just as he warns against overuse of sweetening fruit juices and believes that, with limited exceptions, drinks combining more than three types of alcohol result in little more than a mediocre "taste melee." On points of technique he is unsurpassed and the would-be mixologist should take pains to follow his advice. Measure accurately. Serve drinks arctic cold. Don't mix too many drinks at once. Resist the temptation to buy inexpensive liquor. These are the words of the master.

Of course, *Jigger, Beaker, and Glass* is more than a mere recipe book, and even those few spoilsports uninterested in the art of the cocktail will enjoy setting sail with Mr. Baker. Far more than several dull and scholarly history books we could name, *Jigger, Beaker, and Glass* is a splendid window on some fabulous *temps perdu.* Its author is a vivid embodiment of that sadly vanished type, the dedicated and self-respecting *bon vivant.* Today, it would be hard to imagine anyone drinking one's way around the world with such whole-hearted gusto and so little remorse. But the world of Charles Baker was one in which contemporary Puritanism had little place. It was a world where cigarettes were smoked and martinis drunk, all in quick succession and with very few apologies. It was a world in which Nick and Nora Charles, of *Thin Man* fame, could get falling down drunk, wake with killing headaches, and lose not a shred of their polish. It was a world where the elegant places were also the drinking places, and where one could think of no more stylish place to be than the bar of the Raffles Hotel in Singapore or the American Bar in London's Savoy Hotel.

In this world, bartenders commanded a respect that is unimaginable today. They were not mere assemblers who learned to execute a few set drinks, but innovators who put their signature on each cocktail served. Like today's star chefs, they became famous for their individual versions and creations, their particular techniques and flourishes. The cocktails they perfected became synonymous with the establishments for which they worked, conferring a fame that spanned the reaches of the globe. Thus, in *Jigger, Beaker, and Glass*, we have not only recipes but attributions as well. A Singapore Sling is not just any Singapore Sling but "The Immortal Raffles Gin Sling, Met in 1926 and Thereafter Never Forgotten." The Sahara Glowing Heart Cocktail comes "From the Hands of One Abdullah, an Arab Muslim Wizard Back of Mahogany at the Mena House Bar, Near the Pyramids of Ghizeh, Which are Just South of Cairo, Egypt." The lively competition that existed between barmen can be glimpsed in the book's double entries. In the case of the Million Dollar Cocktail, Mr. Baker includes two from his journeys, the first as mixed by Shideaki Saito of Tokyo's Imperial Hotel, the second the concoction of the celebrated Nomura, of the Tor Hotel in Kobe.

In reading *Jigger, Beaker, and Glass*, one often feels that a curtain has been pulled back to reveal a golden era of large drinking and even larger living. History books tell us that most of the author's exploits occurred during an era of worldwide depression and American prohibition. Yet there are few shortages in evidence. One cannot help but notice that many more liqueurs, flavorings, and ingredients seem to have been available then than are available today. Only recently has our own era rediscovered the joy and usefulness of flavoring syrups, and we can only hope that such exotic-sounding delicacies as Maraschino and Crème de Violette will return to the stage as well.

The existence of a wide array of ingredients seems to have stimulated the creative urge. On page after page, Charles Baker introduces us to friends and acquaintances of widely exotic stripe, nonprofessionals who, whether on the deck of a bobbing sanpan or the balcony of a Tahitian vanilla plantation, were only too happy to invent, mix, and drink their own *specialities de la* maison, usually with great gusto. In setting down their recipes, Mr. Baker gives them as much consideration as he gives the most famous of barmen. This is a happy decision, bringing us the Fourth Regiment Cocktail as mixed by "One Commander Livesay, in Command of One of His Majesty's Dapper Little Sloops of War, Out in Bombay, A.D. 1931" and Shelby Langston's Palmetto Punch, "An Exotic Invented on a Florida Camp Hunt." No mention of the number grouse taken.

In such brief, vivid sketches, Mr. Baker demonstrates the most compelling of all reasons to keep him perpetually in print—the fact that he is, above all else, a marvelous raconteur and a writer of the first order. We read him for the charm of his words and the liveliness of his images. In his company, we have sailed to latitudes otherwise inaccessible to us and met characters long-since vanished from the stage. His large life has given us little lives within our own, freighted with the pleasure of vicarious memories. No one who has read *Jigger, Beaker, and Glass* will ever hear the words *pousse café* with detachment again. Instead, their mention will awaken the image of a bungalow outside Calcutta on a night in 1926, when a group of comrades mixed *pousse cafés* and drank till dawn "on the terrace under the low, hot stars, talking over college days, friends here and there, impending marriage, birth, death, while big bats the size of kittens shuttled back and forth over the level green of the tennis court."

For this delight and many more, we raise our glasses to Mr. Baker.

Susan Waggoner and Robert Markel
authors, *Vintage Cocktails*
January, 2001

# A FOREWORD

ONE COMFORTABLE fact gleaned from travel in far countries was that regardless of race, creed or inner metabolisms, mankind has always created varying forms of stimulant liquid—each after his own kind. Prohibitions and nations and kings depart, but origin of such pleasant fluid finds constant source.

Fermentation and the art of distilling liquors over heat became good form about the time our hairy forefathers began sketching mastodon and sabretooth tiger on their cave foyers. Elixir of fruit juice, crushed root and golden honey date back to the dawn of time and far beyond the written word, to when the old gods were young and stalked abroad upon business with goddesses, when Pan piped the dark forest aisles and Centaurs pawed belly deep in fern.

The Phoenicians, the Pharaohs, the first agrarian Chinese, all ancient races on earth buried jars of wine or spirits with their dead alongside the money and food and weapons and wives, so the departed might find reasonable comfort and happiness in the hereafter.

Go to Africa and the poorest Kaffir cheers life with—and for all of us he can have it—warm millet beer. We just returned from Mexico and can affirm that our Yucatecan most certainly ripped the bud out of his *Agave Americana* and drank the fermented pulque—a fluid which tastes faintly like mildewed donkeys—centuries before Montezuma's parents journeyed southward to the Valley of Cortez. We found additional evidence after three voyages to Zamboanga in Philippine Mindanao—where the monkeys have no tails—that the more agile Moro shinnied up his cocopalm and slashed the flower bud with his bolo; caught the saccharine drip—and an astounding menagerie of assorted squirt-ants—in a fermentation joint of bamboo, long before the Spanish Inquisition or Admiral Dewey steamed into Manila Bay.

In Samoa the loveliest tribal virgin chews the *kava* root for the ceremonial bowl when your yacht sails into her lagoon, and the resultant fluid furnishes a sure ticket to amiable paralysis of the lower limbs.

China and Japan have for centuries had their rice wine and *saki*. The Russian made his vodka from cereals, the blond Saxon his honey mead, the Hawaiian his *okolehao* from roots or fruits. We've been often to the Holy Land and have flown across to Transjordania and the rose-red city of Petra, and can bear witness that those grapes Moses the Lawgiver found in the Promised Land weren't all of a type suitable for raisins.

To any reasonable mind this past and present testimony of mankind through the ages would indicate that some sort of fluid routine will continue for many centuries to come. With adventurers like Marco Polo, Columbus, Tavernier and Magellan, there was a vast national introduction and interchange of beverages. For better or worse both conquistador and native sampled, discarded or adapted an incredible addition of liquid blends and formulae.

Through rigour or amiability of climate, through physical, racial and psychological characteristics of the individuals themselves, from the cocoon of this pristine field work there emerged an equally incredible list of drinks—mixed or otherwise—which for one reason or another have stood the test of time and taste and gradually have become set in form. They have become traditional, accepted in ethical social intercourse. And it is with the more civilized family of these that we are concerned in this volume; not the pulques and warm mealie beer or fermented Thibetan yak milk.

Now at this point we prefer firmly to go on record that we find scant humour in dipsomania, or in potted gentlemen who in their cups beat girl-wives, or in horny-handed toilers of any class who fling their weekly pay chits onto the public mahogany while tearful mates and hungry infant mouths await by a cold hearth. We promptly grant the evils of strong drink just as we concede that stuffing the alimentary tract with French pastry, bonbons, pigs' knuckles and hot breads; with tea, coffee, sarsaparilla or orange water ice, can insure a flabby paunch and fatty degeneration of the heart.

Even though we come from a line of Revolutionary British Colonials whose homestead by the Schuylkill embraced most of what is now Fairmount Park it seemed unprofitable to be secretive that the far-sighted Father of our Country ran up the fattest cellar bill the White House, then or present, ever knew; or that further he operated his own home brew concession at Mount Vernon, with Martha skimming the crocks with her own prim hand. Certainly on a joyful recent summer, sampling our way from inn to inn through the British countryside, as we stood in Jourdans meeting house yard by the grave of William Penn, lying properly beside his two wives, none of his worth was shrunk one jot through meditating that this Puritanical Quaker who dreamed he was almighty God and talked King James out of Pennsylvania and the Indians out of their furs, also showed sound material sense by building and owning the first brewery in the new world.

In our own unregenerate way we prefer honest confession right here at the start. That per hour of elapsed time, man and boy, we probably have been happier when mildly looking into the ruddy cup than at other times. Even granting our lethal morning-after disease we question if willingly we would exchange even our hunting, fishing or blue water sailing experiences for those mellow and gorgeously spiffed hours!

WHAT IMPORTANT adult event, for instance, could ever approach that gorgeous moment when the headmaster of a certain private school, whose name is not pertinent to mention, opened up our graduation gift to him: a stuffed ostrich bought in company with two useless kindred souls out of an Atlanta pawn shop? . . . Or the time we led, carried, coaxed and boosted the Holstein heifer, who proved not entirely neat and very, very expensive, up the spiral stairs to the college belfry after winning a certain crucial football game?

Then how about the time after the Art Students' League Ball on 57th Street, across from licit Carnegie Hall, and we went with a girl who unexpectedly turned out to be painted half in gold and half in silver under her evening wrap; later ending up in our Arab Sheikh's burnous and red turned-up-toe shoes doing telemark turns through the snow to lace a pink satin corset on the front of General Sherman's statue at the Plaza? Does anyone dream that raspberry vinegar could produce a triumph like that?

We also doubt if any lemonade social ever afforded a thrill like the moonlit night in Ceylon when we went to a Hollander friend's beach bungalow out beyond Galle Face, where we swam in the blood-warm Indian Ocean and drank enough of his *Flying Fish* cocktails to do, and lay on the cool sand and listened to Tauber sing *Dein Ist Mein Ganzes Herz* on the gramophone. Then when we swam again we slipped out of our suits to make the water feel better, and finally, when it was very late indeed, we dressed and said goodnight and vowed eternal friendship to our host; then for precisely no reason at all dismissed our waiting carriage with a flourish of gross overpayment and walked all the way back in our evening clothes through a new quiet rain to the jetties and the motor launch, just in time to prevent one of our best American cruising friends from consummating bribery of the Quartermaster on the good ship *RESOLUTE* into letting him hoist a purchased baby girl elephant—whom he said was Edith, and over whom he politely held a Burmese parasol of scarlet oiled silk—from a hired barge onto the forward cargo hatch in a sling!

Then again why should we go starry eyed and clasp a tin dipper of birch beer to our bosom in preference to a blend of Holland gin and fresh lime juice and fine ice and Angostura that we christened *Death in the Gulf Stream* when Carlos the Cubaño head gaffer freshened them for us while fishing giant tuna off Cat Cay with Ernest Hemingway on *PILAR?*

We also doubt what intercourse with strawberry sodas could hope to match another dawn in China, before undeclared wars were stylish and the White Russian princesses were still young in Shanghai; a dawn when we stood with a China-born American comrade on the bridge over the Whangpoo by the Bolsheviki Legation, both of us mellow as casks on *Cossack Punches,* and through his knowledge of dialect we carried on a flowery and mutually instructive conversation with some Son of Heaven who has just risen from the matting shelter of his sampan between a deckload of filled coffins to perform the dual pleasures of morning cigarette and a prosperous call of nature—a mutually serious and respectful conversation on the sorry condition of mankind generally and his own alimentaries in particular; on the cholera epidemic upriver, the high cost of living; a sure *feng-shui*— or good luck charm—against certain diseases, the proper routine for begetting male children and a proven simple calculated to thaw the most arctic woman's heart.

Why on earth should we seek solace in a bankruptcy of sarsaparilla in preference to an evening last month with the Mint Julep goblets frosted about mentionable rye—imagine an Eastern Sho' Marylander using bourbon!—sitting by Hervey Allen's fireplace with more ice and sugar and mint and sweet spring water and the decanter handy, talking half the night about books and men and women and manners?

How in heaven's name could any known liter of ice water since Ponce de León produce such memories as that January twilight up at Juhu Beach, which is out of Bombay on the Arabian Sea and twice as broad as Ormond and four times Waikiki, on the bungalow verandah of two friends in General Motors Export and the American Commercial Attaché? There we lay in rattan chairs, the kind with those swivel arms for ankles to drape over in the breeze, while the three cat-footed Mohammedan bearers refilled our *Gimlets,* reading the month old *New Yorker* and *Time* and talking over our three day beater hunt just finished a hundred miles or so back in the wild Mahratti country. Then the smell of the roasting saddle of *cheetal* venison, the dozen grilling sand-grouse, teasing out from the separate cook house, while a blood red sun the size of a gun turret set between the hundred-foot-high cocopalms and the lateen sails of the homing fisher *dhows* were a strand of flamingo plumes on the horizon. And after dinner sweet Arabian coffee and the tray of liqueurs; Drambuie—our favourite of all—Chartreuse, green and yellow; Cordial Medoc, which is made from peach pits; brandy *fine*, Benedictine, Curaçao, Kirschwasser and Cointreau; and kümmel in a bottle like a bear.

No, here was something precious and fine and very good. Something which began between four men who, until the evening came and the shadows lengthened, had taken no thought of spirits, but which there on that verandah found complement and gracious ease in the whole fragrant array of flasks and queer shaped bottles and pungent savours.

So here between these covers is firstfruit of twenty-one years of international field work in club, hotel and private society around much of the known world. You will find them all here, all the famous ones, and more besides that are now accepted and granted brief through long local usage and tradition. Here are the Raffles *Gin Sling* from far off Singapore, Seaholm and Gerber's *Tiger's Milk* from the historic Wagons-Lits in the Peking Legation Quarter. The proven *Gimlet* of India and South China, the unpredictable *Balloon Cocktail* from Calcutta's smartest restaurant named Firpo's; the truly magnificent *Million Dollar* as mixed by the genius Saito at the Imperial in Tokyo; the impeccable *Gin Fizz Spécial* of Aziz Effendi, monitor of the one and only Winter Palace at Loucqsor, in Egypt—yes, all these are here. And we haven't forgotten Jerusalem's *Between the Sheets* as perfected by our philosophical friend Weber at the Arabian Nights King David Hotel; nor the for-the-ladies *Hotel de la Silva Casino Special,* with the blush of a maid at her first whispered proposal, and having domicile in smart Cuernavaca, where Mexico's Four Hundred spend summer.

The Colombo *Flying Fish,* from Ceylon; Monk Antrim's *Quarantine*—Manila's perennial favourite; and his *Lintik*—Tagalog vernacular for "Lightning"—are not missing. There is the *Grande Bretagne No. 1*—which we consider one of the four finest in the entire world— from Athens, Greece; Bilgray's *Hallelujah* from Colon, Panama. There are rum swizzles and punches and *crustas* that for generations have cooled the parched palates of planters and merchants and dilettantes in Jamaica, Martinique and other hot country islands of the romantic Caribbean.

Readers will find the Rangoon *Star Ruby,* from exotic Burmah; the

*Mood Indigo* from Gould's fantastic Casino *Palais de la Mediter-ranée,* whose purpose is not necessary to mention; and Lord Ruthven's *Tewahdiddle, or Gossip's Cup,* which . . . "exceeds by far all the ale that ever Mother Bunch made in her lifetime," according to His Lordship's *Experiments in Cookereye &c,* London 1654.

All of these are here, and many many more of varying size and type together with authentic ways of manufacturing bitters, syrups, stone bottle ginger beers, which have been well proven by tests of time and peoples. So once again, as in *The Exotic Cookery Book,* we have offered our personal alimentaries to the pleasant and educational task as a sort of liquid proving ground for endless alcoholic formulae before offering this hand-picked collection of lively masterpieces from the *Greater and Lesser Ports of Orient & Occident, & the South Seas.*

And so, before the turned page, we say: *Salud y pesetas, sköl, santé, salute,* and here's mud in your eye!

*Java Head,*
*Coconut Grove, Florida,*
*1st July, Nineteen Hundred Thirty-Nine*

# CHAPTER I

# A DESIGN *FOR* DRINKING

*Being a Brief Dissertation on This Pleasant Subject in General; why Too Many Cocktails Fail through Over-Sweetness & Plurality of Ingredient; why Hot Drinks must be Hot, & Cold Drinks Cold; an Ardent Plea for Accurate Calibration; & finally a Second Invitation to The Mixer.*

As in the creation of *THE EXOTIC COOKERY BOOK*, this setting down in print of the first-fruits of fourteen years' liquid field work naturally credits all readers with fair fundamental knowledge on the subject of mixed potables. In any congregation of exotica there can hardly be room for formulae on such elementary subjects as the ever-present Dry Martini, the Manhattan or the Old Fashioned Cocktail. Our own native Mint Julep was included because it can, and does, stand proudly beside the world's best concoctions; a masterpiece in its own right, a true exotic of the Deep South which has been taken up and deliciously modified in other interesting places as far off as the Philippines.

It is also a physical impossibility to pretend that this volume is a complete treatise on beverages. There are some ninety-seven visible volumes on our own shelves dealing with wines, blended drinks, and tradition obtaining to this gentle art of imbibition—which is our coined word for the sport—and heaven alone knows how many more there must be in print that we've never heard of! Experts have spent whole lives covering one phase or type of wine—of which there are around sixteen hundred listed. We, therefore, will briefly mention which to chill; which not to chill; which types march best with certain foods and courses.

On the truly American matter of mixed drinks we feel we can speak from some slight experience, and with fair authority. Instead of listing a maze of receipts already listed in, and plagiarized from, professional bar lists and previous cocktail books, we will bring you famous liquid classics from odd spots of the world—classics which, through the test of time and social usage, have become institutions in the place of their birth. One volume in our possession naively lists seventeen hundred allegedly authentic cocktails, whereas there cannot possibly be that many *good* cocktails on earth—or a hundred and seventy, for that matter.

All those we list cannot please every reader, naturally. Certain normal friends of ours dislike Holland gin with a passion little short of fanatical. We've yet to meet the female who really likes Jamaica rum unmixed with lighter rums to modify the heavy molasses taste. Absinthe, for instance, can conquer the most desiccated puritan on occasion, but makes the heart of many agreeable folk shudder at the taste. Anisette, kümmel, tequila, Hawaiian *okolehao*—all have their enemies and champions. No, the best we can hope to do is thumb over our battered field book, our odd scrawled-upon bar chits, menus and scraps of notes from bygone days, and construct therefrom a sequence of drinks which for this reason or that, stand out in memory beyond their fellows.

The issue we take with current cocktail books is no reflection on their authors, but on their subject matter. It dates back to the year 1931 when we were headed around the world, and found ourself in the Free Port of Gibraltar. Well, the British pound sterling was down to $3.30 American—then—gold. Being a duty-free port American cigarettes were ninety cents the carton, Johnny Walker *Black Label,* eighteen the case. London Gordon around three dollars, eighty the case. With these few basic figures it proves the possible scope of our laboratory work.

We got back in the last tender out of "Gib," and if she wasn't down to her Plimsoll marks it wasn't through lack of brown paper covered packages destined for the vacant cabin on B Deck next to ours! That night we stowed our pelf—bottle on bottle of it. There was everything the wildest madcap mixer could demand for any known blended potation, fizzes, daisys, rickeys, cocktails, punches, and pick-me-ups.

We had bought the biggest cocktail book in print, and every evening thereafter we went to work. It was one of those thick volumes which sprouted on the damp soil of prohibition like wan, mad mushrooms. Along with two other stout hearts and chrome vanadium stomachs we attacked that plump book every evening for five solid months! We cut no corners; we didn't cheat. We measured accurately, chilled properly. We tasted and drank or promptly flung the abortive fluid out the nearest port hole.

To our naive mind, assuming that all drink receipts in print must have been put there through some sort of tested merit, the disillusionment was immediate and illuminating. By Suez we were groggy; we spent two days in Newara Eyliya, hill station back of Colombo, Ceylon, to get our breath. By Singapore we were cellars-dry, and bought again. We literally drank our way across Siam and Cambodia. We, along with our other fellow-scientists, popped corks and gulped our triple-threat through the Dutch East Indies, Java, Bali, Borneo, and Makassar to Zamboanga, to Manila, then to Hongkong in South China. On the Bund in Shanghai our heads were groggy but unbowed, and we bought again. By the time we quit Honolulu the baldfaced conclusions were plain as the nose on our face—much of that welter of mixed things with fancy names were the egotistically-titled, ill-advised conceptions of low-browed mixers who either had no access to sound spirits, or if they did have, had so annealed their taste buds with past noxious cups that they were forevermore incapable of judicious authority. It was no wonder that, like the originators of the latest parlour story, their originators would invariably hide incognito. We measured with laboratory accuracy, obeyed every law. Here's the verdict.

1. Out of all the thousands of cocktails listed in all books there are too many drinks calling for gin and vermouth. We admire vermouth in its place, but that simply isn't in 60% of our cocktails.
2. Entirely too many cocktails specified too much Italian vermouth and French vermouth with fruit juices. It is an evil combination, productive of evil enzymes and tastes.

3. Too many cocktails of delicate base specified too much of Italian vermouth, with result that the latter drowned out the basic and better flavour. Like absinthe, Italian vermouth is a dominant taste; and we must watch it.

4. Many cocktails seem to get into books more because of a trick or "cute" name—heaven only knows why!—than for the chemical soundness of its *raison d'être*. Calling a drink a *Widow's Kiss,* or a *Horned Toad,* really isn't any ticket to liquid immortality; for no inferior blend ever lasts out the night of its evil concoction.

5. Except for flavouring cocktails, and one or two rare Exotics like the Hongkong *Rosy Dawn,* immortal to our memory, no mixed drink having more than 3 main alcoholic ingredients but which becomes hoist on the petard of its own casual plurality. . . . In other words, barring Pousse Cafés and other feminine threats, no drink calling for 1 part gin, ½ of cherry brandy, ½ Curaçao, ½ apricot brandy, and ½ rye whisky, can ever prove out into anything but the taste melee it is. However it is possible to point up a drink with a *dash* of this and that upon a basically sound foundation.

6. Watch using liqueurs or cordials in cocktails. Most of these are very sweet and not only can make an otherwise good mix too sweet, but lose their own character through dilution.

HAVING come through this test by liquid, still sound in wind and limb, or as Fritz (*Alone in the Caribbean*) Fenger would say "unfrayed at either end," we are still heartily of the opinion that decent libation supports as many million souls as it threatens; donates pleasure and sparkle to more lives than it shadows; inspires more brilliance in the world of art, music, letters and common ordinary intelligent conversation, than it dims—as even a brief glance into the history of our finest lyric poets, musicians, artists, authors, and statesmen, will attest—right from the day of Wull Shaksper to our own generation.

We view the subject with clinical interest, continued joy and extreme toleration. We feel that so long as it is an existing part of human life, too strong and too important for prohibition, we should make the enjoyments as apparent and as controlled as possible; the tastes crisp, the compounding as intriguing as far ports of the world can afford.

In the collection of this volume's data we gradually came to realize that the great drinks around the world, like the ethics of draw poker, the length of ladies' skirts and width of men's pantaloons—the *accepted,* the proven, thing is the right thing; the best thing, and all of these proven experiences march here.

Each one of them fetches joyous memory of some friend, place, or adventure; is flanked with happy memory of a frosted glass, a smile, the sip of something which is perfect. No, nothing shall ever pirate away those memories, or the recorded history of these two hundred and more drinks. We are faithful to them, Cynara, after our fashion!

AN EARNEST PLEA for THREE METICULOUS OBSERVANCES in the CONSTRUCTION of any MIXED DRINK—and ESPECIALLY that of the COCKTAIL

1. Measure accurately, and don't be betrayed by that insidious temptation to pour with a "heavy jigger." It is undeniable hospitality to wish guests to get their ample share of spirits, but don't force the amount. More drinks are spoiled through being too strong than being too weak.
2. Serve cold drinks *arctic cold*. Chill bottles and glasses, to speed up the process. . . . Serve hot drinks *steaming hot*. . . . Compromise in either of these events is merely bargaining with fault and disaster.
3. If there are guests present who appreciate decent cocktails, let's do the mixing ourself. The amateur will always take infinitely more pains than any houseboy or butler. Trust him for such usual fare as whisky-and-soda, the Tom Collins, and so on. They are easy. But the crisp pungency of a proven cocktail demands infinite care in observance of the simple mixing requirements. It is such a brief step from excellence to mediocrity.
4. Don't try and make decent cocktails out of cheap, briefly aged liquors. Stick to highballs, or else do the job up right. We can no more build a fine cocktail on dollar gin than Whistler could paint his mother's portrait with barn paint.

WORDS to the LIQUID WISE No. I, URGING all GOOD AMERICANS to LIFT a PROUD HEAD & MEET the WORLD EYE to EYE, when IT COMES to MAKING MIXED DRINKS

Your Britisher may scorn ice in his whisky-sodas, your Indian Colonial may insist on cellar-warm ale, your Frenchman may know all his wines by their maiden names—but remember that the American has invented, and always will invent, more of the world's good mixed drinks than all the rest of humanity lumped together. . . . Just read the pages of history. There they are: juleps, cocktails, cobblers, fizzes, daisys, sours, rickeys, coolers—these and more all originated in America, reached their highest technique here in America. . . . Whether the rest of the world cares to admit it or not, we started these drinks in circulation, just as we started the telephone, submarine, phonograph, incandescent light, electric refrigerator, and decent bath tubs. Oddly enough, outside the continental boundaries of the States the best drink mixers are American-trained Chinos, Cubans, Filipinos, Japanese, Swiss, and officers in His Britannic Majesty's army and navy!—not native English, French, or Italian citizens on their own soil.

## A SECOND INVITATION to THE MIXER

Just as in the volume on cookery, we again remind our readers that a decent electric mixer is just as necessary on any well-equipped bar these days as a horse in a stable. Of course most cold drinks may be mixed, or shaken, by hand. Of course underground tunnels may be dug by hand, but modern machinery saves hours of wasted time and effort. There are also several so-called Tropical drinks, notably the new style Daiquiri, which simply cannot be shaped up by hand at all. There is no wrist strong or deft enough to make any mix of liquid and cracked ice turned into frosted sherbet-like consistency so essential to these examples.

The Ramos Brothers used to have a battery of eight ebony black bartenders to shake their famous fizzes to perfection—each one working fiercely and passing the shaker to the next, when weary. The Waring Mixer is not being revived again here in this drinking volume in any spirit of commercialism. As explained before, we do not even know Mr. Waring, but we like his music and his Mixer. It is fairly expensive, but is assembled of as fine materials as man can make—to give hard professional service; to last. There will probably be imitative, cheaper electric mixers. There will also be violinists who imitate Messrs. Heifetz and Kreisler. For cooling Daiquiris, gin fizzes, making grenadine juice from pomegranates, for a dozen and one unexpected uses, we find this deft gadget indispensable. If this slight paean of appreciation and gratitude to Mr. Waring for his aid to the mixing profession should make even one person beat a trail toward him seeking his mousetrap, that result is amply deserved—just as correctly as the Frenchman who thought up the drip coffee biggin, the chap who fabricated the first double boiler, the first deep fat kettle for the preparation of food.

Future reference to this mechanical unit will refer to it plainly as The Mixer.

AND NOW a COMPANY of 200 & 67 ASSORTED POTATIONS from AMATEUR & PROFESSIONAL HOSTS about the WORLD

AN ABSINTHE COCKTAIL, as MIXED for Us by an ITINERANT RUSSIAN PRINCE on the OCCASION of OUR USUAL MORNING PILGRIMAGE to HARRY's AMERICAN BAR, which Is in PARIS

During several weeks domicile in Hotel Daunou over Ciro's across the Rue Daunou, we often groped to Harry when visibly withering on the vine—seeking aid and comfort. On this especial occasion a Russian gentleman spied our ambulant corpse, took pity, bowed Harry aside in his spotless white coat, and in a small frappe shaker compounded the following life saver. We advocate putting it in The Mixer for a jiffy with finely cracked ice.

Absinthe, 1½ jiggers

Anis or anisette, dash

Water, ½ jigger

Sugar or *gomme* syrup, ½ tsp or less

Orange & Angostura bitters, dash each

White of egg, 1 tsp

Twist of lime or lemon peel

This is an excellent appetizer and tonic. Twist bit of peel to insure getting oil on surface of the drink. Must be very cold.

JUST a WORD on the LARGELY MISUNDERSTOOD SUBJECT of ABSINTHE in GENERAL; & CONCERNING an ABSINTHE DRIP from LE PERROQUET, in Saigon, French Indo China, & an Absinthe Frappe from the Heliopolis Palace, in Cairo

Technically absinthe is a highly toxic liqueur running between 70% and 80% alcohol, with an aromatic characteristic flavour of a kind of wormwood known as *Artemisia absinthium,* blended with little items like angelica root, sweet flag, dittany leaves, star anise fruits, hyssop and fennel. In other words it is a strange herb-alcohol brew acting potently on the nervous ganglia. Too much can cause hallucinations,—what we have lightly come to call D. T's. And other things not judicious to mention.

In mixed drinks absinthe has a flavouring value all its own. Usually a very small quantity should be used, as the taste is potent and will dull many other more delicate flavours.

Due to French mishandling of the liquor, and the sorry plight of her addicts, its manufacture was banned in the republic. For years the old French Quarter in New Orleans turned out a good type, and now the Swiss seem to have an inside corner on the market. Pernod is the *capon* near-absinthe made in France now, with much of the taste but little of the lift—due to many simples being ruled out of the formula.

THE ABSINTHE DRIP as Properly Fabricated in Saigon, or anywhere Else, for that Matter

One of the charms of so many far eastern colonies is that many of the old world laws, tabus, taxes and other civilized nuisances are tossed overboard at Suez. If there is any prohibition of absinthe in *Indo-Chine* we failed to see it, ever, and, barring corruption of natives and conspiring against France, there is little prohibition of any kind. In Saigon we found a diverse and international parade of people, none of whom apparently had anything urgent or immediate to do, except the coolies tugging their burdens. A Siamese aristocrat strolled by our lower window in the shade of a parasol held by a servant. He was wrapped in a smart white silk coat, pipe-clayed sun topee and a purple silk diaper twined between his sturdy brown thighs. A merchant from Rangoon in a blue and crimson skirt. Chic flexible Chinese girls with their trim, exquisite figures poured into the scabbard-like split dresses of pastel silk that so elegantly suit their type. A brace of snipe-legged little Japanese men with f. 2 Leicas swinging around their necks, half-inch thick eyeglasses, flat straw hats, muttering urgently at each other without the slightest trace of facial expression. A Javanese girl-mother with her naked brown babe swinging in a butterfly tinted sarong tied above her hips and tucked in with a cunning woman's twist. A Buddhist priest from far back in the wild hill country back of beyond, in his funny hat and worn robe dyed three centuries ago in a yellow hue which would be mellow and fair a century after its present owner was dust. Two short, plump, short-skirted French girls giggling, looking us squarely in the eye before continuing other inspection—totally without self-consciousness or inhibition as they audibly speculated on our origin, age, marital state and capitalistic solvency in a machine gun undertone of rapid French. This is just the briefest vignette of Saigon.

Before quitting this subject of absinthe perhaps we had better explain that taken in steady doses over a considerable period of time, it does nibble the keen edge off the brain until a man becomes a sorry sort of thing; aimless, listless, and generally—shockingly—lacking. This, and the habit it forms under constant usage, of course accounts for its ban in France. Actually, too, it happens to be one of the few liqueurs which more or less definitely stimulates the cavaliers riding herd about the altar of Aphrodite.

An Absinthe Drip isn't one of the black arts at all; nor something confined to Maupassant, and mystery, and low and devious dives all coagulated with *apaches,* and their *grisettes,* and sitting around all hours of the night with drooping cigarettes in the corners of their mouths, and long hair drooping in their eyes, and long knives up their sleeves. . . . The cute, almost doll-like Annamese bar-man took a small thin tumbler, nearly the size and shape of our Old Fashioned Cocktail glass. This he centered up with 2 cubes of sterilized ice, a lump of loaf sugar. Onto this he turned a jigger of absinthe. A tiny pitcher of cold water was supplied, this to be poured in 1 drop at a time, or at guest option, ladled in with a small teaspoon. . . . Under this routine the pearly, almost opalescent, sheen of the absinthe is even more apparent than in the Frappe; also its potency.

AN ABSINTHE FRAPPE from Heliopolis Palace, Cairo, in 1931
Here is one of the most bizarre and startling hotels in all the world. We found it, and not doing so well, back in 1926; but later on, in funds, it drew the fashionable crowd out near the race track. . . . This drink was mixed in small silver cocktail shakers holding enough for 2 guests; fetched to table with chilled glasses of champagne saucer type. . . . Merely turn 2 glasses of finely cracked ice into a chilled small shaker, add two 2-oz jiggers of absinthe and 1 tsp *anis del mono,* or French anisette. Shake quickly and hard. Pour out, ice and all; and a short straw, bright green in hue, is the final touch. This again produces a pearly white fluid at odds with the greenish liquid in bottle.

Please don't ignore this small shaker, iced shaker, iced glasses business. When making drinks especially in small amount this is essential to chill cold enough—*but mainly to prevent much ice melting to dilute and injure the tone of the finished drink.*

WORDS to the LIQUID WISE No. II, STILL further INSISTING that SHAKER & GLASSES ALWAYS BE CHILLED—ESPECIALLY when MAKING COCKTAILS for a VERY FEW GUESTS
Mixing 2 cocktails in a huge, room-temperature shaker, and pouring them into room-temperature glasses, is careless business. The ice melts rapidly, dilutes the drink, and the whole mix warms so fast that instead of being really chilled the final outcome is also not far from room temperature. . . . A warm cocktail is like half-way objects in life—neither this nor that, and often a reflection on the judgment and discretion of those present.

*ADIOS AMIGOS,* ONE from the Army-Navy Club in Manila, & One to be Watched *SEÑORS!*

| | |
|---|---|
| Bacardi, 2 ponies | Cognac, 1 pony |
| French Vermouth, 1 pony | Lemon, juice, ½; or lime, juice, 1 |
| Dry gin, 1 pony | |

Shake well with lots of cracked ice, pour into a large flat champagne glass, and send for the Marines!

## J. PIERPONT MORGAN'S *ALAMAGOOZLUM,* the PERSONAL MIX CREDITED to that FINANCIER, PHILANTHROPIST, & BANKER of a BYGONE ERA

This might conceivably be a punch, if handled like a Planter's Punch; just as it could be stirred in a pitcher. To tell the truth this is no exotic from a far land, but is such a tasteful and sound cocktail that we append it here, standing on its own legs and its own merit. To serve about 5 cocktails: take 1 jigger each of Jamaica rum, *gomme* syrup, and yellow or green Chartreuse; add ½ pony yellow Curaçao and ½ pony of Angostura bitters. Add 2 scant ponies of Holland gin, the same of water; donate ½ the white of an egg and shake hard with lots of cracked ice. Serve in a Manhattan glass.

## THE AMER PICON "POUFFLE" FIZZ, from the BAR-LOG of an EDITOR FRIEND DOMICILED for a SUMMER & WINTER on the FRENCH RIVIERA, at ST. JACQUES CAP FERRAT, & in a VILLA & THINGS

This is a very odd and fascinating affair, we can assure everyone. Simply turn a jigger of Amer Picon into a shaker with plenty of cracked ice, donate the white of 1 recent egg, and a scant pony of grenadine. Shake well, put into a goblet containing a lump of ice and fill to taste with best club soda available. Add ¼ tsp Angostura; stir.

## THE ANTRIM COCKTAIL, ONE WE FOUND in the QUAINT LITTLE OVERSEAS CLUB in ZAMBOANGA, on the ISLAND of MINDANAO in the YEAR of GRACE 1931

This classic, being invented by "Monk" Antrim in Manila 5 or 6 years before, had found its way down into Moro country, many hundreds of miles to the south. We will bring more news of "Monk" later, meanwhile this is his own special origination, later blended for us by his own Chino *barmeister* in Manila.

Use 1 pony each of good French cognac and port wine; toss in ½ tsp of sugar; shake with lots of cracked ice and serve in a Manhattan glass. This is a slow creeper-upper, so *prend garde!*

THE ASTOR HOTEL SPECIAL, from SHANGHAI, during a TRIP around the WORLD in the YEAR 1926, & on the OCCASION of OUR BECOMING MAROONED in that CITY, with OUR OWN SHIP & PERSONAL BELONGINGS GONE on to HONGKONG, & with a DELIGHTFUL YOUNG MAIDEN by WHOM WE WERE LATER REJECTED in MARRIAGE, & WHO LATER DISTINGUISHED HERSELF by ESPOUSING a VERY NICE GENTLEMAN WHOSE MAIN CLAIM to FAME IS that HE WAS once KIDNAPED by KARPIS prior to the LATTER'S ENTERING HIS SUITE in ALCATRAZ

That whole trip around the world was the fault of GRS stock because it went up over 200 points before we sold; and our epidemic of missing steamboats began in Shanghai and was the fault of this very blend—sitting in the charming old Astor, with fog setting in, and a big party given out at the Majestic if we'd stay. The formula is noted directly from the Astor's Number I Chino mixer.

Cognac, 1 jigger
Maraschino, 1 tsp
Egg white, 2 tsp

Absinthe, ½ jigger
Lemon juice, strained, ½ tsp
Club soda

Shake well with cracked ice, strain into a tall wine goblet, then top off with just a little chilled soda.

THREE VERSIONS of ATHOL BROSE, an ODD SCOTTISH INSTITUTION which, LIKE MANY THINGS SCOTTISH, IS FOUNDED on MIGHTY GOOD REASON, & IS GUARANTEED to PROFIT ITS USER

ATHOL BROSE No. I

This potation, like our favourite cordial, Drambuie, was coined far up in the misty Hieland country where two-fisted Scottish swordsmen swung two-handed claymores for Bonnie Prince Charlie, Mary o' Scotland, or their own feudal Laird. It is the traditional drink with that weird meat lusty, the Scotch Haggis. We personally prefer Athol Brose served hot on wintry nights, although this is not following custom. Please don't attempt to use any young Scotch whisky—use the best the shelf affords.

Really old Liqueur Scotch whisky, 1 part

Clear strained honey, 1 part
Cream, 1 part

Mix well, warm slightly to make smooth. Then cool and sample, or heat and sample while still hot, to insure a mix to taste. Drink cold. Never boil cream or milk in a Brose. "Milk boiled is milk spoiled," runs the Scottish proverb.

## ATHOL BROSE No. II
Put a heaping tsp or so of strained honey into 4 jiggers of liqueur Scotch whisky, turning this into a tumbler. Fill tumbler with milk, heated beforehand. Cool before drinking.

## ATHOL BROSE No. III
This is still another ancient blend: Use 1 part liqueur Scotch whisky, ½ part strained honey, 1 part thick cream. Heat carefully, as before. Serve cold.

WORDS to the WISE No. III, BEING an EARNEST PLEA NOT to SERVE an OVER SUPPLY of RICH CREAMY COCKTAILS before any DECENT MEAL
Being more or less of a meal in itself, this sort of rich creamy drink cannot whet or build appetite. For this reason it really should be served on other occasions than immediately preceding a notable dinner. This applies to Pink Ladies, Alexanders, and all their nourishing kin.

THE AUNT EMILY, a CREATION of SLOPPY JOE's, in HAVANA, YEARS before HIS SPOT GOT to BE a SORT of HALF WAY HOUSE for EVERY ITINERANT AMERICAN on the ISLAND
Try and use good aged *Calvados*—fine French apple brandy—for best results in this creation,—not the usual, fairly new applejack. We have found under these improved conditions that it is a memorable cocktail well worthy of notation. . . . Mix ½ jigger each apple brandy, dry gin, dry apricot brandy, and orange juice. Add 1 dash

grenadine for colour. Shake hard and serve in a tall cocktail glass with stem.

THE BAGUIO SKIN, being a VERY SIMPLE yet VERY UNUSUAL EXOTIC from OUR BEAUTIFUL HILL STATION away up in the IGOROTE COUNTRY among the HIGH MOUNTAINS of LUZON

Baguio happens to be the world's first and only *planned* hill station, beautifully laid out by Cameron Forbes. Beside it the Topsy-like British India hill stations at Mussoorie, Gulmarg, and Simla—that "jest growed"—are straggling, casual affairs with no organization or scenic plan other than that endowed by an ever-generous Almighty. Baguio is the summer, rainy season retreat of civil and military Manila. We found this drink there, 7000 feet up, sitting before an *open fire* at the Country Club, looking out through the windows while the cloud slowly came down and tucked the 18th fairway under its wing.

In a tall-stemmed wineglass put 1 tsp of sugar dissolved in a trifle of water; then 1 dash or so of orange bitters. On top of this place 2 thin slices of green lime—or lemon—3 ice cubes, and then add 2 ponies of *Carta de Oro* Bacardi. Stir briskly with a bar spoon and serve as-is, with a final dusting of grated nutmeg on top. We consider this one of the finest possible, and find that 1 pair of orange or jasmine blossoms starred in each glass lends the true tropical, the fragrant, touch that guests like.

BALAKLAVA SPECIAL No. I, as BREWED for Us by ONE CAPTAIN FERGUSON, SHIPMATE of Ours around the WORLD in 1926, & LATE of HIS MAJESTY'S BENGAL LANCERS, ONE-TIME STATIONED in the PUNJAB, NORTHERN INDIA

This very unusual cocktail is dedicated to the spot made famous by the charge of the Light Brigade which was a spectacular, tragic, and rather unnecessary military gesture. . . . Fill a small-stemmed wine goblet brimming full with shaved ice—or very finely cracked ice. Into this pour 1 jigger each kümmel and cognac. A dash of any red syrup like grenadine is optional and pretty.

## BALAKLAVA SPECIAL No. II, when LADIES ARE PRESENT

Just why handsome women prefer sweet and creamy cocktails has always troubled us, but they do; and anyway a lot of things about handsome ladies have troubled us, so why get tweaky about the business at this late date? . . . Put 1 jigger of kümmel, ½ jigger each of absinthe, cognac and *kirschwasser,* into a shaker. Add ½ tsp orgeat syrup and 1 to 1½ tsp of thick cream. Shake briskly and serve in a tall-stemmed cocktail glass. And for heaven's sweet sake don't think this snake-in-the-grass drink is a harmless and gentle lady's affair just because it has cream in it!

## FIRPO'S BALLOON COCKTAIL, the CALCUTTA CLASSIC

Our college mate C. Byron Spofford, at the time American Commercial Attaché in Calcutta for all of India, Burma and Ceylon, once gave a dinner celebrating the farewell of a very opinionated pair of men wished on him from Russian Famine Relief Headquarters by Herbert Hoover. We seem to recall their names as being Sabine and Renshaw, but that doesn't matter—it didn't then, and it certainly doesn't now. The thing that does matter is that Firpo mixed us a special round of Balloons—named because the 5th one consumed is guaranteed to set us bobbing about up under the ceiling. Firpo's is Calcutta's one smart night spot. It was all very gay in spite of the Hoover sycophants. . . . To 1 jigger of really good rye whisky add the same of Italian vermouth and absinthe—substituting Pernod Veritas lacking the true wormwood spirit. Now donate 2 dashes of orange bitters, or Angostura if preferred, and 1½ to 2 tsp of egg white. Shake well. Serve in a big saucer type champagne glass. This is another one to watch cannily lest our pedal extremities fold up at some totally inappropriate moment.

## THE BARRY COCKTAIL, from MANILA, and MET FIRST in 1926, then again LATER. As MIXED at the ARMY & NAVY CLUB

This is included through clinical mixing interest. It is exactly the same as a Martini, but using Italian vermouth instead of the dry French type; adding Angostura bitters rather than orange, and trimmed with ½ tsp creme de menthe, floated on at the last. Twist a curl of lemon peel for its oil. It is stirred in a bar glass and must be cold indeed.

BERTITA'S SPECIAL COCKTAIL, *con HABAÑERO,* Being an Exotic We Have Personally Fetched Back from Taxco, which is Back in the High Hills of Mexico, where Artists from America Congregate for Varying Reasons, & with Varying Success

Bertita, diagonally across the southwest corner of the public square from de la Borda's matchless cathedral is a dingy but mildly celebrated place, noted twice in this volume. This is a potent drink poured with a heavy hand, as we found during a stay in Taxco in February 1937. . . . *Habañero* incidentally, means any of the light Cuban rums properly distilled from sugar cane by-product, and aged in the wood. Properly they should be called rum brandies, we imagine. Bacardi is the best known, but down there in Mexico the citizens blot up an amazing count of Cubaño rums we never even heard of, like *El Caney* in its slim Rhine wine style bottle. . . . To 4 jiggers of light Cuban rum add the strained juice of 2 limes, the strained juice of 1½ average sized oranges, 2 tsp of grenadine, or sugar or *gomme* syrup. Shake vigorously with lots of ice, serve in big champagne glasses—for 2 people. As we recall it Bertita served it with cracked ice still in the drink. It would pan out well in The Mixer, incidentally. Personally we float on 1 tsp Jamaica, atop the finished drink.

WORDS to the WISE No. IV, on the WISDOM of ADDING a VERY LITTLE JAMAICA RUM to ALL COCKTAILS REQUIRING FRUIT JUICES of any KIND
This is our invariable rule now, as 1 tsp of Jamaica adds a definite something to all fruit juice drinks; and especially to those based on Bacardi or other light rums, which are so delicate that their virtues are cloaked in the more usual fruit juices themselves.

JERUSALEM'S BETWEEN the SHEETS, from the Bar Book of Weber at the King David
Like the American Side Car, and other truly worthwhile cocktails

this invention is totally sound, and is already quite famous throughout the Near East. We ran into it one dank day of sleet and rain in early January, just after the first Arab-Jewish riots which started with a murder of a poor old man stoned to death in a Haifa melon patch, between halves of a soccer match! and had just reached a climax beside the Dome of the Rock mosque—which has religious significance to both Arab and Jew, and unfortunately overhangs the famous Jewish Wailing Wall. We won't go into the politics of the thing, but it was a nasty mess, with British Tommies in the streets finally, and machine guns and barbed wire entanglements—all the modern civilized show. . . . We were disillusioned at all this wholesale murder in Christianity's own heart city, sad at the sight of a fifteen year old Arab girl—the daughter of a fine Arab friend—crushed under a heavy slab of masonry tossed from a rooftop as she returned from worship after the end of *Ramadan*—the Mohammedan Easter—and we were wearied at the thought of the drawn knives, the murder from ambush which would follow all this blood debt throughout Palestine. We had both sinuses pounding, were coming down with definitely *something,* as well—when in the weird, almost Egyptian-looking sanctum of the King David Weber took charge; first with a hot rum toddy, then—on evidence of renewed life—with the following origination.

Of cognac, cointreau, dry gin and lemon juice—strained—take equal parts. Shake briskly with lots of cracked ice and serve in a Manhattan glass. Cut down the cointreau to make "dry," to taste.

THE JAMAICAN BLACK STRAP, from the FORMULA of an AMERICAN FRIEND WHO INHERITED a MOUNTAIN PLANTATION on JAMAICA'S WINDWARD SIDE, not too FAR from PORT ANTONIO

This is a strange drink, and will arouse a lot of interest among strangers, only better be sure they admire Jamaica rum—many ladies don't, for instance! . . . Take 2 jiggers of old Jamaica rum, add 2 tbsp ice water, 2 tsp blackstrap molasses, and 1 dash Angostura, or 2 dashes of orange bitters. Shake with lots of cracked ice, and garnish with a thin stick of fresh pineapple.

THE JAMAICAN BLACK STRIPE, another HEARTENER from that TROPICAL PARADISE, that MAY BE SERVED either HOT or COLD

If served cold: work 2 tsp strained honey into 1 tbsp boiling water until well dissolved. Add 1 jigger Jamaica rum, shake with cracked ice, pour into stemmed cocktail glass and dust with nutmeg. Furnished us by Emerson Low, Esq., gentleman, student, Rhodes Scholar, author and delightful dilettante, who, now that he is married and possessed of child and responsibility, is not nearly so diverting, it pains us to say.

THE BAVARIAN "BRIDEGROOM'S CUP," a MEMORY from the GAY DAYS when THERE WAS TIME in which to LIVE a LIFE—& LAUGH, & LOVE, & SING, & DANCE, in MIDDLE EUROPE

We have a lovely friend, a girl, who married a Bavarian "von" who is our idea of what a "von" ought to be; and at their wedding in New York he introduced us to this delightful drink—which is doubly nice on a hot summer's day. . . . Take the biggest crystal goblet we can find, then chill it. Fill it 1/3 full of ice and turn in ½ bottle of good Rhine wine—well chilled—and 1 jigger of *kirsch*. Stir for a moment with a silver spoon, then garnish with a handful of crushed lightly sugared ripe strawberries—also chilled; only put them in with a spoon —3 tbsp total. Bedeck with a sprig of green mint, if in the mood. There we have it.

THE BROKEN SPUR, a CLASSIC FOUND in the PERGOLA of LEON ELLIS, 2d SECRETARY of the AMERICAN LEGATION in PEKING, in the YEAR 1932, and before a BUFFET DINNER of UTTER CHARM

Imagine Peking then, just before Japan had screwed up brass enough to defy Britain, and the rest of Europe's Legations, and ours too by the way!—and had quietly occupied most of Imperial North China while everyone sat back like a lot of spineless ostriches with head in sand, and another lot of spineless men who violated their own sacred signatures behaved like a lot of schoolboys playing grownup around the League of Nations table at Geneva throwing dice with an unfortunate and *colorado maduro* gentleman named Haile Selassie, whom no one much had ever heard of before. Imagine getting there on our third trip, and knowing people, and with a fiancée who had already agreed to the banns, and the plum blossoms frosting the Summer Palace gardens where Old Buddha once strolled, before we re-entered our motor cars and went to the foot of Western Hills where Ellis had sedan chairs and coolies waiting for the madcap, swaying, almost perpendicular climb to the very topmost ridge, past the American Minister's temple, and the other Buddhist temples the Europeans rent, through this connivance and that with the willing priests—to Ellis' Grotto of the Propitious Pearl. And there in back of his living quarters was a cave in the hills, where he has to let the pilgrims go day or night, and where the mummy of a famous saint sits lifelike, covered with some sort of plaster and tinted like real flesh. Imagine the view at sunset of the distant Tartar walls of Peking, just barely visible through the golden light, with everything powdered with Peking dust which is older than time itself. Picture an impossible grinning combination of Fu Manchu and Houdini who bowed and smiled and produced miraculous things from vast wicker hampers which had, through some other Oriental magic, transported themselves before us to this place. There between the 500 year old red lacquer columns of that Buddhist pavilion we sat and thought things about Jenghiz Khan, and fiancées, and sipped big 3 oz Broken Spurs served in hand engraved crystal champagne glasses.

To ½ a jigger of dry gin add the same of Italian vermouth; then 1 jigger of port wine, 1 tsp *anis del mono* or anisette, the yolk of 1 fresh egg. Shake briskly with big lumps of ice and when cold serve in a champagne saucer glass, dusting the top with a pinch of powdered ginger at the last.

THE BARBADOS BUCK, Being a Fine Refreshener We Ran into One Early January Afternoon upon Introduction to the British Club that Clings to the End of the Dock at Bridgetown like a Determined Spider

Tom Hartnett and Larry Stucky and I had been lying naked on a sugarwhite beach, talking about Gilbert & Sullivan, and about the days we used to play baseball against each other at Yale and Trinity, and then we went in to town for a quick one before all the West Indies cruise passengers had to be lightered off to the *RELIANCE* anchored out there, and a friendly British Lieutenant suggested this cooler, which is also a bracer. . . . Put a large lump of ice in the biggest tumbler in sight—and 16 oz size is proper. Now add 1 jigger Barbados rum (any dark rum will do) and the same of Bacardi, the juice of 1 small green lime, 1 tsp sugar; stir this friendly group to mix thoroughly, then fill the big glass with ginger beer, or some good ginger ale like imported Cantrell & Cochrane. Stone bottle ginger beer is best, buyable now in America.

WORDS to the WISE No. V, on the MODIFICATION of JA-MAICA RUM when LADY GUESTS ARE PRESENT
Never forget, please, that only 1 lady in 12 really likes the Jamaica rum taste. Therefore dilute the rum this way: 3 parts white Cuban type to 1 of Jamaica. The aroma will be there and the full round Jamaica flavour too, but in a tempo inoffensive to the most rabid Jamaicaphobes.

THE CAFE de PARIS COCKTAIL from "MONTE," a PLACE WELL-MENTIONED ALREADY in OUR PREVIOUS VOLUME on FOODS; SAMPLED FIRST in 1931
To 1 jigger dry gin allow 1 tsp anis or anisette, ½ the white of an egg—very fresh please—and 1 tsp cream. Shake well and serve in the tall style cocktail glass with a stem. Ladies like it!

CASTLE HARBOUR SPECIAL, a MID-OCEAN COOLER from LOVELY BERMUDA
We've always loved the more outlying parts of this island since our first stay there of several weeks, back in 1928. In those days most of the islands in Castle Harbour were unsettled and we used to sail over there in a small boat, and swim the white and pink beaches in utter seclusion except for our companion, and the screaming nesting sea

birds. Gosling Brothers brought out the liquid necessaries to our little hotel, and here are the proportions. Mix the following in a bar glass: 4 small dices of ripe pineapple, the juice of 1 small green lime, 1 tsp grenadine, 1 tsp of sweet pineapple soda fountain syrup, add 1½ jiggers Barbados, Demerara, or Martinique rum, ½ jigger white Bacardi. Stir with a lump of ice and either strain out as-is, or better still —as we found—turn into a small goblet half filled with cracked ice. The pineapple syrup gives the touch, and grenadine may be omitted, to taste. We find the pineapple much more important as a sweetening agent, and there is no conflict of delicate tastes.

FIVE DELICIOUS CHAMPAGNE OPPORTUNITIES, which ARE not to be IGNORED

CHAMPAGNE COCKTAIL No. I, KNOWN as the MAHARAJAH's BURRA-PEG

The word *Burra* in Hindustani means "big," "important," or "big-time," as the case might be; and "peg" throughout Britaindom means a "drink"—more often than not a Scotch-and-soda. This particular champagne affair was broken out on the eve of our departure alone across India, after a month with Spofford in his big Calcutta bungalow show in the fashionable Ballygunge section down Chowringhee, beyond Lower Circular Road. This Burra-Peg is to the ordinary Champagne Cocktail what Helen of Troy was to a local shepherd maiden. . . . We got aboard the Bombay Mail with our tail between our legs and lunged across Central India, and later on found ourself in Jaipur —already mentioned in Melon, *Orientale,* Volume I. And here in this amazing town in Rajputana, with its modern government and 120 ft. wide streets, where tigers are protected so the Maharajah may shoot without fatiguing travel much beyond city limits, where we found Ambar—India's most marvellous deserted city—and got mixed up in the yearly Festival of the Sun, starting from the Gulta Pass, and with more elephants, *fakirs* and jugglers than a three ringed circus; here we found probably the lonesomest Standard Oil man we'd ever seen.

So we joined forces, and of evenings we would sit on the rooftop of his bungalow, and while the sun set through the sherry-brown dust cloud that broods over Central India throughout the dry season, would listen to the vain male peacock's scream, and watched the Rikki-tikki-tavis—or mongooses, or mongeese, or whatever the hell they choose to call those trim little animals that would sooner fight snakes than live—scuttling about their mongoosing business among the bushes in the garden. And we would sip various tall things, including—on Washington's birthday of course—a quartet of Champagne Burra-Pegs, and he would recount to us certain toothsome bits of "under-the-punkah" tales about Maharajahs and people; and how, actually, the young new one we'd just met preferred one wife to the regiment of 400 or so his dad had thoughtfully left him!

Duplicating our experience we suggest: the largest chilled goblet in sight, at least 14 oz, and 16 oz is better. Into this turn 2 jiggers of good well-chilled cognac, drop in a lump of sugar doused with Angostura, fill up with chilled dry champagne and garnish with a spiral of green lime peel.

CHAMPAGNE COCKTAIL No. II, which with MODESTLY DOWN-CAST LASH WE ADMIT Is an ORIGINATION of OUR OWN, & which WE CHRISTENED the "JIMMIE ROOSEVELT"

Last spring we had the pleasure of turning our house into an oasis, between planes, for Colonel Jimmie Roosevelt and Grant Mason of the Civil Aeronautics Commission. No citizen—Republican, Democrat, Socialist, Townsendite, or any other political breed, can meet Jimmie and not at once be taken with his smile, his sense of humour and affable charm. It was warmish, and being a sort of Nephew-in-Law of Paul Garrett, dean of all American Vintners, and present "father" of Virginia Dare, we brought out 2 chilled bottles of Garrett Champagne, and created this one.

Fill a big 16 oz *thin* crystal goblet with finely cracked ice. In the diametrical center of this frosty mass went a lump of sugar well saturated with Angostura, then 2 jiggers of good French cognac, then fill the glass with chilled champagne, finally floating on very carefully 2 tbsp of genuine green Chartreuse—no pineapple, no mint sprig, no cherry garnish. It is cooling, refreshing, invigorating, a delight to eye and palate.

CHAMPAGNE COCKTAIL No. III, in the Charming Style of the Jocky Club in Rio de Janeiro

Choose a large tapering champagne cocktail glass; inside of this build a tower of 4 ice cubes, crown it with a lump of sugar saturated with 4 dashes of orange bitters. Against the sides of the glass lean 2 sticks of ripe fresh pineapple, encircle the ice tower with a spiral of green lime peel, and fill with well chilled champagne, medium dry, and not too acid in type. Now as the crowning gesture carefully float on 1 tbsp of cointreau.

CHAMPAGNE COCKTAIL No. IV, the Correct Name of which Is the Imperial Cossack *CRUSTA,* and One of the Most Startling & Intriguing Drinks in the Far East

We stumbled into this classic, as we did several other items of precious interest, in the French Concession of Shanghai long before the days of undeclared wars, and at the house of a friend whose name it is not seasonable to mention. It is an expensive cocktail as cocktails march, but now and again we find occasion to celebrate this thing or that, and no guest can fail to be favourably impressed by the appearance, size and taste of this formula—which came out of White Russia when Russia was Russia—and Kolchak wasn't retreating in Siberia ahead of that breaking tide of Reds; the prey of cowardice, politics and corruption.

Take a large champagne cocktail glass, and ice it well. Split a green lime, or lemon, lengthwise and rub its combined oils and juices over the whole inside of the crystal, and then on out and down a full ½″ below the rim. First dip this lip into powdered sugar, then fill the whole glass with the sugar—emptying it out and permitting what sticks to remain. . . . Now add 2 dashes of orange bitters, 1 jigger of cognac and ½ that of kümmel, stirring for a moment in a bar glass with 3 ice cubes. Empty this into the goblet, fill with chilled dry champagne, toss in a scarlet rose petal and think of slender, pliable Russian Princesses and things!

*ILE de FRANCE* SPECIAL, Being Champagne Cocktail No. V

The bar *maitre,* one Reynauld, on this somewhat amazing craft has found that picker-uppers have to be even better than putter-downers the night before. Long devotion to his art has evolved this delicate appeal to the intellect, thus causing the numbed nerve centers to nod closer and closer together until they, at long last, touch—and the day is begun!

Into a large champagne glass put a half teaspoon fine sugar, a half pony of good cognac, fill with very cold dry champagne, and top off with a dash or two of yellow Chartreuse. The pungent herbs greet the nostrils, then the cool quenching of the viney bubbly. . . . This being passed along by an Ile de France habitual crosser, and not from the usual personal imbibition, naturally arouses our suggestion that two dashes of any good bitters would help tone the inner man—orange preferred—and not injure flavour or bouquet in any manner.

WORDS to the DRINKING WISE No. VI, EMPHASIZING the SPECIAL NEED for the CHILLING of GLASSES in MAKING any CHAMPAGNE COCKTAIL

One of the sharp charms of this drink is its icy coldness. The glass itself makes an efficient radiator, drawing much more heat against the liquid than the ordinary sized cocktail glasses. Therefore let's always chill our glasses. Warm champagne is a foetid thing, of brassy taste, astringent to the throat, an insult to the nostrils. Also never use tumblers for champagne cocktails, use stemmed goblets or champagne cocktail glasses. The heat of the hand soon warms a tumbler's contents.

CHAMPAGNE VELVET No. I, Being the "Meriveles" from the Manila Polo Club

Meriveles is an extinct volcanic peak cooling its heels across Manila

Bay to the westward, and when they set the tables out on the grass terrace just before sunset the gunsight notch in the dead crater frames the sun. It is a pleasant spot, this terrace, one of the loveliest, in fact, in all the tropics. For there is always a bit of breeze, the shaded lights lend an air of intimacy to each rendezvous of the moment—and man how they do rendezvous in those island tropics! There is even a miles-long plume of bats that exit from some distant mountain cave, and drift like a strand of smoke across the far off sky. The Polo Club not only produces crisp polo between service and civilian teams, but has always taken especial pride in the precision, the quality and service of its drinks. As Monk Antrim once said, "This Meriveles Velvet is an expensive sort of drink, but when you think everything over, it's worth it!" It will save life, nourish, encourage and induce sleep in insomniacs.

Chill dry champagne well, chill a bottle of Guinness Stout. Get a big goblet and pour these two liquids in 'arf-and-'arf. Stir gently, and there we have it.

CHAMPAGNE VELVET, à la MARMION, INVENTED ONE MEMO-RABLE CRUISE up LONG ISLAND SOUND to the CUP RACES off NEWPORT in the YEAR 1934
Repeat this same process only use Bass Ale instead of the heavier, more bitter Guinness. Chill everything very cold.

THE PARISIAN CHERRY RIPE, ONE of the VERY FEW FRENCH COCKTAIL INVENTIONS worth ITS MEASURING TIME
This one we met eye to eye, and under circumstances not relevant to this work, on returning through the Bois de Boulogne from a view at the current vintage of Davis Cup tennis, not so long ago. It is po-tent, dependable, but one of the most foetid conceptions ever to come out of shaker when served improperly chilled—for then it is vilely sweet. Chill long and vigorously. . . . Take a jigger of dry gin, and half that both of *kirsch,* and cherry brandy of the French type. Better mix with shaved ice and put in The Mixer. Float 1 tsp cherry brandy

on top of the frozen product. Garnish with 1 green and 1 red maraschino cherry. Delicious and pretty, both at the same time.

THE COLONIAL COOLER, which We Met in Sandakan, British North Borneo, Some Fourteen Years Back

The water was so shoal there that the big steamer had to anchor fourteen miles out, and the two main motor lifeboats were lowered, and started towing the regular lifeboats. And after half an hour running both motors conked out, and a Borneo *prahu* with a sail like a striped butterfly and a gent in a G-string and a headdress that looked exactly like an American overseas cap, only made out of wine coloured velvet, was squatting right on top of the blunt, low mast supporting the big lateen sail, and the thing steering itself. Somehow we managed to convey the idea that we were not wallowing there on a glassy sea with a molten brass sun striking like a sword across our necks, because we wanted to. So he disappeared down wind and then two hours later a stuffy little British North Borneo Company tug came out and saved the day, and pretty soon we saw the raw, red cliffs back of Sandakan, and landed in a maze of godowns and Chinese "Loan Farms"—pawn shops to America—and fantan dives.

We first went out to the Sandakan Club—there'd be a British Club on Mount Everest if 2 Britishers could stand the cold there!—and had these Coolers, through courtesy of an American who was sentimental enough to fetch a mint root out with him. Then our last and most vivid memory, outside of the headstones in the little cemetery listing the violent causes of death—cobra bite, blow-pipe arrows tipped with gum from the deadly *ipoh* tree, fever, cholera—was the 12 foot hamadryad, or king cobra,—stuffed thank God!—in the museum. This thing had a head as big as a tennis racquet and with enough coil to strike there was still six feet of him off the floor—staring us coldly in the eye.

To 1 jigger of dry gin add the same of Italian vermouth. To this base donate 1 dash each of Angostura and Amer Picon, and 1 tsp of orange Curaçao. Stir with a goodly lump of ice in a small highball or sour glass, and top off with a squirt of soda, garnished with 2 sprigs of mint and a stick of ripe pineapple.

CREOLE CONTENTMENT, an INSIDIOUS PLEASANTRY from that CHARMING HOT-BED of INTRIGUE & CULTURE which Is the PULSE of the GREAT DELTA COUNTRY—NEW ORLEANS

This hazard and liability to consistent maidenhood came to our desk through office of a friend whose father once was Episcopal Bishop of Washington, and who writes books about pirates. Don't treat this one lightly, *mes amis.* . . .

Of cognac, Madeira wine and maraschino, take 1 pony each; turn this into a bar glass with ice; toss in 1 dash of orange bitters, stir well, pour into a big Manhattan glass or saucer type champagne, and garnish with 3 maraschino cherries: red, green and white. . . . Our personal experience is that it is better to cut the maraschino down by half, stepping up the cognac in that ratio. That business of the 3 cherries, while no doubt a pretty and chivalrous gesture to the feminine victim is, of course, sheerest swank. It is a good drink and needs little trimming.

THE *CUBA LIBRE*—or "FREE CUBA"—ANALYZED & IMPROVED

This native Island concoction started by accident and has caught on everywhere throughout the south, has filtered through the north and west. Last summer, for instance, we ran into Kooba Lee-brays 5000 feet up in the North Carolina Mountains at High Hampton, the year before in Mexico City and Seattle. Last week in Palm Beach and Cat Cay. The only trouble with the drink is that it started by accident and without imagination, has been carried along by the ease of its supply. Under any condition it is too sweet.

What's to do? . . . After clinical experimenting for which our insurance carriers heartily dislike us, we tested several variations of the original, with this result: the Improved *Cuba Libre* consists of 1 big jigger of *Carta de Oro* Bacardi, the juice of 1 small green lime, and the lime peel after squeezing. Put in a Tom Collins glass, muddle well to get oil worked up over sides of the glass, add lots of ice lumps, and fill up with a bottle of chilled coca cola. Stir up once, and *salud y pesetas!*

THE BAKER *CUBA REFORMÉ,* an ORIGINATION with the AU-THOR, which WE HAVE TRANSMITTED WARILY to OUR FRIEND VESEY RAINWATER, WHO AMOUNTS to THINGS in COCA COLA, & which WAS PRONOUNCED GOOD

While not an exotic from Singapore, any drink originated after a Miami-Nassau Ocean Yacht Race that ended up with all sails blown out in a gale and lying stormbound for a week back of Cat Cay, is possessed of its own spurs in any company, we believe.

Fill a big goblet with very finely cracked ice, turn in 2 jiggers of good imported sloe gin, add the juice and spiral peel of 1 green lime—then stir vigorously to work the rind oil about, and fill with all the coca cola the glass will hold. A mild and delicious cooler, but is sweet enough that it *must be very cold indeed* to be good.

THE CUERNAVACA SPECIAL, from the FILES of ONE MANUEL who PRESIDES behind MAHOGANY at the HOTEL de la SILVA CASINO BAR

As we have indicated, Cuernavaca is Mexico City's summer resort for people who matter, a habit begun by Cortez himself after the conquest; and here small modern palaces rub elbows with 16th Century affairs built by the great Conquistador. Hotel de la Silva, until President Cardenas took the reins, was an unbelievable Mexican Monte Carlo—an incredible place of *moderne* cellophane drapes, exotic murals—*not* by Diego Rivera, praise be!—a vast pool of limpid mountain water outside for swimming, and roulette wheels, and every known device for acquisition of cash, inside. Manuel talks of the good old days now, but he has a twinkle in his eye, and originated this bit of genius as he expressed it—*por los señoras.* It is a nicer drink than the old favourite Pink Lady. Test it out next time.

Take 1 jigger each of cognac and dry French vermouth and put in a shaker with 2 tsp of *Crème de Cacao,* 1 or 2 tsp of grenadine to taste; the white of 1 fresh egg and 1 tsp of thick cream. Shake hard and pour into a big Manhattan glass letting a little of it foam prettily over lip of the glass. Garnish with sprigs of tender mint, hang a split red maraschino cherry over the glass edge too. Take 2 short scarlet cellophane straws, touch their lower ends onto the glass foot and press the top ends against the overflowed foam where they stick cleverly to the outside of the glass. A nice gesture with all fancy cream-egg cocktails, too, by the way.

WORDS to the WISE No. VII, OFFERING up an EARNEST PLEA for RECENTNESS in ALL EGGS to BE USED in COCK-TAILS or DRINKS of any KIND, for that MATTER

A stale or storage egg in a decent mixed drink is like a stale or storage joke in critical and intelligent company. Eschew them rabidly. If really fresh eggs can't be had, mix other type drinks, for the result will reflect no merit round the hearth, no matter how hospitable it may be.

*DAISY de SANTIAGO,* a LOVELY THING INTRODUCED to Us through the GRACIOUS OFFICES of the LATE FACUNO BACARDI, of LAMENTED MEMORY

The Bacardi people were always mighty nice about taking visiting yachtsmen and other travelers through their factory, and the result was always amazingly gratifying in several ways. As many of us know they have erected a special small skyscraper in Havana, too, where visitors may go for free Bacardi drinks, and we must confess that our name appears in four places on pages of their guest book in a brilliant modern bar smart enough to make New York jealous. To our mind, along with the immortal Daiquiri, this is the best Bacardi drink on record.

Take a big thin goblet and fill to the brim with shaved ice. Take a bar glass and put in 1½ jiggers Bacardi, the strained juice of 1 green lime, 1 to 1½ tsp of bar syrup, optional. Stir well and pour onto the ice, stir up once, garnish with green mint and fresh fruit, and float on

½ jigger of *yellow* Chartreuse. Personally we find the Chartreuse brings all the sweetening we need, and a squirt of charged water adds a sparkle. A lovely thing indeed.

AND NOW, *MESSIEURS et MESDAMES,* the One & Only Tropi-cal Daiquiri

We honestly believe that more people have boasted about the origin of this happy thought than any modern drink. We have had to smile quietly on at least 4 occasions; once overhearing 3 Cuban gentlemen who had never been out of Havana, 1 alleged German title on a West Indies Cruise, 1 Racquet Club Member on a fishing trip—why is it that so many German alleged titles and fancy club members seem to talk very loud and authoritatively?—and 2 female frequenters of the New York Colony Club. All of these assorted folk either had helped invent this drink or had been like *THAT* with the ones who had in-vented it!

The whole business is tommyrot, unless these persons knew a cer-tain 2 officials of the Yankee-run Cuban mining firm taken over dur-ing the great war by Bethlehem Steel, and which operated in the mountains not too far out of Santiago de Cuba, where the firm of *Bacardi y Cia.,* had, and has, its being. The invention was simple, as so many good things in life are simple, and right smack after the Span-ish-American war, too. In those days not 1 American in 10,000 had ever heard of *Ron Bacardi,* much less invented drinks with it.

There was fever. Doctors still thought that a lot of yellowjack malaria cases came from drinking water and swamp mists. They couldn't turn off the swamp mists but they knew that diluted alcohol was a disinfectant against germs. So they put a little rum in their boiled drinking water. This tasted pretty bad so some bright citizen squeezed a lime into the thing, and a little sugar to modify the acid. Ice made from distilled water took the tropical blood heat off the thing. The 2 originators were my friend Harry E. Stout, now domi-ciled in Englewood, New Jersey, and a mining engineer associate, Mr. Jennings Cox. TIME: summer of 1898. PLACE: Daiquiri, a village near Santiago and the Bacardi plant, Cuba. Hence the name "Daiquiri."

Like the Martini, Manhattan, Side Car and other immortals, the Daiquiri marched straight around the world, and we have tried them in many places and circumstances—including the old Plaza, the Habana Yacht Club, Country Club, Hotel Nacional—between revolutionary bombings—Sloppy Joe's, La Florida, the Bacardi Building, and factory in Santiago; and other spots in Cuba. In spite of all the loud speeches on the subject we claim there is no "best" place for Daiquiris. The only thing that can go wrong, besides insufficient chilling, is that it is often made too sweet. Technique progressed from the days of drinking with 1 lump of ice in a tumbler, to the flute cocktail glass with the finely cracked ice left in; then came the electric vibrator mixer and the screen strainer to improve the thing further —and it became called the "Tropical" Daiquiri. Now that The Mixer is available, it frosts beautifully, in a few seconds.

The original Harry Stout–Jennings Cox mixture for the Original Cuban Daiquiri was: 1 whisky glass level full of *Carta Blanca,* or *Carta de Oro* Bacardi rum, 2 tsp of sugar, the juice of 1½ *small* green limes—strained; and very finely cracked ice.

Either shake very hard with finely cracked ice and pour ice and all into a tall flute cocktail glass, or put the same things into The Mixer, and let frost into the delicious sherbet consistency we so admire nowadays. . . . Never use lemon juice. And remember please, that a too-sweet Daiquiri is like a lovely lady with too much perfume. Sugar should be cut down to 1 tsp, to our belief, and a Manhattan glass is less likely to tip over, in steady service!

ERNEST HEMINGWAY'S REVIVER on Mornings after Anything, Made of Hollands & other Things, which We Called "Death in the Gulf Stream," but Found Most Valuable

Drinking Holland gin drinks is like the fanciful *cliché* about eating olives—when you like one you always like them. For many years we had hated the stuff with a passion, holding its taste to be like fermented radishes mixed with spirits of turpentine. One January 2 years back we took *MARMION* in a howling no'theaster along with the, then, 4 year bride, a companion, and an insane steward, and pointed her down to Key West to get some receipts from Hemingway for the cookery book. We fished the Gulf Stream by day, and ate and drank and talked half the night. Even by the second day we were withering slightly on vine, and along with raw conch salad, or "souse," listed in *Volume I,* we got Hemingway's other picker-upper, and liked it.

Take a tall thin water tumbler and fill it with finely cracked ice. Lace this broken debris with 4 good purple splashes of Angostura, add the juice and crushed peel of 1 green lime, and fill glass almost full with Holland gin. . . . No sugar, no fancying. It's strong, it's bitter—but so is English ale strong and bitter, in many cases. We don't add sugar to ale, and we don't need sugar in a Death in the Gulf Stream—or at least not more than 1 tsp. Its tartness and its bitterness are its chief charm. It is reviving and refreshing; cools the blood and inspires renewed interest in food, companions and life.

## FRITZ—FREDERICK ABILDGAARD & *ALONE-in-the-CAR-IBBEAN*—FENGER'S DOMINICA *TOPET*

When Fritz was sailing his sliver-size canoe *YACKABOO* and making his 50 and 60 mile open water ocean hops from Trinidad up to the Virgin Islands, he annexed this liquid threat to his log book; and double checked during the cruise of *DIABLESSE* several years later. "This drink," Fritz shouted with his fanatical look, which is a combination of a revivalist preacher and a cloven hoofed satyr, "is a drink for those of not too Scotch descent, and detailed instructions may be deciphered on Page 243 of *The Cruise of the Diablesse* (Adv.). So to fabricate 4 *Topets:*

"Take 5 ponies of any good medium dark rum, and in this soak the spiral of a sizeable green lime, muddling about to extract the essential oils. Now add an equal part of cold water, and the strained juice of the lime. Next put ½ tsp *gomme* syrup in each glass. Now carefully flow in the lime-rum mix, being careful to float it on so it doesn't blend with syrup. More carefully still flow on the Angostura bitters—at least a good ⅛" thick on top of everything. . . . It is a sort of Pousse Cafe in appearance, but far more artistic in results, and in the island of British Dominica it is served as an appetizer, before a good dinner, by the discriminating.

EAST INDIA COCKTAIL, which CAME to OUR DEVOTED ATTENTION also in FIRPO's, in CALCUTTA

It is mild and appetite-inspiring in hot weather, and is now known everywhere, but we append it just the same. Into a bar glass turn 1 jigger each of dry French vermouth and really good *really dry* sherry —the usual sweet American sherry just won't serve. Add 2 dashes of orange bitters, plenty of big-lump ice, then stir with a bar spoon and turn into a Manhattan glass. Garnish with green cherry or not, to preference.

THE EAST INDIA HOUSE COCKTAIL, BEING ONE for ANY MAN's BOOK, & GARNERED in THE ROYAL BOMBAY YACHT CLUB, INDIA, 1932, while the—then—FIANCÉE SIGHT-SAW across INDIA to DELHI, AGRA, BENARES & FATEHPUR SIKRI, & CALCUTTA

Take 1½ jiggers of cognac, 1 tsp pineapple syrup—the soda fountain kind—and put in a shaker. Add 2/3 tsp maraschino, 1 tsp orange Curaçao, 3 dashes of orange or Angostura bitters, according to preference. Shake with lots of fine ice and strain into a Manhattan glass, twisting a bit of lime peel on at the last.

THE CLAN McGREGOR EGG NOGG, BEING a LOVELY, FORCEFUL THING BASED on BRANDY, BACARDI, & FINE OLD SHERRY, from SCOTLAND

There are a hundred and one Egg Noggs about the world, and many of them already set between the covers of books, but this Scottish institution was rare enough to be the only one we include in this collection of exotica. It is a milder mix, which we consider a blessing.

Also, having no cream, it is more refreshing and not so likely to be gastrically disastrous as the over-rich customary formulae we have consumed on certain festive occasions.

This mixture needs simply to be multiplied for any company, and serve in thin 12 oz goblets, not the usual thick punch cups. . . . ½ pony of good cognac, 2 ponies of good Spanish *dry* sherry, ¼ pony of *Carta de Oro* Bacardi; 1 tsp or so of sugar, to taste, the yolk of an egg and 1 cup or so of chilled milk. . . . First put egg and sugar into the bar glass and beat well, then add spirits and 4 lumps of ice. Stir or shake briskly, strain into goblet, add cold milk and dust both nutmeg and cinnamon on top.

A FAREWELL to HEMINGWAY, Being a Sort of *KIRSCH* Collins We Invented on the Night We Saw Hemingway & Bull-fighter Sidney Franklin off on the Plane for New York, & Loyal-ist Spain

There is no reason to this drink. It just happened because Ernest prefers *kirschwasser,* and it was a muggy, half-breathless sort of night. The cherry syrup sweet, of course, can be varied to taste. . . . Take 1½ jiggers of *kirsch,* ¼ pony of cherry syrup—again the drug store kind—and the juice of 1 big green lime. Shake this mixture with 4 ice cubes, turn ice and all into a collins glass of at least 14 oz capacity, drop in a spiral peel of green lime, and fill glass not quite full with good chilled club soda. . . . We've later found that raspberry syrup is very decent, also.

MEXICAN "FIRING SQUAD" SPECIAL, which Is a Creation We Almost Became Wrecked upon in—of All Spots—*LA CUCU-RACHA* Bar, in Mexico City, in 1937

Now and again we found ourselves just a little fed up with rather casual Mexican mixes, and the guidance of 2 young Mexican *cabal-leros* whose parents mattered in official circles in that city of Mexico. We were herded into fancy, rather dull places, served too warm drinks. And finally on 1 occasion we broke off by ourself, sought out this bar,

—where an aristocrat native oughtn't to be seen!—ordered things in our own way.

This drink is based on *tequila,* top-flight distillation of the *Maguey* plant. Use a tall collins glass and snap fingers at the consequences. . . . Take 2 jiggers of *tequila,* being sure to purchase a good brand, for there are many raw distillations. Add the juice of 2 small limes, 1½ to 2 tsp of grenadine, or plain *gomme* syrup. Add 2 dashes of Angostura bitters. Chill the glass, pack with finely cracked ice, turn in the mixture and garnish with slice of orange, 1 of pineapple and a red cherry.

THE COLOMBO "FLYING FISH" which WAS TAKEN into the FOLD on a MEMORABLE NIGHT in CEYLON, under CIRCUMSTANCES PARTLY RELEVANT to MENTION, & already FRACTIONALLY DESCRIBED in the FOREWORD to this VOLUME

Take 1 jigger of dry gin, put in 1 dash of peach bitters, ½ pony of yellow Curaçao, ½ tsp of maraschino; then shake with plenty of cracked ice and serve with proper flourish in a Manhattan glass, garnished with a slice of orange. We have found that when peach bitters are not too readily available that a parallel, and most delicious alternative is to ignore the Curaçao and bitters idea entirely, substituting ½ pony of Cordial Médoc—a lovely French liqueur based on peach pits and other delicate Gallic interpretations. It is readily procurable at any spirits shop, and Americans should make its acquaintance—not merely stopping with benedictine and cointreau.

THE SPANISH ORANGE FLOWER COOLER, or *REFRESCO,* CALLED *FLOR de NARANJA, SEVILLAÑO*

From lovely Seville.

Oranges aren't absolutely essential, as fresh grapefruit juice will do —provided we carefully add what nature lacks in sweetening. Actually it is a modern Sevillian origination along the American cocktail route, and isn't bad at that. Use a 2 oz jigger, not one of those scant

1½ oz affairs which squeezes four or five extra drinks out of every bottle for our up-to-date barkeeps!

| | |
|---|---|
| Chill glasses, dampen edge and dip in powdered sugar | 2 jiggers dry gin |
| | 2 tsp orange flower water |
| Put a small spiral of orange peel in each | Sugar to taste |
| | Juice of 2 oranges |

Use pretty large glasses, as the ice must do a bit of diluting for us. Fill large shaker with lots of ice; frappe vigorously. Pour out and twist a bit of peel over each to add the fragrance of flavour of the essential oils to the ensemble.

THE FOURTH REGIMENT COCKTAIL, Brought to Our Amazed Attention by One Commander Livesey, in Command of One of His Majesty's Dapper Little Sloops of War, out in Bombay, A.D. 1931

This, we discovered finally, was merely a Manhattan Cocktail made in 4 oz size, spiced with 1 dash each of celery, Angostura and orange bitters—but why the last was included we never have understood as the Angostura dominates. Chill very cold and garnish with a twist of green lime peel squeezed so as to deposit oil upon the waters after the drink is poured.

LA FRAISE d'AMOUR, another Tentative Adventurous Offering from One of those Quiet Spots in the Bois de Boulogne, Referred to before, from Time to Time

Another spring, it was in 1926, we sat out under the trees and dined and danced and discussed matters that were old when Marie Antoinette rode to the guillotine in her tragic tumbril, or when du Barry passed in her royal carriage. This Fraise d'Amour, my dear friends, is not a woman's drink in the usual concept of the word; but, on occasion, can be very apt to a charming lady. It is a deceiver; mild-tasting, insidious, slow to act, but thorough at the last!

Into a bar glass put 1 pony of fresh ripe strawberry juice after being strained. Add 2 dashes of maraschino, 1 dash of orange bitters, then 1½ jiggers of good cognac. Stir and pour into a thin crystal goblet—not too large—filled with shaved ice, stir once and garnish with 1 dead-ripe strawberry teed up in the precise center.

GABY des LYS COCKTAIL, One from Old New York Pre-Prohibition Days when Diamond Jim Brady Was Alive, & the Winter Garden Was New York's only Smoking Theatre, and the Immortal Gaby Was Playing with Al Jolson & Harry Pilcer

Gaby the lovely, Gaby the delightfully mad, Gaby the free soul—who died too young and gave a fortune in pearls to the Paris poor! Gaby is gone, and Bustanoby's old Beaux Arts is gone, and the first Rector's is a memory, but her memory marches on—and this cocktail named in her honour.

It is very simple, crisp. To 1 jigger of good dry gin add ½ pony of orgeat syrup and 1 tsp of absinthe, or a trifle less. Frappe very cold indeed or it will tend to over-sweetness, and serve in a Manhattan glass.

THE FAR EASTERN GIMLET, Classic Now All over the Orient—from Bombay to Hongkong, & Further

Why on earth this stroke of genius stands unheralded and unsung in this fair and allegedly free land of ours shall, to us, always be a mystery like who it is that designs expensive radio cabinets, why all cinema stars long to ruin themselves playing highbrow roles, and why good prize fighters want to write fiction. . . . Throughout the whole swing of the Far East, starting with Bombay—down the Malabar Coast to Colombo; to Penang, Singapore, Hongkong and Shanghai, the Gimlet is just as well known as our Martini here.

The main thing in its favour is that, unlike most cocktails, it is not "warming" in hot weather, and in fact is a good cooler. It is simple, without fancy fizzings, and is one to experiment with until the precise amount of lime cordial is found, to taste. . . . This last is a British invention based on a similar essence to Rose's Lime Juice—which comes in the slender decorative bottle we see back of most good soda fountains—but is not quite so pungent. Soda fountain lime syrup also would do in a pinch. We have approximated it with fine results by diluting it with equal amounts of water. . . . Take a big saucer champagne glass, put in 1 jigger either of dry or old Tom gin, 1 tsp *gomme* syrup or sugar, ½ tsp—to taste—of lime syrup or lime cordial. Fill up with chilled plain water, add 1 ice cube and thin slice of big green lime. Don't use soda water, please.

GIN & BITTERS, the GIN *PAHIT*—PRONOUNCED *PIE-EET*—of JAVA, the "PINK GIN" of INDIA & POINTS EASTWARD where BRITANNIA RULES

This of course has long since gone round the world, but it forms such an important part of men's drinking life in the colonies that we append it here. Either dry or old Tom gin is proper, and the latter appeals most to us. Take a thin, stemmed cocktail glass. Shake in 4 or 5 dashes of Angostura, tip the glass like the tower of Pisa and twirl it between thumb and fingers. Whatever Angostura sticks to the glass through capillary attraction is precisely the right amount, although a lot of old India hands whose stomachs are lax find that a lot more Angostura than that is in order to stimulate appetite. Gently pour off the extra bitters that do not cling. Fill glass with gin. That's all. Superfluous bitters go back in the bottle, on the floor, or out the port hole or window—depending upon who, where and what we are.

## COMMANDER LIVESEY'S *GIN-BLIND*

We shall never forget the courteous open-hearted wardroom hospitality of the British navy in Indian waters, and Commander Livesey —together with his charming Australian wife—least of all. Along with another very mentionable discovery Livesey's head-bearer—a High-Caste high-binder in the Mohammedan priesthood on feast days, was a wizard with the shaker. . . . Livesey's words were: "We don't prescribe this just before target practice, gentlemen."

Gin, 6                           Curaçao, 3
Good cognac, 2                   Orange bitters, dash

Mix with lots of ice, shake vigorously and serve in a Manhattan glass. A twist of yellow orange peel is optional, to add oil.

GIN & QUININE WATER, or "GIN & TONIC"—ORIGINATED to COMBAT FEVERS, REAL or ALLEGED, & which LATER BECAME an ESTABLISHED DRINK in INDIA & the TROPICAL BRITISH EAST, & STILL LATER BECAME ACCEPTED over HERE by AMERICAN HOSTS WHO WANTED to IMPRESS FOLK with HAVING COMBED the ORIENT

This is merely a gin highball, using dry or old Tom gin—either 1 or 1½ jiggers—and filled up with chilled quinine tonic water. All Americans, and some Britishers not so hidebound as to insist on brassy, half-warm drinks, added 2 lumps of ice, and a twist of lime peel. We like the latter style better, but must warn all those who embrace this drink to remember it is a medicine and not primarily a stimulant only. On more than one occasion we have temporarily showed aberration on this subject, with the result that our ears rang unmercifully and next day we felt like Rameses II, réchauffé. We suggest from 2 to 4 drinks of gin and tonic as being plenty for any one sitting.

GIN FIZZES, to the NUMBER or ELEVEN, which SHALL BE REMEMBERED LONG after THEIR SPONSORS ARE DEAD & GONE, & WHOSE GENIUS WE RANK alongside that of the INVENTORS of the MINT JULEP, & other TRULY IMMORTAL DISCOVERIES

FIRST of ALL the AZIZ SPECIAL, BEING the IMPECCABLE GIN FIZZ of AZIZ EFFENDI, MONITOR of the ONE & ONLY WINTER PALACE HOTEL, which IS in LOUCQSOR, in EGYPT, up the NILE FOUR HUNDRED EIGHTEEN ENGLISH MILES by RAIL, & FOUR HUNDRED FIFTY by DAHABEAH

Those of us who have journeyed up the East Bank of the Nile by train, Imperial Airways flying boat, or *dahabeah*—one of those odd, romantic looking and amazingly luxurious river sailing craft with their pointed lateen sails curving half moon style against the cloudless sky—to Loucqsor know the Winter Palace and Aziz Effendi; know his superb gin fizz. It is a wonderful thing to sit on the terrace of a wine-clear evening, pleasantly wearied from a day of marveling in incredible Karnak, and after our drive in a carriage down the Avenue of the Sphinxes, with a 14 oz example of Aziz' art in our hands. Actually what he has done is to take the original New Orleans Silver Fizz, and through meticulous chilling and the use of fine Schweppes club soda instead of carbonated city-main water, has immortalized the thing like a graceful imported, expatriated, work of art, and set it up again in the Valley of the Nile. It may be commanded with London dry gin or old Tom—to your wishes. The orange flower water is stepped up probably because the whole amazing East adapts perfume to many more uses than the American office of making lovely ladies smell like bowers of roses. . . . Using a big glass the call is for more gin than usual.

Put 1 to 1½ tsp of sugar into the shaker, add 2 jiggers of dry or old Tom gin—to preference—the juice of 1 small lemon, 1 pony of thick cream and 1 tbsp of fresh egg white. Put in lots of finely cracked ice, *shake hard and long,* turn into a big goblet leaving a few ice lumps floating. Add 2 or 3 good dashes of orange flower water. Now fill up with chilled Number 1 grade club soda. Stir once. Serve immediately and drink soon thereafter, since no gin fizz gains virtue even from brief neglect.

THE BIRD of PARADISE, a Colourful, Eye-Filling Experience We Found in Signing Our Names to the Book at the *STRANGERS CLUB*, Colon, Panama

This strange little club has many famous names in its logbook, Robinson of the *SVAAP*, Alain Gerbault, poor Dick Halliburton whom we first met in Singapore before he flew to Sarawak in 1932, sitting at table with Ruth Elder and Walter Camp. We always have found a welcome there during the 10 or 1 doz times we have been in the "Zone" going west to east or vice versa. . . . Actually this Bird of Paradise Fizz is Aziz' Special to which 2 to 3 tsp of raspberry syrup have been added instead of the sugar, and juice of 1½ limes instead of the lemon. Float on a red rose petal, or any scarlet small tropical blossom, like bougainvillea, as a final garnish. *Shake hard and long.*

THE CREOLE FIZZ, Being a Latter Day Hot Weather & Milder Variation of the Original New Orleans Silver Fizz, & Employing Sloe Gin to Lend Its Shy Blush to the Colour Scheme

Lyle Saxon gave us this one away back in 1930 during a visit to New York, telling us about his acquisition of the old French Creole house on Royal Street. . . . Take either the Aziz Special or New Orleans Fizz and substitute an equal amount of good imported sloe gin, and cutting cream down a trifle. Garnish with a sprig of fresh green mint and that's all.

THE GIN FIZZ *TROPICAL,* Being One More Sound Bit of Liquid Nourishment from where, to Our Routine Mind, Exists the Best & Most Consistent Group of Mixed Drinks—& Mixed Drinks Mixers—on Earth: Manila, P.I.

This again is an affair based on the New Orleans Fizz background but using pineapple syrup up to 3 tsp instead of sugar, and juice from 1½ green limes instead of lemon. Jim Steele introduced us to this one—he's Tourist Association head for the Islands—on our trip to the Pagsanjan—pronounced "pack-san-han"—River for the dugout canoe trip down the rapids through a stupendous wild mill-race flung through a rocky gorge of towering walls hung with weird tropical growths, peopled with gibbering monkeys and vivid unnameable birds; a feat for which we now possess a fine illuminated parchment diploma. Thermos carafes, ice cubes, hampers of civilized fodder both liquid and solid, made odd contrast to all of this primeval setting, to the native boatmen—2 to a canoe. Fresh green mint is the garnish, a few tender leaves, recently broken off and stuck in a round and fragrant rosette there right under the drinker's nose. Don't use a straw; the closer the mint comes the nicer.

## THE MID-OCEAN HIGHBALL, which CONTRARY to NATIVE TITLE IS a LEGITIMATE FIZZ, BEING an EXOTIC from BERMUDA

Not so long ago we went to this charming island with St. Georges as a base camp. We pedalled, sailed, fished and golfed. Swam naked as Adam off small isolated islands with beaches like faintly rose-tinted granulated sugar. The Mid-Ocean Country Club had a gentleman back of mahogany who, then at least, took his art seriously. Actually he called it a "cocktail." Burt MacBride—Associate Editor of *Cosmopolitan*—who flew down on the first Bermuda Clipper with Pan-American Airways and first told us about the drink, called it a "highball," but in spite of this odds-on risk we call it a "fizz" still.

Take 1 jigger of old Tom gin, and ½ jigger each of cognac and French dry vermouth. Donate 2 dashes of orange bitters. Shake well with cracked ice, strain into a highball glass and add chilled club soda to taste. Twist on a bit of green lime peel.

## THE NEW ORLEANS ORIGINAL GOLDEN FIZZ

This is simply the usual New Orleans Silver Fizz, only instead of using egg white the yolk of 1 egg is used; or a whole, quite small, egg. Fresh eggs are imperative, let us repeat.

## NEW ORLEANS FIZZ No. I, with DRY GIN & a TOUCH of *KIRSCHWASSER*

This, to our mind, is the best New Orleans Fizz of the original type. It also may be used with old Tom gin, of course. . . . Take 1½ jiggers of gin, 1 pony of thick cream, the white of an egg, juice of ½ lemon, 1 to 1½ tsp sugar and 1 tsp *kirsch*. Shake hard in lots of cracked ice, strain into goblet and top off with chilled club soda, or seltzer, to taste. Orange flower water of course is optional. We feel that where *kirsch* is used that the two bouquets will neutralize each other. *So omit the orange flower water if kirsch is mixed with the drink, use it when not.*

THE AMER PICON "POUFFLE" FIZZ, Something Native Originally to Paris, & Encountered at the Cafe du Dome, where in Spite of the American Inundation of Pseudo-Bohemians Is Still a Moderately Consistent Rendezvous for other Americans over There Who Do Things with Their Brains & Hands

Simply turn 1 to 1½ jiggers of Amer Picon into a shaker, add lots of cracked ice, the white of 1 fresh egg, ½ jigger of grenadine, shake, then turn everything into a big thin goblet and fill up with club soda to suit taste. This is a fine stomachic, and inspires interest in foods.

THE ORIGINAL GIN FIZZ which Was Long a Secret of the Brothers Ramos, and which Was Given out by Them, in a Fit of Generous Aberration during Our Alleged & Ridiculous Drouth of the Prohibition Era

The Ramos Fizz has long been synonymous with the finest in all the New Orleans art. Thinking that the formula, like any history dealing with the dead arts, should be engraved on the tablets of history, it was given to the world after the now rejuvenated Ramos bar closed for the "dry" era. The main secret of excellence was the platoon of 8 or 1 doz blackamoors who passed the shaker over shoulders to the next, after each had literally shaken his heart out chilling the drink. . . . Iced glasses, and iced soda, also were vital factors of excellence.

To 1 jigger of old Tom gin add 1 tsp sugar, 3 to 4 drops of orange flower water, white of 1 fresh egg, 2 tbsp cream, and the juice—strained—of ½ lime and ½ lemon.

The shaker is first iced with a tumbler of finely cracked ice, then ingredients go in, then the shake—which when done by hand should last at least 1 full minute. Serve strained in a thin goblet and top off with chilled club soda of best grade, to taste. . . . Here again we earnestly recommend The Mixer, only using about ¼ goblet of fine ice. This Mixer reduces ice to powder, changes consistency of main drink to a sherbet; then the soda, added and stirred, reduces this first frozen consistency to a creamy, slick, chill loveliness. We always use this method to save overheat from physical exertion. It changes the tempo of the drink slightly, due to a trifle of ice still remaining in it after final soda goes in; but like the present "Tropical" Daiquiri thus frozen in The Mixer, it is an improvement over the old manual shaking method.

FIZZ, *à la VIOLETTE,* a Cairene Innovation Served Us in the Home of Ahmed Soliman, whose Family for 400 Years Has Made & Marketed Perfumes & Perfume Essences in the Same Spot in the Khan el Kalili Bazaar, Cairo

Ahmed we consider one of our best friends in the Near East. He it was who arranged a duck shoot for us up in the Oasis Lakes in 1932, at Fayyoum; who sent us Ambar cigarettes on the occasion of our marriage, and other kindly gestures too numerous to mention. Long may his shadow extend—this man who numbers every crowned head among his clients—and thanks for this lovely Fizz, incidentally.

Omit the orange flower water from the Ramos Fizz, adding instead 1 pony of imported French or Bols *Crème de Violette* liqueur, or *Crème Yvette.* Mix everything else in exactly the same way, touch the outside of the crystal glass' lip with the glass rod in the flacon stopper of a bottle of *violette* perfume or essence. Serve with garnish of 1 or 2 violet blossoms floated on top. It is a pretty thing to look at, to taste, to smell. It has caused more than one bachelor to become heralded, with cause, as a stoutly clever fellow perennially capable of the right, the judicious, thing! . . . In our own practice—not trusting the value of taking perfumes internally, we supply 2 short purple cellophane straws, and touch the perfume to their upper one-third just beyond lip reach, yet close to the nose tip for fragrance.

THE JAMAICA "GINGER" COCKTAIL, from the Guest Book Record of a Friend Wise Enough to Winter on the Shores of Lovely Montego Bay; & Discovered, a.d. 1930, under Circumstances Unimportant to this Work

Take 1 jigger of dry gin, ½ jigger of claret or Burgundy, ½ jigger of strained orange juice, and 3 good dashes of Jamaica ginger extract.

Shake with cracked ice and pour into a Manhattan glass. . . . We find this a good picker-upper, a stomachic *par excellence,* a carminative of prompt efficiency, for ladies or gentlemen troubled with any of the various ailments from lack of appetite to plain old pre-war stomach ache or collywobbles.

## THE IMMORTAL SINGAPORE RAFFLES GIN SLING, Met in 1926, & thereafter Never Forgotten

There are other good Gin Slings in the East. Spence's Hotel, a small one in Calcutta, frequented rather than the Grand or the Great Eastern, by business gentlemen who like good food, well mixed drinks, has the best in India—outside of those blended by amateurs at home. But the Singapore name clings to this famous drink, and along with the famous Shepheard's in Cairo, Hotel Raffles is probably the best known of any in the Orient. The Brothers Sarkies are canny managers with whom we have had some moderately large booking accounts on 2 occasions. Singapore stands at the cross roads of the East, and whoever has been to Singapore knows the Raffles. Here we can sit and watch steamers, warships, *prahus,* sampans, yachts, and God knows what else riding in the Roadstead off Collyer Quay. Just looking around the terrace porch we've seen Frank Buck, the Sultan of Johore, Aimee Semple McPherson, Somerset Maugham, Dick Halliburton, Doug Fairbanks, Bob Ripley, Ruth Elder and Walter Camp —not that this is any wonder.

We've had many Gin Slings out at Seaview, the summer seaside resort of the F.M.S., and where we found the quite delightful atmosphere marred with a quietly grim touch due to the whole bathing area being surrounded with tough wire netting to dampen ardour and appetite of the sharks infesting those warm seas. But we still concede the palm to the Raffles for the best Gin Sling. Hotel Nederlander, the Harmonie and Concordia Clubs in Batavia, Java, also make good Gin Slings—the Harmonie Club—where we are eating and drinking at table in a lovely courtyard one minute, feel a breath of cool night air, and see one of the most startling sights in the world: a couple of hun-

dred men and women suddenly getting up and sprinting for the quad-
rangle of verandahs before the torrential rains put 4″ of water where
they were sitting 5 minutes before! But the Raffles drink is best, why
we don't know, except that the best Planter's Punch on earth is at the
Myrtlebank in Kingston. When our soft-footed Malay boy brings the
4th Sling and finds us peering over the window sill at the cobra-
handling snake charmers tootling their confounded flutes below he
murmurs *"jaga baik-baik Tuan"*—"jaga bye-bye, too-wan," as it
sounds in English—or "take care master" as it means in English. The
Singapore Gin Sling is a delicious, slow-acting, insidious thing.

The original formula is 1/3 each of dry gin, cherry brandy and
Benedictine; shake it for a moment, or stir it in a bar glass, with 2
fairly large lumps of ice to chill. Turn into a small 10 oz highball
glass with one lump of ice left in and fill up to individual taste with
chilled club soda. Garnish with the spiral peel of 1 green lime. In other
ports in the Orient drinkers often use C & C ginger ale instead of
soda, or even stone bottle ginger beer.

Our own final improved formula calls for 2 parts dry or Tom gin,
to 1 part cherry brandy and 1 part Benedictine. This is dryer, not too
sweet. We also use a trifle more ice in the glass than the Raffles technique. One lump melts too quickly where we live among the coconut
palms!

THE SAHARA GLOWING HEART COCKTAIL, from the
HANDS of one ABDULLAH an ARAB MUSLIM WIZARD back of MAHOGANY
at the MENA HOUSE BAR, near the PYRAMIDS of GHIZEH, which ARE
JUST SOUTH of CAIRO, EGYPT

Watch this one when out under the moon in a desert overnight
camp, riding camels out across the vast dunes, or strolling in the
moonlight around the Sphinx with some congenial young woman
companion. Full many a mere man has gone and committed himself for life under that desert moon after a brace of Glowing Hearts,
as we have seen with these failing and rheumy eyes. The effect on us
was that, along with another American ne'er-do-well, we untethered

all the camels while the Arab boys haggled over some eternal native unimportance, tied them in a line, and mounted most insecurely on a pair of dromedaries of antique perfume, doubtful morals, and the manners of a horned toad, we led them to the Sphinx and tethered them to the claim-stakes of some random excavating party then in operation during daylight hours, between the Sphinx's feet. It didn't make sense then, and it doesn't now, but the row those Arabs and dragomen tossed up when they found the whole mess of camels vanished was something to take down on a sound track.

Take of dry gin, 1 pony, absinthe, 1 pony, dry imported apricot brandy, 1 pony; donate ½ pony of bright rose coloured grenadine. Shake with lots and lots of ice and strain into a large saucer champagne glass, and pray Allah for forgiveness of all imminent and future sins of the flesh.

THE GRANDE BRETAGNE COCKTAIL No. I, Being to Our Ungoverned Mind One of the Five or Six Chief Cocktails of the Whole Wide World

One dank, chilly, and snow-carpeted day in January of 1931 we wore out shoe leather, shins, and temper in the name of "history" and "art," hiking all over the Acropolis in Athens; skidding from the Temple of Diana, around the Parthenon, and back down past the Erectheum and its divine caryatids, and to our motor car and to Athens proper. Here we met Eddie Hastings, now cruise director for the M.S. BREMEN with Raymond-Whitcomb, and he told me about the little Greek barkeep in his tiny bar and his miraculous inventions. . . . This Grecian male had been abarring for over 40 years, man and boy. During that time he had devoted ½ hr daily to the pardonable indoor pastime of testing new and radical mixes all his own. The Grande Bretagne Nos. I and II, were the final result—the pinnacle. Using lime juice we found later is far better than lemon, although lemon is plenty good enough. Use *dry* imported apricot brandy, never the sweet syrupy American copy. . . . No. I: 1 jigger of the best dry gin possible, ½ pony apricot brandy, ½ pony or so of strained lime or lemon juice, 1 tsp of very fresh egg white, 1 dash of orange bitters. Shake with lots of ice and turn into a chilled Manhattan glass. . . . No. II: substitute *kirschwasser* for apricot brandy, omit orange bitters—using 1 dash of peach bitters if available, or 1 tsp *Cordial Médoc*.

The domestic Bridge Table cocktail, the 3-to-One, both copy this Grande Bretagne, but the apricot brandy content is too heavy, and no mention is ever made that unless fine *dry* apricot brandy is used, the result is sweet, abortive, disillusioning in the extreme. . . . It is amazing, though, how such a small amount of *apricot* or *kirsch* comes zipping through to lend bouquet to this brisk drink.


THE BARRANQUILLA GREEN JADE, from a STAY in COLOMBIA in the YEAR 1933, and again in 1934

This amazing jumping-off town for emeralds, oil and gold in Colombian hinterlands, has already been described; how the ancient Spanish town rubs elbows with the most modern American practice. We have fond recollections of one charming hostess in Barranquilla who served us whole shrimps boiled in deep olive oil, bits of popcorn tossed in garlic butter, little fritters of *plantano,* and many strange tropical, chilled, fruits—mangoes, carissas, mangosteens, Surinam cherries, rose apples, mawmees, heaven only knows what else with long Latin names! . . . The Green Jade is a crisp thing, too, fine for hot weather like the Grande Bretagne, the Gimlet. . . . 1 jigger of dry gin, ½ jigger of green crème de menthe, ½ jigger cream and 1 tsp or so of egg white. Shake with ice, strain into a saucer champagne glass, and garnish with 1 green cherry and a sprig of fresh mint. Serve with a green straw affixed with same technique as in the Cuernavaca Special already listed.


THE HALLELUJAH COCKTAIL, a PALATE-TWISTER from the ISTHMUS of PANAMA

This was originated by our good friend Max Bilgray, of Colon, Panama, somewhere around 1929, and dedicated to Aimee Semple

McPherson as a result of an alleged visit to his Bilgray's Tropic Bar and Cabaret, long a gay spot on the Isthmus. Now whether Aimee ever went to Bilgray's under the alias of Betty Adams; and if she went there, whether or not she found anything she wanted, are matters beyond our deductive powers. All we know is that we arrived one night just after this alleged inspection, and that Bilgray was mailing out post-cards, postage *gratis*—as many as we wanted—listing the Hallelujah ingredients. . . . Of course many thousands went out, and a million dollar lawsuit was instituted, and Aimee's mother forgot her squabble with daughter, and rallied to her defense. Even remote, pure and austere sheets like the New York *Times* had special cables, and we thought the whole business hugely amusing—and strangely enough, the drink is good. Quote:

Babylonian Grape Brandy (Cognac) ....................... 1 pony
Ice from the Crest of Mount Sinai ............. Lots, finely cracked
Lemon from the Desert of Sin ................ Lime juice, 4 drops
Gomorrah and Sodom vermouth .................. Italian, 1 jigger
Rum aged in Noah's Ark .................½ jigger; rye also used
Add Cain's syrup from the Garden of Eden ....... ½ tsp Grenadine
You then give it the Hebrew shake and—pop a cherry on top
Say Hallelujah after drinking!

Not that it makes any great difference, but the initial letters of each line spell Bilgray's. Any drink known probably to a hundred thousand people in the last eight or nine years in Panama alone must have had something besides postcard appeal. . . . It should be served in a large saucer type champagne glass.

THE HONEYMOON COCKTAIL, or *LUNE de MIEL,* One of Many Strange Memories from a Place in Paris Known as *CHEZ MA BELLE SOEUR,* under Circumstances not Relevant to Mention, Circa 1926

If the place still exists it can be found, if not we can assure those adventurous enough to be curious that the French *Sûreté* closed its doors upon those precious things of the long evening gowns, the slave bracelets about wrist and ankle; the pendant earrings; rouge, jeweled slipper and tiny fans. . . . It is a strange drink, and for all we know it may have its purposes and its moments. Take a sherry glass and build up as follows: *crème de cacao, parfait amour,* the yolk of 1 egg carefully unbroken, and finally *kümmel doré*—all chilled beforehand. Use about 1 pony each of the liqueurs, or slightly less.

THE MANILA "HOOP PUNCH," another MASTERPIECE from the HANDS of "MONK" ANTRIM's No. I CHINO, FIRST DISCOVERED in 1931

Take 1 pony each of cognac and orange Curaçao, add 2 ponies of port wine, donate 1 tsp of lemon or lime juice. Fill a goblet with finely cracked ice, turn in the mix, stir and serve with short straws—garnished to suit taste. . . . This can also be made not quite so sweet by changing the strained lime juice up to ½ pony and cutting down the Curaçao to ½ pony.

AND NOW SEVENTEEN or so "HOT HELPERS" CALCULATED to KEEP CHILL SWAMP MISTS at BAY, BANISH the MEGRIMS & WARM BODY, HEART & SOUL into a FINE & AMIABLE DISPOSITION

Of all the retinue of drinks listed in this volume, it is certain that Hot Helpers really will be of most grateful use to readers. For when a man is wet and chilled through, blue with cold and long exposure in such voluntary tortures as November duck blinds, the wheel of an ocean-going sailing craft in a winter chance, or in any chilly and depleted situation, a Hot Helper will in 5 short minutes recall him from being a sorry and useless thing into restoration as a warm-hearted homebody, kind to dogs, children, wives and even landlords—as we can surely attest! Out of the endless blends in glass and silver bowl we have listed these as the best and unusual from all over the civilized world.

## FIRST MARCH FOUR BASED upon a MATTER of ALES

AULD MAN'S MILK, a REVIVIFIER from the HEATHER BOUND
SLOPES of BONNIE SCOTLAND; and FETCHED BACK to these SHORES after
RESIDENCE in the BRITISH ISLES in 1932

Take a bottle of Scotch ale, heat it gently in a saucepan and while
it is gaining temperature dust with ¼ tsp of powdered cinnamon, the
same of nutmeg and ginger. Take the yolks of 2 fresh eggs, add 1 scant
tsp of brown sugar; then beat them well. When ale is hot but not
quite boiling, pour this egg-sugar mixture slowly in—stirring diligently. When thoroughly blended, turn in 1 to 2 jiggers of good
Scotch whisky. A fine stout and nourishing drink, this.

YE OLDE GOSSIPE'S BOWLE, BASED on MULLED ALE, and DATED,
ENGLAND, 1622

We, as a matter of principle, despise all titles with "Ye" in it—Ye
Little Giftee Shoppee, and such ilk, but when we ran on the near-
Elizabethan dating of this receipt we forgave all, for it is a grand title
and one of England's oldest drinks—sometimes called *Lamb's Wool*.

Strong ale, two 12 oz bottles, 1    Brown sugar, to taste
   qt; Bass preferred    Roasted crab, or other small,
Good white wine, 1 pint     apples; sugared and spiced
Nutmeg, 1 tsp

Mix ale and wine, add sugar and spice, heat slowly. When piping
hot add the roasted apples, serving in wide mugs if you have 'em. Not
too much sugar on the apples, please. Crabs are best.

LORD RUTHVEN'S "GOSSIP'S CUP," or *TEWAHDIDDLE*, a
CHARMING MIX of ALE, BRANDY, SPICES & SUGAR, & DATED LONDON,
1654

We imagine that this is an older drink even than the Olde Gossipe's
Bowle, given above. And of *Tewahdiddle*—what a name, what a
name!—the immortal Dr. Kitchiner says:

"Before our Readers make any remarks on this Composition, we beg of them to taste it: if the materials are good and their Palate vibrates in unison with our own, they will find it one of the pleasantest beverages they ever put to their lips. . . ."

Lord Ruthven says in his volume *Experiments in Cookery*, London, 1654:

"This is a right Gossip's Cup that far exceeds all the Ale that Mother Bunch made in her lifetime."

Ale, one 12 oz bottle or pint
Brandy, 1 tbsp or a trifle more
Brown sugar, 1 tsp

Lemon peel, 1 curl, yellow part only
Ginger, 1 pinch
Nutmeg, sprinkling

Mix all these and heat on the fire, but do not boil. . . . This drink is a warmer of the heart, and would be a neat one to produce some cold fall or winter's afternoon or evening, before a snapping wood fire.

NOW, finally, DR. WILLIAM KITCHINER's "YARD of FLANNEL," which Is SOMETIMES CALLED an "ALE FLIP," *CIRCA* 1817

This is another hot helper based on ale, and calculated to cheer up any long winter evening while the wind whistles about the eaves.

Ale, 1 qt; or 2½ to 3 12 oz bottles
Eggs, 3 beaten
Brown sugar, ½ cup
Ginger, 1/3 tsp

Nutmeg, 2/3 tsp
Good cognac, or rum, ½ cup
Lemon, yellow peel, ½

Take the yellow peel of ½ lemon, put into the ale and bring to heat; meanwhile beating up eggs with spices, sugar and rum. When the ale steams—but still isn't boiling—pour into a pitcher; then turn the egg-spice blend into another. Now pour back and forth briskly until everything is creamy and smooth.

WORDS to the LIQUID WISE No. VIII, on the SPECIES of
ALE for MULLING

In all receipts calling for heated, mulled, or otherwise spiced ale,
again we recommend English Bass, or any English Musty Ale, most
heartily in preference to our present list of domestic products, and in
spite of the cost made necessary by our ridiculously high tariff duties
on products which we never have made here, and probably couldn't
make as well if we did try.

ONE, now, BASED on APPLEJACK—which Is America's Term
for Apple Brandy, & Called the Jersey Lighthouse

It is rather unfortunate that our prohibition era through its raw
applejack and Jersey Lightning, managed completely to deflect American taste against this fine spirit. Decently aged-in-wood applejack is a
fine thing, just as French *Calvados*—a superfine apple brandy from
Normandy and the orchards of Ausse and Bessin—is a lovely stuff, as
fine in its way as any cognac, especially the brand marketed in the
flask bearing an apple, on a leafy branch in bas relief.

We met the Jersey Lighthouse sitting in the back room of a small
New Jersey inn one horrid winter night, with William Faulkner,
Tony Sarg's puppet maker Bil Baird, and Eric—*Midget Magellans*
and *Blow the Man Down*—Devine, our sailing mate on *MARMION*.
. . . Into a tumbler place 2 lumps of sugar, a dash or 2 of Angostura,
3 or 4 cloves, a spiral of lemon peel. Onto this pour 2 jiggers of ancient
applejack, fill with boiling water, float on 1 tbsp applejack at the last
and serve blazing merrily. Those of us who read Bill Faulkner's *Light
in August* renamed the drink *Light in February*.

A HOT HELPER FOUNDED upon BEER from Denmark &
Called the Copenhagen—Pronounced as Near as We Can Do It,
"Kern-Haben"—Beer Toddy

It is a fine one to use after winter sports, in an Alpine ski-camp, anywhere like that. Take 1 average bottle of good Danish or Bavarian
dark beer, beat 1 to 2 egg yolks well with 1 tbsp of brown sugar; and
after heating beer in a saucepan put beaten eggs into the mug, turn

in the hot beer, stirring diligently the while. A dusting of nutmeg is optional.

## FOUR HOT ONES BASED on BRANDY, or BRANDY-RUM BLENDINGS, the FIRST of which Is the APRICOT, or PEACH, *FLAMBÉ*

This is a delicious and totally different touch from all the others, from the usual hot drink. Take 3 dried apricots or 2 dried peaches—plumped in hot water beforehand; put in a silver cup and add 2 tsp of brown sugar. Pour ½ jigger of cognac, heated, onto this foundation and set alight, blowing out when sugar starts to melt well. Now turn in 1 jigger or so of cognac, stir well, and add very hot water to taste. A pinch of powdered clove, or 3 or 4 whole cloves, form optional touches.

## THE SO-CALLED "ENGLISH BISHOP"—CONSIDERED by the AUTHOR to be ONE of the MOST ATTRACTIVE HOT CUPS ever INVENTED for the AID & COMFORT of CIVILIZED MAN, DISCOVERED in the SUMMER of 1932 in BOXMOOR, HERTFORDSHIRE

Take an orange, stud it thickly all over with whole cloves, dip it in cognac and dust with brown sugar. Now brown well until sugar caramels, either spitted upon a skewer or stick before the fire or under the broiler. Cut it into quarters; now take a saucepan or other vessel, turn in 1 qt of red port wine, simmer tightly covered for 20 minutes, add 2 jiggers of cognac just before pouring. Can be served *flambé* with a little brandy floated on top.

## CAFÉ DIABLE, which Is neither ALTOGETHER BRANDY nor ALTOGETHER COFFEE, nor MERELY A HOT DRINK—but a MELLOWED & DRAMATIC INSTITUTION from the CREOLE DELTA CAPITAL of NEW ORLEANS

This is always an impressive bit of business when dining with a handsome young lady, *chez nous* and *à deux*. Be sure to turn out all the lights before trying it, however, or the effect will be spoiled. The successful brewing of a *Café Diable* somehow instills a bit of admiration for the imminent male in the stoniest feminine breast. It causes her to think that here in truth is a monstrous clever fellow, a man above other men. Don't disillusion her. . . . For this routine have two cups and a fire extinguisher handy.

> Really strong black coffee, 2 cups
> Brandy, (Elaborate but worth it!) 1½ cups or so
> Peel of orange and lemon, both pared off very thin
> Sugar, 8 lumps (Some use four to six)
> Whole cloves, 4; or more, to taste

First warm your silver bowl—for china may crack. Put in peel, spice, and pour in brandy. Light candle and cut lights. Heat ladle by holding beside candle flame—not over it because of soot. Dip up a couple tablespoons of brandy, and put in two of sugar. Set alight and lower ladle into bowl—being sure that neither your Perfect One nor your own eyebrows are too close when it puffs into a blaze. . . . Now dip up a ladle full and let it fall back, then after the proper applause start putting in coffee gradually, ladling busily all the time. Finally the flame will flicker and die, and before our audience's interest flickers and dies, ladle into demitasse cups.

The SHANGHAI COSSACK PUNCH, Come upon at a Most Vulnerable & Romantic Moment, which Shall Never Be Forgotten; and a Fabrication which We Have always Held to Be the Finest Hot Drink Extant

Those of us who knew Shanghai before the red Russians were chased out and the white Russians were dissipated and scattered to the four corners of the globe, remember what we remember. We recall one drizzly afternoon after the races, a house in the French Concession whose host again it is not necessary to mention, and among other interesting selvages of that afternoon—the following, fetched by him from Siberia during those incredible days when Kolchak's army was dispersed. . . . This day it was served hot, in tall Russian coffee glasses.

Good brandy, 1 pint

Curaçao, yellow, ½ pint

Lemon peel, yellow part, 2

Hot tea, 1 quart

Dark rum, ½ pint

Lemon, strained juice, 4

Orgeat syrup, 1½ tsp

Orange flower water

This was simmered up once over a spirit lamp, and poured off steaming to each guest, who sweetened to taste—most adding a dash or two of orange flower water.

HOT HELPERS BASED upon BURGUNDY or CLARET or PORT WINES

THE ENGLISH BISHOP IS FIRST, & MENTIONED under BRANDY DRINKS just above this JUNCTURE & in the SAME CATEGORY, PAGE 54

NOW WE COME UPON a MATTER of MULLED CLARET & PORT, together with COGNAC, SPICES, PEELS & other MATTERS; from a RECEIPT in the TIME of GOOD QUEEN BESS, *CIRCA* 1578

Mix 3 cups of claret and 1 of red port; add ½ cup of cognac, the spiral yellow peel of a lemon, and 2 good pinches each of cinnamon and nutmeg. Toss in ½ doz whole cloves, cover well and heat hot—but do not boil. Take off immediately it is hot enough to suit taste and not a moment longer, an' it please you! Boiling ruins port instanter, evaporates all alcohol and leaves a bitter lees calculated to spoil the best ingredients.

MULLED CLARET, *à la GULMARG,* from the SHOOTING LOG of a BRITISH COLONIAL CAVALRY OFFICER upon the OCCASION of a SHOOT of *CHIKOR* or MOUNTAIN GROUSE, & WILD DUCK—the FIRST in the FIR CLAD SHEER SLOPES and VALLEYS around GULMARG, & the LAST on WULAR LAKE, which IS in the FABULOUSLY LOVELY VALE of the KASHMIR some TWENTY MILES to the NORTHEAST

This must have been something in a Kashmiri mountain hut in late September, nearly 2 miles above the sea, with the perfume of ½ doz plump grouse sizzling before the coals on a rock slab hearth, the air outside clear as wine, and the summit of the nearer Himalayas walking up to the white, deathly still, roof of the world—where only the wind and the snow and the cold could dwell. . . . Then in 3 days back to the heat and confusion of teeming Bengal, to Calcutta 2d largest city in the British *Raj* after London itself; to orchids, and jasmines and Paris frocks and intrigue.

It requires 2 bottles of still red Burgundy, 2 limes or 1 lemon, cut into thin slices and seeded, ½ banana cut into slices. Tie the fruit together with 2 sticks of cinnamon, 1 doz whole cloves and 6 allspice, in a bit of cheesecloth. Put along with the wine into a covered pot, simmering for not over 10 minutes. Discard cheesecloth bag and contents, turn in 1 cup of dark rum, ½ cup of brown sugar to taste, and 1 cup of club soda or seltzer. Stir and *serve foaming,* garnished with curl of lemon peel.

THE TIMKE LOCOMOTIVE from FAR AWAY LUZON, which Is a Smooth, Delicate, Gentle, Hot Reviver, Discreet Enough for the Tenderest Maid, the Most Careful Spinster

Monk Antrim leans over our shoulder again, for he it was who told us about this drink. Also as we have explained elsewhere Baguio, the Philippine hill station, is cool o' nights even though it is right smack in the hottest tropical belt. The formula noted on the back of a Baguio Country Club score card, with a gross not creditable to mention, reads as follows: take a small saucepan or chafing dish, and before putting to fire turn in 1½ wine glasses of good Burgundy or claret, ½ pony of orange Curacao, and 1 pony of honey mixed with 1½ tsp of sugar. Stir well until honey is entirely dissolved, stir in 1 lightly beaten egg, then put over the flame. . . . When it first simmers up pour into a mug or silver julep glass, and with another in the opposite hand pour briskly from one to the other for a final mix. Add 1 thin slice of green lime or lemon, dust with a little cinnamon and that's it. A most unusual blend of flavours; all delicate, and affording total distinctly low in alcoholic strength. A beautiful drink for any invalid or convalescent wearied of usual routine liquids.

AND NOW, FINALLY March Certain Hot Aids Founded on Rums

THE JAMAICA BLACK STRIPE, Being Served as Often Hot as Cold, May Be Found by Turning to Page 18

NEXT MARCHES the BAKER "HORSE COLLAR," Originated by the Author, a.d. 1935, upon Running into Stonington, Rhode Island, ahead of a Howling Nor'easter when Heading South from Lawley's Yard to Florida in *MARMION*

This hotter toddy was invented by these sere and palsied hands, quite through luck and by accident. Our 56 foot ketch *MARMION* having just been discharged with a new and costly main trys'l re-rig from Lawley's Yard, the split-sprit necessary to spreading that fancy triangular bit of canvas became known as the "Horse Collar." On the run from Cape Cod to New York, we stuck our noses into a snoring nor'easter, which added up so quickly that we dropped the hook at Stonington, Rhode Island, rather than be shaken up any more than necessary. It was nearly November and cold as hades. Well that night all hands screamed for hot rum, and we found no lemons in the lazarette—and to many otherwise cultured folk a hot rum without a dash of lemon is like the Democratic Party without the ghost of Jefferson, Tom without Jerry, a Cuban without his mistress. But we had oranges!—and thereby hangs a tale. For suddenly we thought of orange peel—and orange peel roasted with wild duck and how superbly fragrant it can become. Scarcely daring to hope for anything virtuous coming out of the effort we proceeded as follows.

Tin cups for mariners, silver julep cups for fancies
*Carta de Oro* Bacardi, Jamaica, Barbados, or Haitian rum, 2 jiggers
Orange peel, 1 to each cup, cut in unbroken spiral
Brown sugar, 1 tsp per cup
Whole cloves, 6; or powdered clove, ¼ tsp per cup
Boiling water, enough to fill
Butter, ½ tsp, optional

Line cups with spirals of orange peel, first dipping them in rum to moisten. Dust sugar on peel, then cloves the same. Put a jigger of rum in each cup, put cups on hot stove, and after a moment set aflame. Let burn until edges of peel start to brown and sugar to caramel. Blow out. Take off stove, add other jigger of rum, fill up with hot water, give a brief stir and serve—either with or without a lump of butter on top the size of a hazelnut. . . . This sounds complicated, but the whole thing takes only a couple of minutes. Cups and rum must be heated or when set alight the moisture in the peel will come out and smother the flame. . . . The *Horse Collar* thus has four delicious aromatic scents and savours: first the rum itself, then the nut-like perfume of burned oil of orange, then the brown sugar, slightly carameled by the flame, then the toasted spice.

THE OXFORD UNIVERSITY HOT RUM PUNCH, a CLASSIC that Is SIMPLE & SOOTHING & SATISFACTORY, and DATING back into the DIM, DISTANT PAST

Take 1½ bottles of Barbados, or lighter Jamaica, or 1 bottle of Demerara 160 proof; add 1 bottle of cognac, 3 quarts of boiling water, 2 cups of lemon juice. Add brown sugar, to taste, and a handful of whole cloves. Put a spiral of yellow lemon peel in each cup, and there it is. Most excellent for anyone coming down with anything, due to the lemon juice.

EXPLODED OLD ALEWIVES' TALE No. I, BEING a WARNING against OVER-INTRODUCTION of CITRIC JUICES into HOT ALCOHOLIC DRINKS

No matter what dear old Aunt Florina-May Fittich may grumble about how she used to cure Grandpop's cold with hot lemon juice and spirits, let's lend at least ½ an ear to certain master rum drinkers who claim—probably with justice—that alcohol and sugar and lemon juice, *under heat,* work toward an acid condition of the gastric machinery most conducive to spleen and vapours. It is just a thought anyway, and we really don't expect anyone to heed the warning after all.

## HAROLD PETER'S HOT BUTTERED RUM

Anyone who has sailed with Pete—whether around the world on *PILGRIM,* to EUROPE on the schooner *LLOYD BERRY,* or south to Florida from Cape Cod on some ship like our own *MARMION,* as we did, remembers his magnificent tattooed masterpieces, haunch, paunch, back and chest, and his Hot Buttered Rums at the end of a cold, wet, Fall chance. Our first introduction to them was running from Woods Hole to New York, one late October day, with the wind whipping up a dry nor'easter, and our new main trys'l pushing us along close to nine knots.

Into each average sized glass put a teaspoon of brown sugar, a twist of lemon peel, a teaspoon lemon juice, four to six whole cloves, and a spoon. Take a "futt" dish and heat water on the galley stove—and in case we don't remember Pete's definition of that time-honoured bit of New England addenda, a futt dish is the flat tin handleless sort of pan we see on top of bullet heating stoves down east, to keep the air humid. Actually any pot does as well.

To each glass donate two ponies of Barbados, or any stout rum— two full ounces—add boiling water to taste, stir, and with the spoon which has kept the glass from cracking, slide in one teaspoon of butter on top. Drink as butter becomes wholly melted. . . . When getting really fancy for Harbour Furl Company, Pete may float a spoon of rum on top, and set aflame, but not for anyone less than a full Commodore!

WORDS to the LIQUID WISE No. IX, on the EXCELLENCE of ALLSPICE in HOT RUM DRINKS
To vary the usual clove and nutmeg add half a teaspoon of allspice to the next hot toddy. The result is quite aromatically happy.

RETURNING to our RETINUE of COLD DRINKS again WE PRESENT the JAMAICA BUCK, BEING a SHANGHAI BUCK—already NOTED —only USING JAMAICA, or other DARK RUM instead of BACARDI, & ADDING HALF a LIME for FLAVOUR

We found this years ago in Kingston, on a jaunt through the West

Indies, during our editorial days with Doubleday, Doran & Company magazines. Take 1½ jiggers dark rum, turn into a collins glass with large lumps of ice, squeeze ½ lime in and add the crushed lime itself; now comes 1 tsp sugar, and fill up with ginger ale of some decent sort, or better still with stone bottle ginger beer. It is a satisfying cooler. By using ½ dark rum and ½ *Carta de Oro* Bacardi the drink will suit feminine Jamaicaphobes.

NOW, GENTLEMEN, at Long Last Are Eight or so Mint Julep Ceremonies—Being Various Adaptations of this Peerless American Conception from All Parts of the World where It Is Properly Revered

Right from the meaning of the word Juleps have been a spill-and-pelt of contradiction and disagreement. . . . The very name itself never was midwifed on any honeysuckle-bowered southern balcony, but comes from the Persian *gulab,* or Arab *julab,* meaning rose water. . . . No sane Kentucky planter, in full possession of his faculties will yield an inch to any Marylander when it comes to admitting rye is superior to bourbon in a Julep, when actually, a Julep is international and has been international for years—just as the matters of radio and flying are international. It is a drink composed of whisky or brandy —and, of late—rum; sweetened, iced, and flavoured with aromatic leaves of the *mentha* family.

So before the shooting starts let's explain right here and now that there's no more chance of getting the various Julep schools to agree on fabrication of this most delectable of drinks, than we have of getting a proud Atlanta great-grandmother to concede General Sherman a nice, gentle, well-meaning, big boy.

First of all there is the silver cup versus the glass school; the chilled glass versus room-temperature school; the slightly bruised mint versus the all-bruised school; the rye versus the bourbon school; the fruit garnish versus the plain school.

Feuds have begun because someone breathed the possibility that city water would make a Julep as well as water dipped from a fern-draped Blue Grass Country spring. Men have been shot at for heaping fruit juices, slices of citrus, and maraschino cherries on a Julep completed. Families have faced divorcement about the slight-appearing concern of red-stemmed mint.

A gentleman who discards the slightly bruised mint from his drink views another who permits the bruised leaves to remain in glass as one who did not have quite the proper forbearance on the distaff side. . . . And so tell they the tale—

Getting right down to cases, there is no more need for argument of violent nature along such lines than there is that a flashing-eyed Spanish girl is any less useful in life than a lovely honey-haired Scandinavian, than a titian English maid, or a jet-haired and urgent daughter of the Killarney Country.

On this matter of Juleps we can boast to a thorough Julep research, without pride or prejudice, for we have put in some years of mighty clinical home-work on the matter!

We've sipped Juleps on a shaded upper gallery brewed by a genuine Colonel, from Versailles, Kentucky. We've tried Juleps in Charleston, Cape Cod, Toronto, Kelly's in Panama City, and the Royal Hawaiian in Honolulu; we've sipped other Juleps in Nassau, Cumberland Island, Georgia, Seattle, Los Angeles, and that little Overseas Club— or whatever the right name is—that sits up on stilts by the pier-end in Zamboanga; we've tried—of all places—a Julep in Sandakan, British North Borneo. . . . We've buried this inquisitive proboscis in green, spicy-cool mint foliage under king coconut trees, looking out over the coffee and cacao plantations of central Guatemala, in shadow of the Shwe Dagon Pagoda in Rangoon, Burma, on the start of the road to Mandalay—which last is hundreds of miles inland and a mountainous table-land without flying fish, and China isn't across the bay either.

But the best Julep of all, up to date—an' Ah mean that Suh!—was mixed by Monk Antrim's Number One Chino boy at the Manila Hotel, Luzon, P.I., and A.D. 1926. . . . Just *good* bourbon—yes, Manila never was dried up by our experiment and much of the finest bourbon found its way out there—really tender, fresh, red-stemmed mint;

a big glass, plenty of fine ice, a little sugar, a teaspoon of Demerara rum floated between the two ripe sticks of fresh ripe Pasig River valley pineapple, in a big sloping-sided glass holding a full English pint of sixteen ounces. And *lots* of mint, for it takes a real clutch of the herb for fragrance.

But let us inject a word of caution to seekers after this miracle of frosted perfection. No man can rough and tumble his Julep-making and expect that luck must always be on his side, that a lovely arctic frosted thing shall always reward his careless ignorance.

Especially on yachts or boats, for instance, no Julep glass can frost when stood in any considerable wind. Frosting depends solely upon condensed moisture being converted to minor ice through the excessive chill of melting cracked ice and liquids within that glass. Therefore if the breeze whisks it away there can be nothing left to frost. Paradoxically, when the outside of any Julep glass is moist from careless rinsing, handling, or standing about only partially iced in humid weather, frost will be in total lack due to *excess* moisture.

Likewise no Julep can ever frost when caressed by the warm, *bare* palm of an impatient host or guest—not any more than decent frosting can ever result from wet, half-melted cracked ice that is more liquid than solid. Just obey the rules, few but important, and success will crown every amateur effort.

Actually if we would forget all the eternal nonsense about Juleps and obey the few common sense rules, everyone could save their strength for enjoyment of this institution.

1. Chill glasses, whether silver cups or otherwise.
2. Use glasses of sixteen ounce capacity.
3. Use two and a half jiggers of likker for sixteen ounce glass, two for fourteen ounce.
4. Use red-stemmed mint, simply because red-stemmed mint is more pleasantly aromatic. Use fresh mint, and cut stems short just before putting in as final garnish—to make them bleed.
5. Don't bruise that first installment of tender mint leaves more than very slightly. The inner leaf juices are bitter and cannot have profitable

flavour. Bruise one between the teeth, then really chew it up—to find out.

6. Don't expect to get a whacking good Julep out of six months old "bourbon" or "rye." We can't.
7. Don't use coarse ice, use finely cracked ice—very fine.
8. Don't over-garnish with sliced orange and random fruits. With Juleps, and in fact any drink of delicate quality in its own right, don't add anything with a different strong scent—and orange, lemon, and certain other fruits have a very potent aroma. . . . The aroma of a bourbon Julep should be bourbon and mint—not bourbon, mint, and a fruit store. . . .

Garnish simply, then, without trying to gild the lily. A Julep is more than a mere chilled liquid; it is a tradition which is to be respected. The mint itself is a delight to eye, just as we admire parsley against a fine red snapper, or permit feminine associates the use of red nail polish, or grace a mother's table with flowers. So let the Julep feast the eye and nostril properly—not supply unending, edible diversions from the main theme. We don't need to eat all the trimmings, after all—but *we* always do! . . . That is why ripe pineapple is so beneficial—and eaten after the Julep is gone, the marinated fruit is delicious.

## MONK ANTRIM'S MANILA HOTEL MINT JULEP No. I, with BOURBON or RYE

Sugar, ½ tbsp; water 2 tbsp
Fresh mint, tender sprigs, 6
Ripe pineapple, 2 sticks or fingers
Good old bourbon, 2½ jiggers;
   or rye

Fresh mint, 1 bunch
Cherries, 4, scarlet
Demerara or Barbados rum, 1 or
   2 tsp, to smell
Finely crushed ice

Ice glasses, and without wasting any time do the following: toss in sugar, then water, then the 6 mint tips. Muddle *slightly,* being sure that the volatile oils are smeared all over inside of glass. Discard this slightly bruised mint entirely. . . . Pack glass with ice, pour on bourbon—and do not stir, letting wise nature take its course. . . . Then distribute rum slowly in drops. Cut mint stems off *quite short* up to the leaves, and make glass look like a green bouquet, with two pineapple sticks peeping out on opposite sides, and the hot red of the cherries nestling in the mint. . . . Serve with two very short straws, but let stand until thoroughly frosted before handling, and always escort it with a small napkin, to handle the melting frost on outside of glass.

Omit the rum if a Marylander or Kentuckian is present.

MINT JULEP No. II, with BOURBON or RYE

This is another variation, and also good. . . . Simply proceed just as in the Monk Antrim version, only leave the slightly bruised mint in the glass. Half fill with ice, and add a few more sprigs of slightly bruised mint. Fill with ice, and finish exactly as above, only omit the touch of rum. . . . Handle bourbon and rye exactly alike.

MINT JULEP No. III

This would be the same as No. II, only use the tenderest sprigs of mint and don't bruise at all—leaving the herb to be its own delicate prophet. . . . Having tried all ways we find this has least mint aroma of all, and as mint saturating the whole affair is so gratifying to our personal preference, No. III does not include when we are at work.

MINT JULEP No. IV, from SANTIAGO de CUBA, EMPLOYING, NATU-RALLY, BACARDI

This is not the usual Julep, and we don't want any sleep lost over the idea. A Cuban gentleman of parts got it up, likes it still, gave us four and we liked all of them. . . . It isn't a Julep as we know it, but after all who are we?

| | |
|---|---|
| *Carta de Oro* Bacardi, 2½ jiggers | Lime, juice, 1 fairly large |
| Pineapple juice, fresh if possible, 2 tbsp | Grenadine, 2 tsp |
| | Fresh mint and garnish |

Using a fourteen ounce tall glass or goblet, bruise six sprigs of tender fresh mint very lightly, rubbing over inside glass. Pack full of very finely crushed ice. Pour on lemon juice, pineapple juice then Bacardi, and finally the grenadine. Do not stir. . . . Garnish with bunch of fresh mint cut off close up to leaves just before putting in, and add pineapple stick, slice orange, and what not, to taste. . . . Let frost before serving.

## LAMARR PEACH BRANDY MINT JULEP No. V

Down Macon way there are more and better peaches than probably any other spot on this testy globe of ours, and one family named La-marr—of whom we know one of the daughters—seems to part own three whole counties or something, and has probably gazed on larger numbers of acres in peaches than any young lady of our acquaintance. In fact she claimed to have an uncle who was written up in *Fortune* because he developed a machine for taking the fuzz from peaches—a fact the late Mr. Mack, of Moran & Mack, would have been pleased to know. . . . It is therefore we give credit to a Southern lady who told us about this Georgia jollifier and all good men take note. 'Struth and 'tis no drink for weaklings!

| | |
|---|---|
| Cognac, 1½ jiggers | Georgia peach brandy, 1 jigger |
| Bar sugar, 1 tsp | Long thin slice ripe peach |
| 1 doz or so sprigs of fresh mint | Spring, or well, or rain, water |

Put sugar in large silver or glass Julep glass, and add just enough water to make it an oily syrup. When smoothly dissolved break off a couple of the tenderest mint sprigs, and muddle very, very slightly—leaving them there in aromatic harmony. Take six other sprigs and gently crush up and about, that no spot may be overlooked of that glass's inside.

Fill with very finely cracked ice, pack down slightly, and pour in the blended brandies. Garnish with sprigs of mint, and on the straw drinking side, insert a single stick of sliced ripe peach. . . . Do not stir. That prime liquor will percolate through the ice to the very bottom without any trouble. Just sit by quietly and watch the whole lovely process of frosting. . . . Then, and then only, drink!

PEACH THUNDERBOLT, BEING No. VI, a Long-Hoarded
Julep Treasure from Old-Time Georgia
This Thunderbolt business is no quip about the effect, but simply
the name of the place just south of Savannah, where we first stumbled
onto this nectar of the gods, this eyefilling, mild, pleasant debauch of
three senses.

| | |
|---|---|
| *Carta de Oro* Bacardi, 3 jiggers— | Sun-ripe, fresh Georgia peach, 1 |
| yes, we said 3! | Lime, juice, ½ large; 1 average |
| Fresh mint, dozen sprigs | Sugar, 1 tsp |

Take a large goblet and pack it half full with finely shaved ice, put
in half the sugar, a trifle of water, and six tender mint heads. Muddle
gently for a moment, rubbing mint all over interior of goblet. The
flavour thus penetrates better. In the center put in a peeled and stoned
peach, cut in halves and stood on edges. Mix rum, lime and rest of
sugar. Pack glass full and pour in liquids. . . . Garnish well with the
remaining mint sprigs, and serve with two *short* straws so the nose can
browse in it. . . . Don't make the mistake of garnishing with a lot
of other fruit, or using cherries. It is the ripe peach which is picked up
by the rum. . . . We have, however, discovered that a teaspoon or two
of good peach brandy floated on before frosting, helps amplify the
basic flavour of the unit.

PENDENNIS CLUB MINT JULEP, BEING No. VII, & Severely
Ungarnished
Martin Cuneo has for many years manufactured his own conception of a proper mint julep to members of Louisville's famous Pendennis Club—mentioned elsewhere in this volume. There are several
minor variations in the gentle art of Juleping, and his is enough off
the usual track for inscription here—as he does not bruise mint, even
slightly.
Take a sixteen ounce silver Julep cup, or the same in glass. Into the
bottom put a lump of sugar and dissolve it in a little spring or well
water. Choose the tenderest mint sprigs and toss in three—arranging

them in the bottom, and don't crush or bruise at all. Fill the chalice with finely cracked ice.

Turn in two jiggers of the best old bourbon the cellar can afford, and stir once to settle. Add enough more ice to fill; a complete small bundle of tender mint comes next, trimming the stalks fairly short, so as to give out their aromatic juices into the Julep. Place in the ice, and stand aside for a few minutes to frost and acquire general merit.

## MANILA POLO CLUB BRANDY JULEP, Listed as Julep No. VIII, for Alphabetical *not* Quality Reasons

Met out in the Philippines in 1926, in '31 and '32—and never forgotten.

| | |
|---|---|
| Sugar, 1 tsp | Mint, 1 doz sprigs |
| Cognac, 2½ jiggers | Any medium dark rum, 2 tbsp |
| Fresh fruit, *du jour* | Powdered sugar, 1 tsp for garnish |
| Water, 1 pony | |

Use sixteen ounce glass. . . . Dissolve sugar and water, and toss in six tender sprigs of mint. Muddle lightly, pack glass with finely shaved ice, stir once, then turn in the cognac. Decorate with two sticks fresh ripe pineapple, cherries, a slice of ripe peach, or what not. Now float on the Jamaica; dust with the final powdered sugar, and spot in the other sprigs of mint, stems down. . . . Serve with two short straws. Drink when well frosted. We first saw this Julep in a huge tumbler with wide mouth and sloping sides, holding around 16 ounces.

## ADDITIONAL JULEPS, of RUM and BRANDY

Since reither Scotch nor Irish take kindly to julepry, the variations —when those same Marylanders and Kentuckians are absent—can be any sort of rum, and any sort of brandy. . . . In the latter case remember that most fancy brandies like apricot, cherry and peach are very sweet, so mix with cognac half and half. In the former, try and avoid a 100% Jamaica base, as this is a trifle heavy for the average palate. Either dilute Jamaica with white rum like Bacardi, or some medium rum like Barbados. Don't forget that Demerara can be as high as 160 proof!

### WORDS to the LIQUID WISE No. X, on the ABBREVIATION of MINT JULEP STRAWS

The final garnish of emerald mint is not merely to look at. If we must have, or prefer, straws—make them short straws. Just a couple of inches peeping out is correct. Thus the olfactory proboscis must be buried in the fragrant herbage, something not the case with the crude long affairs through which certain folk drink ice cream sodas.

### THE KINGSTON *CRUSTA*, BEING a PARALLEL THOUGHT to the MARTINIQUE *CRUSTA*, on PAGE 74, only from JAMAICA

Hardy Jamaican planters turn this same Martinique drink into something vastly different by the startling addition of ¼ tsp of Jamaica Ginger, or the equivalent of Hell-Fire Bitters, see Page 153. . . . Still hardier Jamaicans even wind this business up further by dusting some cayenne pepper on top.

### *KIRSCH au CAFÉ*—or the FAMOUS BLACK & WHITE COCKTAIL

This revivifier was found in the home of a Cairene resident before going out on the Nile of a moonlight night, and on his *dahabeah*—a luxurious and incredible sailing craft originated and maintained in his case, for no good purpose. . . . Take *kirschwasser* and black very strong coffee, 1 pony each. To this add ½ pony of good cognac, the white of 1 small egg. Shake hard with cracked ice and serve in a tall flute cocktail glass with a stem. *Allah, il Allah!*

### THE KNICKERBOCKER "PUNCH," a MEMORY of the GOOD DAYS of 1915

How many of us remember the Maxfield Parrish *Old King Cole* when it formerly hung—not at the St. Regis at all—in the old Hotel Knickerbocker bar on the southeast corner of Broadway at 42d Street? . . . It smiled benignly down upon all sorts and conditions of men, over a free lunch buffet too rich to be credible—and which saved more than 1 hungry college boy in the days when the Dolly Sisters, the Castles, Gaby des Lys, Bert Williams and Hazel Dawn were stars behind the footlights, on the dance floor; when the late Pauline Frederick was so starkly beautiful in *Joseph and his Brethren;* when deliciously tiny Emma Trentini was imported by our round the world cruising fellow-passenger Rudolph Friml to sing in his operettas; when the old Rectors, Delmonico and Louis Martin weren't just names out of the rosy past. In our college freshman—and financially always debted—days we recall the good old Knickerbocker and the snacks there; and here is one of their specials. . . . Into a goblet strain the juice of ½ a lemon or 1 small lime, add ½ tsp of sugar, a fat jigger of St. Croix or other medium dark rum, 1 pony of water and 2 dashes of orange bitters. Ice with lots of finely cracked ice, stir to chill, decorate with fresh fruit galore, then finally float on 1 pony of still red Burgundy. A sprig of mint and short straws are in order also.

## THE LALLA ROOKH COCKTAIL, a RECEIPT GIVEN US on a TRIP HOME from YOKOHAMA in 1931, by CLYMER BROOKE

Clymer Brooke and 2 or 3 other Yale men set off from New London to circle the globe in their 65 foot schooner *CHANCE,* and Brooke liked it so well in Tahiti he jumped ship and got himself a vanilla plantation on the loveliest island possible: Moorea, across the bay. We met him the day out of Yoko, our ship first bound for Honolulu, when he was headed back to Long Island to marry him a bride, and being "in vanilla" as we might say, through having a South Sea plantation of that orchid vine, the drink was typical. Peerless Theodore, mentioned so often in Volume I, had it specially mixed for us in the *SS RESOLUTE* Grill.

Just why it was called Lalla Rookh is something neither Brooke nor logic could explain. . . . Take 1 jigger of good cognac and mix with ½ jigger of brown rum and ½ pony of vanilla extract. Now add 1 tbsp thick cream. Chill well in a shaker with cracked ice, strain into a flute cocktail glass. Vanilla may be cut down or added to, to taste.

Some people admire ½ tsp of sugar or *gomme*. It makes an insidious drink that ladies prefer, often to their eventual risk, joy, and sorrow.

THE MANILA "LEAP FROG" COCKTAIL, another MEMORY of the CRISP DAYS & COOL NIGHTS up in BAGUIO, back in the IGOROTE COUNTRY of LUZON

Take 1 pony of Bacardi, the same of dry apricot brandy, add the strained juice of 1 small lime or ¼ lemon, colour with 1 tsp of grenadine. Shake with lots of cracked ice and strain into a saucer type champagne glass. . . . After home fabrication of this fine drink we have found very definitely that the original Manila formula may be improved by using 1½ ponies of Bacardi and ½ pony of *apricot,* everything else remaining the same. We must not forget that *apricot* is an insistent and penetrating flavour. We only need a small amount to point up a single cocktail—never 1 pony! Gold Seal Bacardi is best, again; the white lacks flavour.

THE BACARDI "LEAVE IT to ME," from the BAR BOOK of an INFANTRY MAJOR STATIONED at FORT WILLIAM McKINLEY, near MANILA

Fill the shaker ½ way with cracked ice, then put in 1 jigger of *Carta de Oro* Bacardi, 1 tsp maraschino, the juice of 1 small green lime, 1 tsp raspberry syrup. Turn into a saucer champagne glass with 3 or 4 small bits of ice, and hit with a spot of chilled club soda. A pretty, flavourful and refreshing cocktail.

MONK ANTRIM'S *LINTIK* COCKTAIL, which REALLY ISN'T any SPECIES of COCKTAIL at ALL, but a SORT of LIQUID TRIPLE THREAT ORIGINATED for REASONS STRICTLY DISHONOURABLE, but ELECTRIFYING; & in ADDITION a BRIEF SORT of BIOGRAPHY of the GENTLEMAN HIMSELF

We appear to refer to Monk fairly often in this volume, and there is a reason besides his being a careful, almost clinical, student of potable liquids. He happens to be one of the most interesting chaps who ever hit the Islands. When we first knew him Monk lived vividly, to say the least. He had a drink memo book, contents of which had been religiously donated by a series of gentlemen who, at the time of our first trip to the Islands, were either in various sanatoria for alcoholic treatment, had been invalided back to the states as incurable dipso-maniacs, or were dead from probably spirituous causes.

A few years back a chap named Walter E. Antrim showed up from somewhere down in the South Seas, came to the Manila Hotel and got him a job as dishwasher—so sing they, speak they, tell they, the tale—it being Uncle Sam's largest and finest hostelry, and the pride of the Philippines, naturally.

So, as the old silent movies used to say, time passed, but didn't pass Monk by. When we got there first in 1926, he greeted our Cruise Staff at the end of a mile or so of new concrete pier, and we met him then —the *Manager* of the Manila Hotel.

Now Monk knew how to live life in his own way, and he lived it: high, wide, and handsome, making friends as he went along. Monk would roll you, flip you, cut cards with you, for anything from a steam yacht to a thousand dollars gold and never turn a hair. . . . The last we heard he had espoused himself to a handsome titian-haired crea-ture, and vanished from Manila. Why or where?—we just don't know. . . . Anyway we have Monk's letter before us dated March 4th, 1927, passing along several Manila liquids, and calling attention especially to the *Lintik* Cocktail. Quote:

". . . the *Lintik* is the smoothest drink which I've run into lately. . . . *Lintik,* as you may know, being Tagalog for 'Lightning' (Tagalog being the language of a tribe of that name down in eastern Mindanao, the big island below Manila).

"The main drawback to this concoction is that it must be aged for two weeks, then chilled in an ice bucket without ever coming in contact with ice. . . . But the final result is well worth that little bother. . . . Will be seeing you next trip out, and we'll test a few in my laboratory, with Wong to do the mixing!"

Good dry gin, 3 bottles          Lemons, juice 15; peel 10
Water, 2½ cups                   Angostura, 2 full tbsp
                   Sugar, 1¼ lbs

Strain lemon juice carefully through 2 cloths. Boil sugar and water for 2 minutes, strain and cool. Add gin and bitters. Bottle, placing the peel of 2 lemons in each bottle. Store in a cool spot, not too cold, to age. Serve chilled and under no condition add any ice. This will make around 4 to 5 bottles of *Lintik* Cocktails.

## ALFRED BARTON'S SURF CLUB *MANGAREVA* COCKTAIL

If there is an exotic spot on our whole Atlantic Seaboard it is the Miami Beach Surf Club, and Alfred Barton is its guiding genius. His gala nights, incredible affairs, make Hollywood fetes look like modest Quaker meetings. He imports whole circuses, ferris wheels, elephants, clowns and God alone knows what else if he wants a circus; a midway, sideshows, appropriate murals. This *Mangareva* is Barton's *chef d'oeuvre,* along with his staff brain trust, when recently seeking a really unusual drink. Honey has long been a French admiration in certain intimate drinks. *Calvados*—or Normandy apple brandy—and honey would be best, but if not possible use the corresponding applejack and honey available in the open market.

First the container: this being a coconut shell sawed off at the top to a 2½″ opening, and the kernel taken out. Clean up the outside with sandpaper or steel wool. Mount this in a ring of fresh pineapple and garnish with galax leaves, and serve with brightly coloured cellophane straws. . . . Now the mix: turn 1 part *triple sec,* 2 parts strained lime or lemon juice, and 5 parts apple and honey into a bar glass. Mix well and allow 3 oz to each coconut shell. Now fill with finely cracked ice, stir once, close the opening with Pineapple Paradise, *et voila!* Even the cleverest guests cannot guess its formula; furthermore it speaks softly but packs a Big Stick.

WORDS to the LIQUID WISE No. XI, on the EXCELLENCE & DIVERSION of PACKING a COCKTAIL GLASS with SHAVED ICE, ADDING HALF a TEASPOON of STRAINED LIME JUICE, then FILLING with OUR FAVOURITE LIQUEUR

Just try this some day when the taste flags, when ideas run dry or bar shelf is bare of the usual high proof spirits. . . . Try it with

Cointreau, Benedictine, Grand Marnier, Chartreuse, Cordial Medoc, Drambuie, Certosa, or any of the myriad French coloured liqueurs coined for devious Gallic purposes, but each notable for this or that fragrance or flavour. . . . Such drinks are lovely to look at, dry enough through the lime juice, and each one radically different from its neighbour!

THE MARTINIQUE *CRUSTA,* which We Found Waiting for Us in Fort de France on the Occasion of Our First Trip through the West Indies, in 1929

This effective and eventful drink uses no man-made cup, but the reversed skin of a small orange or lemon, first moistened inside and on the lip with lemon juice or rum, then dipped in lots of fine white sugar, until encrusted evenly on inner yellow side of the whole *reversed* skin. . . . Now stand this in any stemmed glass that will fit it.

The other method is to peel off a small orange, or lemon, in a single unbroken spiral. Take a small goblet, moisten inside with lemon juice or rum, then line with the spiral peel, and the whole dipped in fine sugar, leaving what clings, clinging.

Now chill either type of container for a good hour in the refrigerator, and into it strain the following, after shaking well with cracked ice.

| | |
|---|---|
| St. Croix or other Martinique rum, | Maraschino, 1 tsp, scant |
| 1½ jiggers | Angostura, 3 dashes |
| Lime, juice, 1 average size | *Gomme* syrup, 1 tsp, to taste |

Garnish with a stick of fresh pineapple, a slice of orange, or anything that suits.

MI *AMANTE,* which Means "My Beloved," and Was Given to Us by Two Young Gentlemen from the Argentine, from B. A., & Who Own Polo Ponies, Ranches & Things

Our young Argentine knows how to live life we can assure you, and does. He is smart, modern, full of fun, often as not a superior athlete. He knows American cocktails, and originates quite a few on his own account. . . . We tried this during a recent local heat wave with results entirely at odds with the first reaction to its written formula.

Take of the best gin possible, 1½ jiggers, of coffee ice cream, 1 cup. Put into a chilled shaker and shake well, or better still in The Mixer. Some people add a few lumps of ice to help the chill—straining the latter out in serving. Pour into large saucer type champagne glasses.

TWO ACCEPTED VERSIONS of the WORLD FAMOUS ONE-&-ONLY MILLION DOLLAR COCKTAIL, which Is ESPECIALLY FAMOUS throughout JAPAN & the PHILIPPINE ISLANDS

MILLION DOLLAR COCKTAIL No. I, as MIXED by SHIDEAKI SAITO, No. I BAR BOY at the IMPERIAL HOTEL, TOKYO, JAPAN, 1926, 1931 & 1932

First fill shaker 2/3 full of cracked ice then put in 1½ jiggers old Tom gin, ½ pony of Italian vermouth, 2 tsp pineapple syrup, 1 tsp of grenadine for colour, 2 tsp strained lemon juice, 2 tsp of thick cream and ½ the white of a fresh egg. Shake hard, strain into a big opulent-looking saucer champagne glass, and that's that. . . . Vermouth content is immediately varied by Saito to suit the palates of his various Million Dollar clients in Tokyo—running from 1 pony down to ½ pony. Some prefer French dry vermouth, but the standard blend calls for Martini & Rossi.

MILLION DOLLAR COCKTAIL No. II, as MIXED by NOMURA, the No. I BAR BOY at TOR HOTEL, KOBE, DATING from 1926, to 1931 & 1932

His formula was exactly the same as Saito's masterpiece except the vermouth was stepped up to 1 pony, and the lemon juice to 1 tbsp, strained of course; then 1 tsp grenadine.

THE MIYAKO HOTEL SPECIAL
From Kyoto, Japan, during the Cherry Blossom Festival, April 20th, 1932.

Japan is heart-breakingly beautiful enough by itself, and Kyoto was its ancient Capital. Being there for a third time was romantic enough surely, but being there for the great festival was something else still— especially with a fiancée by our side. . . . Well, we were all of these, and our bland friend Mr. S. Suda, bar baron at the Miyako Hotel, concocted this after considerable thought, and added his blessing on our whole picture. . . . The results were benignly immediate.

| | |
|---|---|
| Dry gin, 1 jigger | Cointreau, 1 jigger |
| Fresh pineapple juice, 1 pony | Lemon or lime, juice, ½ pony |

Shake with finely cracked ice, and pour into a tall four ounce cocktail glass with stem. It is fairly sweet, so step up lemon a trifle and cut down pineapple, if preferred.

## SLOPPY JOE'S *MOJITO*, which Is a BACARDI COLLINS, PLUS

Cubans and snobbish *Americanos* can sneer all they please at Sloppy Joe's, the fact still remains that there are as good, and better, and more varied cocktails suitable to our somewhat exacting taste than any other spot in Cuba. Granted that the Vedado Club, the Country Club, the *Nacional, La Florida*—all have their known specialties, still Sloppy Joe's assortment is not with them.

This is a greatly improved rum collins, and is best made with *Carta de Oro* Bacardi, or any good medium light Santa Cruz, Haiti, or Barbados rum. If Jamaica is used, don't use it straight, mix with white rum, one part to four of latter.

Put several lumps of ice into a 16 oz collins glass, toss in 1 tsp sugar or *gomme,* insinuate a spiral green lime peel about the ice, turn in 1½ jiggers of Bacardi; white, or Gold Seal, and the strained juice of 1 small green lime—not a lemon. Stir once, fill with really good club soda and garnish with a bunch of fresh mint. . . . If for a lady, use grenadine instead of sugar.

WORDS to the LIQUID WISE No. XII, on the PRETTY SENSE of USING VARIOUS COLOURED FRUIT SYRUPS for SWEET-ENING ALL SORTS of COLLINS DRINKS
Mix the usual Tom or John Collins, only instead of using sugar use

raspberry, strawberry, mint, cherry, or other soda fountain syrups. They add a slight bouquet and taste, make a pretty looking drink. Vary by using stone bottle ginger beer for soda.

THE MOOD INDIGO, BEING another ONE from another YEAR'S CRUISING, FOUND at GOULD'S CASINO, in NICE, FRANCE, in 1932

Once again we happened into the *Palais de la Mediterranée,* accompanied by a young and fluent maiden, to look about, to risk our top limit of 20 dollars—then—gold on roulette. That Gould's Palace really is something—and to our mind a modernistic dream conceivable only by a hybrid of Nero, Alice Foote MacDougall, and our friend Donald Desky. As the French maitre d'hotel told us—quoting from the book —*"Tous les Galas de la Saison attirent-ils une assistance d'elite dont l'elegance et la chic eclipsent les plus eccalantantes societes mondaines."*

Be that as it may Gould's made the over-publicized and faintly funereal Casino at Monte Carlo look like a shabby country cousin— they are reviving its sinking fortune with Keeno now, imagine it!— and someone suggested a Mood Indigo, and we wondered if it were a liquid compliment to Duke Ellington's music, and ordered 2—one of which we introduced to the young maiden, who then introduced herself to us. . . . Take 1 jigger of dry gin, ½ pony of cognac and anywhere from ½ to 1 pony of *crème de violette,* or *parfait amour.* Adding 1 tsp of egg white is optional, and usual. Shake viciously with lots of cracked ice, serve promptly, and drink vis-à-vis. *"Et quel dommage, M'sieu et Ma'mselle?"* . . . A violet blossom is the prettiest garnish.

EL MOROCCO, which Is a COCKTAIL from NORTH AFRICA, not any PRODUCT of NEW YORK RESTAURANTS of SIMILAR NAME

This is from the field notebook of a trusted friend on a Mediterranean cruise in 1938, and dated from Tangier, North Africa. Take 1 pony each of cognac, red port wine and ripe pineapple juice, putting it in a shaker with lots of cracked ice. Flavour further with 1 tsp each of grenadine and orange Curaçao; and make tart with 2 tsp of lime juice, strained. Shake and strain into a tall flute cocktail glass with a stem. . . . Personally we have come to omit all grenadine. The port gives it all the sweetness needed, also pretty colour.

WIL P. TAYLOR'S *HOTEL NACIONAL* SPECIAL, which, along with the TROPICAL DAIQUIRI & the SANTIAGO de CUBA MINT JULEP IS ONE of the THREE FINEST BACARDI DRINKS KNOWN to SCIENCE

Who, who knows his Havana, does not know, or has not heard of, Wil Taylor. We met him back in 1931 when in charge of World Cruise Publicity for Hamburg-American Line, and got into Havana one time in 1933 just after they had mighty near blasted a marvellous hotel off the map, to get at those Machado-phile officers hiding there. And Taylor kept right on managing just as if it had been old times! . . . But that time with pineapples sounding off all night along the Prado, we elected to stick to the old downtown Plaza, what with wife and child, but that did not prevent our remembering with great pleasure Taylor's own Bacardi concoction. . . . It is "mighty lak" a Mary Pickford, but still not, as the latter omits her limes.

*Carta de Oro* Bacardi, 1 jigger        Fresh pineapple juice, 1 jigger
Lime, juice ½                            Dry apricot brandy, 1 tsp

Shake with cracked ice, strain, serve in a tall cocktail glass with a stem. . . . We indicate Gold Label Bacardi for the simple reason that *Carta Blanca* is so delicate in flavour it barely comes through any rich drink.

THE *OKOLEHAO* COCKTAIL, KNOWN out in the ISLANDS as the "OKE"

Having made three visits to these enchanted isles, both during and after prohibition, we have seen, smelled and tasted some pretty strange beverages out yonder. Actually *okolehao* is a spirit made from a certain root, fermented and distilled. During her very strict prohibition administered by a lady who apparently got as much joy out of life as a newt or an eft—see Webster—Hawaii's "oke" was made from fermented pineapple juice, from the bud sap of coconut palm, from taro, from sweet potatoes, sugar cane, and heaven alone knows what else. Now the original native liquor is legal once again, here's the accepted island cocktail for them as likes it. . . . Take 1 jigger each of *okolehao* and fresh ripe pineapple juice, add ½ jigger of lime juice, properly strained, and shake with lots of ice. Garnish with any sort of bright, small, tropical-appearing blossom.

## THE PARISIAN COCKTAIL, Being a Fine Appetizer & Tummy Toner

We got to like this rather odd tasting beverage after a stay in Paris. It is simple and worth noting. Take 1 jigger of Byrrh wine, add the juice of 1 small green lime, strained. Shake with lots of cracked ice briskly and serve in a Manhattan glass with no further trimmings at all.

## SHELBY LANGSTON'S PALMETTO PUNCH, which Is an Exotic Invented on a Florida Camp Hunt

Perhaps our readers have noted a fairly persistent mention of sour oranges in *Volume I*. It seems high time that Americans lucky enough to live in the Deep South should realize what a truly wonderful flavouring agent they are—this wild descendant of the original bitter rind Seville oranges brought to Florida and West Indies by Columbus himself, has flavour both in juice and peel so delicious, so exotic, so superior to other sour citrus fruits, that it should be much more appreciated. The Cubans know it, and their Steak *Bigarade* is listed in *Volume I*, on Page 138. . . . Our good friend Shelby Langston, like ourselves, has shot quail, wild turkey and deer along the great headwater hammocks and marshes of the St. Johns River, in Florida, and squirrels in Nawth Ca'lina. Sour oranges can be found in many old deserted clearings, and his discovery in camp of this mixture should rank in Florida with our friend's invention of the world-famous Daiquiri, noted on Page 30.

The proportion of sour orange juice to that of sweet depends on the sweetness of the sweet oranges. It will only take a few trials to learn what suits personal taste—and here's to you lucky Floridians. No one sells sour oranges, they give them away, for not one person in a thousand thinks they are worth picking off trees.

| | |
|---|---|
| Old Tom gin, 1 part; (Dry gin will do) | Sour orange juice, 1 part |
| | Sweet orange juice, 2 parts |

Shake quickly and hard with lots of ice, pour through strainer, and twist a small piece of sour or sweet orange peel over each glass to get the oil of orange aroma and flavour.


PAN AMERICAN CLIPPER, from the Notebook of One of Our Pilot Friends Who—when Off Duty—May Seek One

| | |
|---|---|
| Applejack, 1 jigger; *Calvados* apple brandy is better still | Lime, juice, 1 scant pony |
| | Grenadine, 1 tsp |
| Absinthe, 1 dash | |

Shake with cracked ice and serve in Manhattan glass.


PANCHO VILLA COCKTAIL, another Classic from the Philippines that We Absorbed in 1926, for the First Time

The late Filipino gentleman of this name was probably the greatest man for his inches that ever drew on a pair of fighting gloves. In Manila he is still a national hero, his monument is impressive, and when Monk Antrim's Chino Number One whipped this one up in his honour, it proved more than good enough for us to insert here.

| | |
|---|---|
| *Carta de Oro* Bacardi, 1 pony | Dry gin, 1 pony |
| Dry apricot brandy, 1 pony | Cherry brandy, 1 tsp |
| Pineapple juice, 1 tsp | Stuffed olive |

This is a sweet one and must be very cold. Fill shaker with fine ice and pour into a big champagne glass. It is one of the very few cocktails calling for several conflicting ingredients that is worth its own weight in bicarbonate of soda.

THE PENANG COOLER, a New Tropical Exotic We First Met in Penang, Prince of Wales Island, F.M.S., Following a Swim in the Milk-Warm Waters of the Straits of Malacca

After a swim at the Aquatic Club, we came back to town and ran into this, unexpectedly proposed by a semi-Chino barkeep at the Eastern and Occidental Hotel. The mint gives it coolness, bite, and character.

Dry gin, 1 jigger                     Fresh pineapple juice, 2 jiggers
Green crème de menthe, 1 pony

Shake with shaved ice and serve with it in a tall cocktail glass with stem. A flat glass was used out there, and ice was strained out—but the more modern technique is best, using an electric mixer and leaving ice in.

THE PENDENNIS CLUB'S FAMOUS SPECIAL

To 1 jigger of dry gin add ½ jigger of the best dry apricot brandy procurable. Squeeze in the juice of 1 lime or ½ a small lemon, strained of course, and trim with 2 dashes of Peychaud's bitters which has been made for generations in New Orleans. . . . Split a ripe kumquat, now available during the winter in most big grocery or fruit stores; take out the seeds and put the 2 halves in a Manhattan glass. Stir the drink like a Martini with lots of cracked ice and strain onto the golden fruit. This is a sweeter Grande Bretagne, see Page 47.

TWENTY and SEVEN PICKER-UPPERS for the Nineteenth Hole, which Can not only Enable Us to Greet the New Day Undismayed but May—on Occasion—Save a Life

There are times in every man's life when, through one reason or both, a man feels precisely like Death warmed up. In such sorry plight there is but one thing to do if we do not wish to sit and suffer through a whole day waiting for the cool hand of normalcy to stroke our dry and fevered brow—a Picker-Upper.

This little list of variegated hairs of the dog, has been hand-culled from quite a few joustings of our own with this sort of human withering on the vine. We have, from sad example set by several friends, come to distrust all revivers smacking of drugdom. It is a small, tightly vicious circle to get into, and a bit of well-aged spirits with this or that, seems much safer and more pleasant than corroding our innards with chemicals of violent proclivities, and possible habit-forming ways.

For years before our ignoble experiment, civilized man had been trying to civilize his drinking, and when we think back just yesterday—as world's time is measured—man's one drink was a crudely fermented affair: juice, seeds, saps, and the like.

Now take an eye filling look at any well-stocked oasis, and consider progress in colour, taste, bouquet, and result. This early civilization in America—except in the main centers like Charleston, New Orleans, Philadelphia, and New York—with the possible exception of the matchless julep, commanded hard likker with a chaser, if any. Now since the insanity of the nineteen-twenties man is studying his spirits sanely and with revived artistic interest in their possibilities.

The field of the great gray Morning After is one which this same civilized mankind is trying to graduate from undiluted hair of the dog that bit him, to something less regurgitative, and shocking to the whole mental and nervous network. With this thought in view we quietly suggest any of the following.

WORDS to the WISE No. XIII, on the NECESSITY for GOOD SPIRITS for MAKING PICKER-UPPERS

Just as we don't serve mediocre acid red wine to the delicate sensibilities of a prize gourmet friend, neither do we give the timid and demure morning-after tummy a turn with raw, new, bilious atrocities. Here, if ever, the smart host will have a special cache of a few prize jewels—for his very own sake. The vile odours arising from improperly aged spirits are just about all a chap needs to set him to withering on the vine permanently. . . . Use only the best ingredients, for after all we don't do these things very often, and it's better to be safe than sunk.

FIRST on the LIST MARCHES CHAMPAGNE, although It Has already Been Dealt with Sympathetically under Champagne Cocktails, Page 21, *et sequitur*

A plain chilled pint of champagne per person with two or three simple biscuits is probably the finest picker-upper known to civilized man. The champagne must be *very* cold, and can either have bitters, a little added brandy, or both.

The Maharajah's *Burra-Peg,* and the Imperial Cossack *Crusta,* are the most magnificent examples of this we have ever known.

Champagne in this role is somewhat more expensive than any of the other remedies collected, but when we think back there is stark realization that the time comes to every man when relative expense means little; and rather than risk a "turn" from sight of raw egg, or taste of sweet ingredients, the refreshing, chill tartness of the bubbly is a dispensation straight from heaven.

## ABSINTHE FRAPPÉ and ABSINTHE DRIP

These two picker-uppers are already given on Page 8, *et sequitur.*

## ABSINTHE PHOSPHATE

There is no doubt about this one working. . . . Simply put two dashes of lemon phosphate in a bar glass, add a jigger absinthe and a pony of Italian vermouth. Stir for a moment and pour into a claret glass filled with finely cracked or shaved ice. Vermouth can easily be cut down slightly to taste.

## BARRANQUILLA PICK-ME-UP

Barranquilla, as has already been pointed out, is the residential center of near-coast Colombia for many of those Americans who do things in oil and emeralds. And here, we found, a man can need a picker-upper just as well as anywhere else.

| | |
|---|---|
| Cognac, 3 jiggers | Angostura, 2 dashes |
| Dubonnet, 2 jiggers | Egg, white 1 |

Shake well with cracked ice and serve in a tall glass with stem.

## CAROLINA PLANTATION BRACER

After dancing the night through, or possibly a gentleman's game of draw poker—nothing wild—until the wee sma' hours, our tide-water blade knifing his way about the selvages of Charleston's society was wise in his pick-me-ups. This suggestion from Bill Heyward, schoolmate of years back, given between boats one winter afternoon is something to note, lest we forget.

Cognac, 1½ jiggers                  *Gomme* syrup, 1 tsp; optional
Egg, 1                              Jamaica or Barbados rum, ¼ tsp
Port, 1½ jiggers

Shake with cracked ice until busily frothing, and pour into a tall cocktail glass with stem. . . . Other neat flavour touches can double for the Jamaica: Curaçao, Cointreau, Cordial Médoc, Drambuie, Benedictine, Chartreuse, Grand Marnier.


## PARISIAN "GOOD-MORNING"

Absinthe, 1 jigger                  Yellow chartreuse, ½ tsp
French vermouth, ½ tsp              Lime or lemon, strained juice, 1,
Bar sugar or *gomme* syrup, 1 tsp       or ½
                    Anis or anisette, 1 tsp

Frappe with cracked ice, strain into old fashioned glass, add small bit of ice, and a little soda or seltzer, stir and pote.


## HARVARD CLUB PICK-ME-UP

This, as Frederick A. R. Thompson, the then Managing Editor of *THE COMMONWEAL* informs us, is the brain-child of former British naval officer now, for this reason or that, Head Factotum behind mahogany in the New York Harvard Club. The request is to serve them three ounces at a time, and as cold as may be with chilled glasses. . . . Three of these have been known to change a blue, murky,

Monday morning into a nascent glowing thing, all rose and mother of pearl.

> *Good* rye, Pernod Veritas, Italian Vermouth, 1/3 each
> Two dashes Lemon Phosphate, per drink

Frappe well, and strain.

## HOLLAND RAZOR BLADE

This rather rugged bit of canine fur was introduced to us by a Hollander who brought body and soul within hailing range on the occasion of certain dawn flight from Batavia, via Semarang and Soerabaja, to Bali, in the year of Grace 1931. . . . It is for those who can stomach Hollands and is one of the promptest.

| | |
|---|---|
| Holland gin, 1½ jiggers | Dust with cayenne just before |
| Lemon, juice, ½, or juice whole | drinking |
| lime | |

This may be shaken with broken ice, or not. We would say yes.

## THE ISLE de FRANCE SPECIAL, BEING in FIRST ANALYSIS a CHAMPAGNE COCKTAIL, as well as ONE of the FINEST PICKER-UPPERS KNOWN to FRAIL FLESH, IS CONSEQUENTLY LISTED on PAGE 24

## KILROY'S BRACER, LONG an ACCREDITED MORNING-after REJUVENATOR EVERYWHERE

| | |
|---|---|
| Cognac, 1½ jiggers | Angostura, 3 dashes |
| Lime or lemon juice, 2 tsp | Anis or anisette, ½ tsp |
| Egg, 1 | Shaved ice |

Shake well, turn into a goblet with some of the ice, and fill to taste with well chilled seltzer or club soda.

## LEFT BANK SPINE STIFFENER

Dated Paris, 5:10 A.M. May 6th, 1926, and well remembered, too!

> Cinzano, or good Italian vermouth, 2 jiggers
> Absinthe, or Pernod Veritas, 1 jigger

Shake with fine ice until well chilled, turn into a whisky glass and top off with a trace of seltzer, leaving in three teaspoons of the fine ice to keep the chill edge on.

## BIARRITZ "MONK-BUCK"

Something to cause nerves to join and coordinate for that morning-after—and rather chill (we've found) swim which characterizes the Mediterranean when we got there too soon, one spring.

Simply throw two and a half jiggers of cognac in a sixteen ounce collins glass already lined with a long spiral peel à la horse's neck. Pack half full of fine ice, fill with the best ginger ale or ginger beer the place affords, float on a couple of tablespoons yellow chartreuse, and let it settle to the bottom. . . . Don't plan on more than one, for a little while.

## MORNING GLORY No. I

| | |
|---|---|
| Dry gin, 1 jigger | Egg, 1 |
| Lime, juice, ½ | Green crème de menthe, 2 tsp, or so |

Shake with cracked ice, serve in a tall cocktail glass with stem.

## MORNING GLORY No. II

| | |
|---|---|
| Good rye, or bourbon, 1 jigger | Orange bitters or Angostura, 3 |
| Gomme syrup, 1 tsp | dashes |
| Curaçao, 1 tsp | Absinthe, 1 tsp |
| Cognac, 1 jigger | |

Mixing technique seems torn between stirring in a bar glass with ice, straining into a whisky glass, and adding a little seltzer topped off with a twisted lemon peel—or stirring in the same bar glass, and turning into an old fashioned glass with a lump of ice, a squirt of club soda, and a twist of peel. . . . Some sane folk merely shake with ice and a jigger of soda or seltzer. The latter works more suddenly than the more diluted drink. . . . Absinthe is difficult to recommend to suit others—increase or decrease to taste. Pernod Veritas will do.

## MORNING "DOCTOR"

Take 1½ to 2½ jiggers of good brandy, a trifle over a cup of very fresh milk, and a teaspoon of sugar, and beat the whole business with an egg-beater.

## OLD PEPPER

This is nothing for children to toy with, but for action and plenty of it we report that little is lacking on that score.

| | |
|---|---|
| Good rye, 1 jigger | Good bourbon, 1 jigger |
| Lemon, juice 2/3 | Worcestershire, ½ tsp |
| Tabasco, 3 drops | Chili sauce, ½ tsp |

Frappe hard, and serve in any sort of fireproof glass.

## PORT ANTONIO PUNCH, from JAMAICA

This is a mild and delicious tropical invention which is very easy to make, and which—unlike so many Jamaica drinks—doesn't insist on one hundred per cent rum in its spiritual makeup.

Squeeze and strain through a sieve juice of two lemons, one orange
Donate a pony of old Jamaica rum, 4 jiggers of cognac
Stir in two level tablespoons of brown sugar
Two bottles Rhine, or one quart chablis
One bottle of iced club soda
Sliced fresh fruit *du jour*

Simply ice, shake, and garnish. This is utterly delicious, but be sure and use fresh pineapple slices, not canned—and ripe pineapple at that!

## PORTO FLIP

From the Army & Navy Club, Manila, P.I., 1931

| | |
|---|---|
| Port wine, 2 jiggers | Sugar, 2 scant tsp |
| Egg, fresh essentially, 1 whole | Chartreuse, 1 tsp |
| Thick cream, 1 pony | Grated nutmeg |
| Cognac, 1 pony | |

Send this up on the breakfast tray of the tweakiest and most jangled week-end guest on the casualty list, and watch the smiles wreathe— and be sure it goes down on an empty tummy for best and most soothing effect.

Simply mix everything with a lot of cracked ice, shake hard and serve in a small goblet, floating chartreuse on top with spoon, and adding a good dusting of grated nutmeg.

## THE SO-CALLED PRAIRIE OYSTER

We once had a shipmate who insisted on a morning dip in Long Island Sound even in November; just so we have other hardy friends who eat enormous cream oyster stews for mornings after, or toss off prairie oysters, which seen eye to eye would simply mean one gyration of our adam's apple and a free ticket to a marble slab in the morgue. . . . However, for such hardy souls, we might as well set down its precise preparation.

| | |
|---|---|
| Egg yolk, in its unbroken state, 1 | Ketchup, 1 tsp |
| Salt, good pinch | Vinegar, ½ tsp |
| Lemon juice, 1 tsp | Tabasco, 1 drop |
| Worcestershire, 1 tsp | Cayenne, pinch on top |

Shut eyes, open mouth, murmur prayers for the soul, pop in and swallow whole. . . . This *has* been administered for the evening before, but its benefits have proven to be base canard, a sorry snare and delusion.

## RANGOON STAR-RUBY, a Picker-Upper from Burmah, on the Road to Mandalay

This affair is properly listed among the exotics from Far Ports, on Page 126.

## SAINT MARK'S MIRACLE, Annotated One November Day in Seattle, after a Washington-Stanford Football Game, at the Advertising Club

This name is of doubtful origin, and all we know is that the receipt found its way to England across Europe, from the Venetian canals, where it has an enviable record of revivition after the unwise cup on a night before.

Champagne *fine,* which of course is liqueur brandy of great age, 2 jiggers
Angostura, ½ tsp

Yellow Curaçao, 1 pony
Lemon, juice, ½
Orange bitters, ½ pony

Shake briskly and strain into any sort of glass best calculated not to fall from our numb and listless clutch.

SWISS YODELER, which We Employed Once at Villa d'Este, which Is on Lake Como

We always wondered what made those Swiss alpenstock wielders such staunch and hardy fellows, so consider this for a warmer-up of waning flesh. The egg white is heavier than most absinthe cocktails.

Absinthe, 1 jigger          Anis, or anisette, 1 tsp          Egg, white 1

Shake well with cracked ice and pour frothing in tall cocktail glass with stem.

WHITFIELD SMITH'S *SUNDAY MORNING COCKTAIL,* No. I, & this One's a Darb!

This is another contribution from Fritz Abildgəard Fenger, and should be served in a 4 oz glass, same as a proper West Indian Swizzle. This makes four drinks.

Put 2 fresh egg yolks in 4 oz glass, and fill with ice water. Add one and a half more glasses water, and add a teaspoon of sugar or *gomme* to taste. To this contribute 4 teaspoons Angostura, swizzle—or shake in shaker to break yolks—and add four ponies of rye or bourbon whisky. . . . In go 2 oz—½ a cocktail glass—of cream, and a little Crème de Cacao or Benedictine, to taste. Swizzle again and grate nutmeg on top. . . . If no cream handy, use water.

Note: Our suggestion would be to omit sugar if any sweet liqueur is used, or it may be too sweet.

## SUNDAY MORNING COCKTAIL No. II

Cognac, 1½ jiggers      Egg, 1 whole
Port wine, ½ jigger      Sugar, ½ tsp, to taste
Black coffee, 2/3 pony

Shake and pour in tall cocktail glass with stem.

## THE PEKING TIGER'S MILK No. I, from the Private Files of M. Gerber, the WAGON-LITS, Legation Street, Peking

This we consider the most amazing milk drink we ever tasted. Its formula—not known to many—and its history are noted on Page 130.

## TIGER'S MILK No. II

This variation was accumulated by us from the Siamese Head Bar-Boy at the Phya-Thai Palace in Bangkok, Siam, in the year 1932, after a trip up-country from the Siamese port of Pak-Nam. Turn to Page 131.

## TIGER'S MILK No. III

This is a West Indian picker-upper from the Windward side of Jamaica, and dedicated to our friend, gentleman and Rhodes Scholar, Emerson Low, who lived there. Use Jamaica rum & No. II.

WORDS to the LIQUID WISE No. XIV, on the EARNEST PLEA for a BIT of OUTDOOR EXERCISE to those HUMAN VICTIMS of the "MORNING-AFTERS"

Science has just recognized that with the tummy linings well saturated with last night's ethyls or methyls, it is best remedied by increased natural circulation removing much of this condition. Therefore, after any Picker-Upper, let's not lie supine and bewail hard and unjust fate, but take a walk, play pingpong—any physical activity not inducing actual death, and no matter how slight or brief, cannot but help; and is urgently recommended!

## "PINEAPPLE MILK" or *LECHE PREPARADA PIÑA*, Collected in the Lovely City of San Salvador, Capital of the Central American Republic Bearing the Same Name

This is a truly delicious beverage first brought to my attention by a lucky friend who stumbled upon it on a trip we made down the central American coast, in 1934 in the quite amazingly modern capital of San Salvador. All the ingredients are easily found.

Pineapple, sun-ripened until good and soft, juice and pulp, 1
Vanilla bean, 2 inch long piece; or 1 tsp extract
Good sound liqueur brandy, ½ cup or so; or white Bacardi
Milk, 3 cups
Sugar, brown, to taste; white will do

Pineapple is topped, pared and sliced off core. Then either chopped into small pieces or crushed in a mortar until almost a pulp—saving all the rich juices. Blend everything together, let be for two hours, and serve well chilled and garnished, if in the mood, with incidental slices of orange, pineapple, sprigs of mint, or maraschino cherries. It is a grand hot weather potation, and has been known to cause chronic invalids to take up their—and other—beds and walk.

## PINK LADY No. I, from Miramar Club, out by Old Panama City, Panama

We've sat and swum from Miramar Club seven or eight times on different trips across the Isthmus. The Pink Lady there is enough different from the usual to make it well listable here.

| | |
|---|---|
| Old Tom gin, 1 jigger | Sloe gin, 1 jigger |
| Lemon, juice ½ small; or 1 lime | Absinthe, 2/3 tsp |
| Orange bitters, 3 to 4 dashes | French vermouth, ½ jigger |
| Beaten egg white, 1 tbsp | Grenadine, 1 tsp, to taste |

Half fill shaker with cracked ice, add egg, then the rest. Shake well and serve in goblet. This is a drink of considerable shocking power, and after consumption keep out of the sun, and in touch with friends.

## CURAÇAO "PONTOON BRIDGE"

We snupped this during the spring of 1933 when circling the Caribbean for reasons not pertinent to drink-mixing. After a few hours in the perfume and other bazaars, we sat on the antique upper balcony of a little sort of Stranger's Club overlooking the odd steam-donkey-engine-driven pontoon bridge connecting Willemstadt with our part of the city, and a traffic policeman sitting in a high chair under a huge umbrella advising us of the fact that the only honest shop in the place was this or that. . . . Having sampled all colours of Curaçao liqueur until it was virtually oozing from our pores, we still stuck to our guns, and were treated to the following—which having no name, we called the Pontoon Bridge.

Fill a large glass with shaved ice, then mix two ponies cognac with one pony Curaçao, juice half a lime, and a dash of orange bitters. Pour over ice, and garnish with a stick of really ripe pineapple. Cherry is optional. We found no cherries in Curaçao.

## A RAKISH FAMILY of SIXTEEN *POUSSE CAFÉS*, INCLUDING a SQUAD of ANGELS WHO NEVER HAD WINGS, BEING VARIOUS & SUNDRY PRETTY LIQUEURS COMBINED in this FASHION or that—for a PURPOSE

A liqueur, technically, is any alcoholic beverage sweetened and variously flavoured with aromatic substances: oils, herbs, and so on. . . . A *pousse café* is an arrangement of one or more liqueurs originally designed by Gallic progenitors as a "coffee-pusher"—hence the name —to be drunk with the after dinner cup, but like many other French ideas started out for one purpose, it has been diverted into other, and rosier, fields where dalliance may be made more pleasant and profitable through quiet absorption of these pretty rainbow-hued drinks.

Now we are great believers in the Up-and-Doing, Derring-Do, and Go West, Young Man. There's no nonsense back of our inclusion of this seductive list of jewel coloured drinks here. We include them for their original purpose of pushing coffee down, and leave criticisms to the judgment of Jurgen's discreet Tumble-bug.

Actually we do think *pousse cafés* have been slightly diverted from their original coffee-pushing intent, for if anyone can imagine following a good demitasse of strong black Mocha with half a dozen sweet cordials roosting on the yolk of an egg, we pass! . . . Some of these affairs may seem to have rather strange names but, like many other things which have gained recognition through the usage of years, we feel it only the stout thing to do to write them as they are called, and not drop the modest lash to hide our possible blushes.

WORDS to the LIQUID WISE No. XV, on the NUMBER of RINGS in a *POUSSE CAFÉ*

For reasons known only to barkeeps and their ancient patrons, a proper *pousse café* should contain seven, five, or three, contrasting rings of different coloured liqueurs. Just why these numerals are sacred we have never quite learned—any more than why seven and eleven count profitably on the first roll of dice, or why folk like Haile Selassie had three-decker parasols.

The liqueurs are poured in ever so carefully with a spoon, and sit each on top of the next, unmixed, brilliant each in its own right. The successive sips give varying taste thrills.

ONE CAUTIONING TALE about the Gentle but Unsafe Amateur Art of Breeding *POUSSE CAFÉS*

We first got this idea in Spofford's big bungalow out in Ballygunge, Calcutta, one pre-monsoon evening in 1926. A tremendous Bengali curry, then coffee on the terrace under the low, hot stars, talking over college days, friends here and there, impending marriage, birth, death, while big bats the size of kittens shuttled back and forth over the level green of the tennis court. . . . Then the idea, we would get every cordial and liqueur in the place, and brew bigger and better *pousse cafés*—and each time one went bad—mixed up hopelessly instead of remaining in distinct jewel-sharp layers, the culprit responsible had to toss it off bottoms up. When a successful one was brewed with five layers or more, the result was shared.

To be exact this whole affair is a matter of precise specific gravities as we tried it then, for instead of flowing each layer on carefully out of a teaspoon, we poured direct from bottle—so that any heavier liquid sank at once into the lighter, and mixed results were usual.

All memories of that especial evening faded into a tropical after-glow by about eleven o'clock, when Chidsey the Dodge agent tells us he came over hoping for a spot of stud poker, and found the two of us, heads bloody and almost bowed, still muttering and mixing with exaggerated care more and bigger *pousse cafés,* while a brace of Mohammedan bearers peered at us through doorways, and marvelled at the madness and triviality of certain white Sahibs who would thus procure child's size glasses into which they continued to pour the same pretty coloured liquids.

Recalling this in Havana last month, we made it a point to collect types from the best *cantinas* and fancy tourist bars, to see if there might be anything new in the routine. We found a couple of fancies, which appear below, each in its proper place, and now turn the whole busi-ness over to readers, depending on their judgment and decorum to the last.

## FIRST A BRIEF COMPANY of SIX ANGELS

Aunt Belladonna Fittich may blink a bit at this short list, but when things have been going on as long as this "angel" business it belongs to history, whether or no. We have our own personal idea, not con-venient to mention, of just why angels were born; but be that as it may, full many a lusty swain has screwed up his courage to the stick-ing point and proposed honourable marriage to the maid of his choice while either—or both—were being swayed by the gentle caress of an "angel." . . . They are too sweet for serious consumption, and all end up with a nominal amount of thick cream—whipped, or from the bottle. Ladies and gentlemen we give you: The Angels.

## ANGEL'S BLUSH

Pour in ¼ each of the following: Maraschino, *Crème Yvette,* Bene-dictine, thick cream.

ANGEL'S CHERRY, a Nominal Risk We Met Successfully in Mentone, near the Italian Border, on a Spring Day in 1932
This addition, whose title meaning is debatable, is a newcomer to the fold. Those of us who take the trouble can find Damiana in any decent wine merchant's shop, and a perusal of the label illustration alone should be worth the price of admission. . . . *Pour la Patrie!*
. . . Needless to say Damiana is alleged to possess certain properties which wise men have sought for many centuries, with greater or less result—mostly less. . . . Benedictine, Damiana, and cognac, 1/3 each. Top off with a tablespoon of thick cream, center with the largest and reddest cherry the neighbourhood affords, and be about our business.


ANGEL'S DREAM
Omit the Benedictine, and use 1/3 each Damiana, *Crème Yvette,* cognac and heavy cream.


ANGEL'S KISS
This heavenly, and hypothetical osculation has scant value as an historical beverage here or abroad, but as long as we are going in for items of more or less serious nonsense, it shall not pass.
Float in, and on, 1/5 each of the following: Damiana, *Parfaite Amour,* yellow chartreuse, Benedictine, cognac, and beaten egg white. On this is superimposed a layer of thick cream, and on it ginger, clove, or nutmeg—a slight pinch—depending on the perquisites of the occasion.


ANGEL'S TIT, No. I, Being the Original Formula
First encountered on one of those Canadian week-ends at Niagara on the Lake when many nice people seemed to forsake these United States seeking oasis for reasons of their own, during prohibition.

Maraschino, ¾                      Whipped cream, ¼

Garnish with scarlet cherry in location diametrically exact.

ANGEL'S TIT, No. II

A Parisian indication of chancey origin, but of definite value.

Damiana, or *Parfaite Amour*, ¾        Whipped cream about ¼″ on
Cognac, ¼                                top

A similar cherry, accurately teed up in traditional style.

TEN MORE which ARE NOT CALLED ANGELS

PARIS' *ARC-en-CIEL*—the WORLD-FAMOUS RAINBOW

This is probably the most famous *pousse café* ever conceived, and is not only beautiful but logical—as it takes the whole seven colours of the spectrum and places them before you in all their jewel colours to be sipped pensively out of a glass, one layer at a time, and experiencing the gamut of seven delicious tastes. Simply spoon in one-seventh each of the following: *Crème de violette, crème de cassis,* maraschino, green *crème de menthe,* yellow chartreuse, Curaçao, cherry or other red coloured brandy.

EVE'S GARDEN, from a *FOLIES BERGÈRE* ENTR'ACTE, in a not-too-DISTANT SPRING, in PARIS

One third each Damiana, *Crème Yvette,* and dry apricot brandy—all finished off with a spoonful of thick cream and a *green* cherry in center. . . . Cognac is also indicated for the apricot, and to our thought is much better, as the drink is sweet enough anyway. . . . This sort of thing only goes to show what grown men will do to keep from devoting their time to something constructive in life.

FRENCH TRI-COLOUR

One third each of: Grenadine, maraschino, *Crème Yvette.*

THE JERSEY LILY, which INCIDENTALLY, CAME from FRANCE

Into the usual cordial or *pousse café* glass pour in half a jigger green chartreuse, then with a spoon float half jigger cognac, finally ten drops of angostura or other, preferred, bitters. First the bitter, then the strong, then the pungently sweet—that is the order of drinking tastes. Something like the *Dominica Topet,* already noted in proper order.

*L'AMOUR TOUJOURS,* Being Not Precisely a *POUSSE CAFÉ,* but rather a *POUSSE l'AMOUR*

Build layers as follows, and very carefully: 1/3 maraschino, egg yolk, 1/3 Benedictine, 1/3 cognac. Build this one in the conventional sherry glass. *Et bon chance, mes garçons!*

LIQUID SYMPHONY

Into a wine glass of shaved ice add the following in order mentioned: *Crème de rose,* yellow chartreuse, *crème de menthe,* and finally some well-aged brandy. Garnish with two red cherries on top.

LOUIS MARTIN'S FAMOUS POUSSE CAFÉ No. I

Take a large cordial glass, with stem, and mix in order given the following amounts and types:

> Yellow curaçao, about ¼ full
> Kirsch, same thickness layer
> Green chartreuse, a little thinner than the others
> Yellow curaçao, enough to fill glass

In the old days Louis Martin's was New York's premier night spot. As we recall it Vernon and Irene Castle started there, as well as being the rendezvous for important folk of all sorts.

*LUNE de MIEL,* which of Course Means "Honeymoon," Has already Been Noted on Page 49

*POLSKI POUSSE CAFÉ,* Straight from the Polish Corridor, and the Supposedly Free City of Danzig at Its End

Into a sherry glass put a quarter of chartreuse, the yolk of a smallish egg, and fill to the brim with *Dantziger Goldwasser,* that amazing liqueur in which tiny bits of pure gold leaf arise and sail gracefully about each time the bottle is agitated. . . . This drink is to be held up, studied, and taken in one or three gulps—the latter preferred, so the curaçao can seal with its sweet and citric kiss all hint of egg.

## HAVANA RAINBOW *PLUS*

Another of Sloppy Joe's specialties, and although the colour sequence isn't too scientific, the reaction upon guests is guaranteed true to form.

One-seventh each of: Grenadine, anisette, *Parfaite Amour,* green *crème de menthe,* yellow curaçao, yellow chartreuse, Jamaica rum.
. . . Serve with rum flaming, and make peace with thy neighbour!

## LA ZARAGOZANA'S *NE PLUS ULTRA,* Noted in Havana, February 24th, 1937

This restaurant, frequented mostly by wiser Cubans is one of Havana's leading places for seafood, and especially Morro Crab, see Pages 67 and 68, *Volume I.* It hasn't the atmosphere of some of the older spots, but *amigos,* what red snapper, what *langostas,* what *saumon*—the Habañero name for the rare, delicious, mackerel-like ocean runner, "salmon."

Apricot brandy, benedictine, chartreuse, cointreau, cognac, and *crème de cacao*—1/6 each. . . . Then a dash of *anis del mono,* or any good anisette. Frappe quickly and serve promptly. . . . A really delicious blend. *Anis del Mono,* or "anis of the monkey's head" is a specially good and dry Spanish anis, their favourite morning eye-opener.

## THE POMPIER HIGHBALL, a French Concession Sometimes Called Vermouth *CASSIS*—the Latter Being the Juice of Currants

Sitting under awning at any Parisian sidewalk cafe we can see all sorts and conditions of men seated at small round metal tables, and drinking various things for all sorts of reasons. The average Frenchman is a funny chap who confines his plain and fancy drinking to 3 grooves, 2 of which are the eternal wine with meals, and to stimulate hunger. . . . This Pompier Highball falls into the latter class, and besides all this it is very cooling and refreshing, has a sharp tangy taste due to the herbs and simples in the vermouth. Take ½ jigger French dry vermouth and the same of *crème de cassis*. Put in a couple of lumps of ice and fill the glass with club soda or seltzer. Serve in a tall thin glass and only fill ¾ full, please.

### THE HABANA *PRESIDENTE,* now Known to Many, but Sound Enough in Its Own Right for Listing in any Spiritual Volume

This has long been one of Cuba's favourite drinks and every visiting Americano should go to La Florida and get one from headquarters. The mix is simple and satisfying. . . . Just put 1 pony each of Bacardi Gold Seal, and dry French vermouth, into a bar glass with cracked ice. Donate 1 tsp grenadine and the same of curaçao. Stir and serve in a Manhattan glass with a scarlet cherry for garnish. Finally twist a curl of yellow orange peel over the top so that the oil strikes the surface of the drink, then drop the peel in. . . . Sloppy Joe's own Special is merely the *Presidente* with the juice of a small lime added, and the twist of lime peel handled as above.

### RITUAL of the PUNCH BOWL

This inheritance from the Orient and Europe—and especially from old England—is probably interwoven with more tradition than any other form of drinking. From those grand days when landlords really did fill the flowing bowl, before and after riding to hounds, on feast and saints' days, or holy days; at weddings, births, yes and even death—the cheering and soothing bowl was all part of the affair.

Oddly the word itself is another Oriental derivation like "toddy," and comes from the Hindustani *panch,* meaning five, and indicating the number of ingredients employed by the wily Hindu: Toddy or arrack, lemon or lime, tea, sugar and water.

Anglicized, it is literally any drink made of rum, whisky, brandy, wine or other liquor, in combination with water, fruit juice, and sugar—or of fruit juices and the rest without any spirits at all—and properly served, either very hot or well iced, from a larger or smaller bowl, into cups or glasses.

For centuries this sort of thing has been concocted in the Far East of varying materials to suit head, stomach, temperature, and heart. In England it soon trickled its way into fine society, possibly in the effort of the British East India Company to attract notice of the world to tea and other Oriental importations of the Empire.

Besides all of this tradition which came to us few things in life are more kind to man's eye than the sight of a gracefully conceived punch bowl on a table proudly surrounded by gleaming cohorts of cups made of crystal or white metals, enmeshing every beam of light, and tossing it back into a thousand shattered spectra to remind us of the willing cheer within. . . . The colours too are delightful—the purple of the grape against silver or crystal, the scarlet and gold and green of fruits, the tawny ambers of other wines, the fragrant scent of sugar cane, sun-ripe grapes, apricots, grain, peaches, what not—all are a challenge to eye, nose and lip; all blended into a perfect and harmonious whole.

The very amplitude of the bowl itself suggests hospitality, and an invitation to quench thirst, which no service of single small glasses can ever effect.

In place of the eternal afternoon tea, a really unusual punch not only delights guests, but saves the hostess the usual maze of questions about who takes lemon, or cream, or sugar. There is no conceivable occasion which cannot be served with a good punch—whether we prefer it with or without the spirits.

It takes a little imagination and ingenuity to make a visibly attractive punch, but we have tried to confine ourselves to punches which not only taste well, but look well also.

### RULES for a DECENT PUNCH ARE FEW—but INFLEXIBLE

1. Use fresh fruits, for although canned fruits will do, as a general rule they lack the pungency, the aroma, of fresh.
2. If sparkling water, wine, ginger beer, or ginger ale is to be added— wait until the very moment of service. The whole object of a sparkling punch is to have it sparkle—and as bubbles soon escape into the atmosphere after pouring in bowl, save that pouring until the last second.
3. Don't use small ice, except in emergencies requiring quick cooling—or

in Planter's Punches and West Indian Swizzles, treated on Page 109.
. . . . Fine ice melts rapidly, dilutes the punch. Dilution beyond a certain point courts sure disaster through loss of flavour, weakness and anaemia of otherwise prime ingredients. . . . Use a single fairly large block of ice.

4. Chill all ingredients at least an hour or two before putting in the bowl, if a punch is to be served cold. Pouring room-temperature liquids on any sort of ice is a withering shock to the ice itself, requires a great deal of refrigeration in a very short period of time, and can only succeed in too-rapid ice melting. . . . A big block of ice in pre-chilled punch will last a long time and melt slowly.

WORDS to the LIQUID WISE No. XVI, BEING THREE ORIGINAL TOUCHES in GARNISHING or FLAVOURING the PUNCH BOWL

Those of us who have a large freezing drawer under the ice cube section of a mechanical refrigerator can add a colourful and dainty touch by adding a little harmonious colouring matter to the water before freezing into cubes. . . . We can also add fruits like cherries, strawberries, and the like, to the water, thus freezing them visibly in the ice. . . . Instead of ice we can use water ice or sherbet flavouring with the basic taste of the punch like pineapple, grape, orange, and so on. This should be put in a little bit in each cup when serving, and makes things very cold. . . . Grate a little fresh coconut kernel, have it in a gravy boat, and dust a teaspoon on each cup when served. This adds a delicate, nut-like flavour which brings out the other tastes, only don't use the ordinary shredded coconut. It simply won't do as well.

A HAND-PICKED LIST of TWENTY & SIX PUNCHES from MANY GAY LANDS, & INCLUDING SOME ELEVEN WEST INDIAN PLANTER'S PUNCHES & SWIZZLES BASED on FIVE CRUISES through that FASCINATING CHAIN, & NOTES from YACHTSMEN FRIENDS on CRUISING to the OUT ISLANDS

FOR THOSE WHO ADMIRE HOT PUNCHES, a BRIEF SELECTED LIST MAY further BE FOUND under *HOT HELPERS,* STARTING on PAGE 50, onward

FOR THOSE WHO WISH to MIX NON-ALCOHOLIC PUNCHES

We have carefully selected several very original, fragrant, and flavourful punches as a relief from the eternal orange-lemon-fruit scramble which has hog-ridden us for generations. These are listed in a separate group under *TEMPERANCE DELIGHTS,* on Page 139.

## BENGAL LANCERS' PUNCH

Captain Ferguson, late of His Majesty's Cavalry in upper India, gave us this one back in 1926, and it was a specialty of his Colonel on quite special occasions.

| | |
|---|---|
| Champagne, 1 qt | Lime juice, ½ cup |
| Orange juice, ½ cup | Cointreau or curaçao, 3 ponies |
| Fresh pineapple juice, ½ cup | Charged water, 1 pint |
| Jamaica or Barbados rum, 3 ponies | A little sugar, to taste; and keep |
| Claret, 2 pint bottles | it dry and not too sweet |

Ice as above, and garnish with very thin slices of green lime. This is a particularly delicate punch, and Barbados rum is less likely to overpower the delicate wine flavours than Jamaica.

## PUNCH *à la DUC de BOURGOGNE*

| | | |
|---|---|---|
| Red burgundy, 2 qts | Lemon, juice, 2 | Fine sugar, ¼ lb, or so |
| Red port, 1 pint | Cherry brandy, 1 cup | Orange, juice, 2 |
| | Charged water, about 1 qt, or a trifle more | |

Ice as above and garnish with pitted red cherries.

## FISH HOUSE PUNCH, Dating from 1732, the State in Schuylkill Classic

This is America's most famous punch receipt; at least it is known by reputation to more people than any other. The mix has come from 1732 right to this date—practically 200 years, unchanged and unimproved for the simple reason that it could not be improved upon!

| | |
|---|---|
| Jamaica Rum; Barbados, Haitian; or ½ Bacardi and ½ Jamaica, 2 qts | Water, 2 qts; spring water is indicated |
| Cognac brandy, 1 qt | Lemon juice, 1 qt; lime would be even more delicate |
| Loaf sugar, ¾ lb | Peach brandy, 1 wine glass |

Put sugar in bowl, put on enough water to dissolve completely, then contribute the various spirits and liquids—stirring diligently. Center as big a lump of ice as may be in the bowl, permitting the brew to stand unmolested for a couple of hours. . . . Our alternate suggestions are in no way intended as heresy, but simply indicate what substitutions, if any, are possible. Many entirely worthy folk both on the Schuylkill River and the Mississippi, don't happen to care for Jamaica rum. All our male parentage having come from Philadelphia or Germantown or the Chester Valley out the "Main Line," we know a bit of how Philadelphia tradition, good or poor, carries on serenely in the midst of an otherwise crude and bustling world. . . . Also bear in mind that while many Jamaica rums come in full quarts, both Bacardi and Cognac invariably seem to come encased in fifths, so calibrate accordingly. . . . Warning: there are a horde of so-called "Fish House Punch" receipts that include benedictine, curaçao, bourbon, and God knows what else. Eschew them. There is but one receipt, unwavering, invariable. This is it.

## KIRSCHWASSER PUNCH, à la ARLÉSIENNE

Kirsch, as we keep emphasizing so often, has the peculiar faculty of enhancing other delicate flavours—both in drink and food. Its ratio here with maraschino is suggested as being the best balance, although sometimes the amount of the latter is cut down slightly, and the kirsch stepped up to the point where there is a ratio of three to one of maraschino, and in some cases the maraschino is left out entirely.

| | |
|---|---|
| Kirschwasser, 1½ cups | Maraschino, ½ cup |
| Rhine or sauterne, 2 pint bottles | If Rhine is used, add 1 extra tbsp |
| Fresh pineapple juice, 4 cups | sugar |
| Sparkling water, 1 pint | Sugar, fine, ½ lb |

Ice ingredients first, then mix in bowl with large lump of ice, and garnish with bits of really ripe pineapple, and grapefruit pulp. . . . A sprig of mint in each cup is a nice touch.

LATIN AMERICA PUNCH, from a Mᴏᴜɴᴛᴀɪɴ Pʟᴀɴᴛᴀᴛɪᴏɴ Hᴏᴜꜱᴇ
out of Sᴀɴ Jᴜᴀɴ, Pᴏʀᴛᴏ Rɪᴄᴏ

*Carta de Oro* Bacardi rum, 1½
   cups
Rhine wine, 2 pint bottles
Lemon juice, 1 cup
Thin small slices fresh pineapple

Orange curaçao, ½ cup
Champagne, 1 qt
Orange juice, 1 cup
Sparkling water, 1 pint

Ice for two hours beforehand, pour in bowl with large lump ice,
have a gravy boat filled with fresh grated coconut kernel, and sprinkle
a level teaspoon on each glass as served. *Don't* use shredded coconut—
that is only for cakes and so on.

FRITZ FENGER'S PINEAPPLE "BOLA," which Is a Pᴜɴᴄʜ of
Pᴀʀᴛꜱ

Fenger's dossier has already been given at some length, and we will
merely state here that both the wording of this receipt and spelling
of the word "Bola" are his—this last presumably an anglicized version of the old German word *Bowle,* or *Wein-Bowle.* The change
from "It" to "Her" is also interesting.

"For evening use: Right after breakfast stalk a ripe but unblemished
pineapple, and when agreeable, snatch it off its perch and take it home
where—in the intimacy of the butler's pantry—we remove first her head,
toes, hard heart, and finally her spiny corset.

"Dice her up very fine indeed and heap pieces and juices in a large punch
bowl and cover with powdered sugar. Pour on a bottle of good bourbon
or rye—not Scotch—and leave her lay *all day,* covered and safely beyond
reach or range of the great dane. Meanwhile you can go back to your legiti-
mate work, if any.

"After dinner sculp a piece of ice, at least 8″ on a side, place it in the
center of the bowl and over this pour slowly, bottle by bottle, scads, shoals
and lashings of chilled dry champagne to the number of 3 or 4 at least—
when a bit hard up use ½ champagne and ½ charged water, or 2/3 Rhine
or Moselle and 1/3 charged water—only don't tell any Nazi I recommended this last!

"Now with a judicious ladle stir gently, just a trifle, to mix with the whisky-sugar-pineapple foundation. Dip in and drink. But when serving best put her smack in the middle of the table with chairs noosed all around; break out tobacco, musical instruments and yarns; for although this Bola does not make one intoxicated as we know the word [Note: We resent this! *Author.*] it does take your legs away, very thriftily."

Author's Note: Having tried this business out once our only suggestion would be to ignore all thought of ice and replace it as a cooling agent by 2 or 3 quarts of fresh pineapple sherbet or water ice. The unusual thing about this punch is that it requires no rum of any sort, for strength or flavouring.

PINEAPPLE MILK, or *LECHE PREPARADA PIÑA,* from SAN SALVADOR, C.A.

This mild, and almost startlingly delicious pineapple-milk-brandy-and-other-things punch is inscribed on Page 91.

TIGER'S MILK, Nos. I, II, & III

These successive formulae from Peking, Bangkok, and finally the windward coast of Jamaica, and which we consider the most amazing milk drinks extant, are listed on Pages 129, 130, 131, & 90.

NAPOLEON II PUNCH, sometimes CALLED PUNCH *à la l'AIGLON*

Time this so it will be made when wild cherries are ripe, barring that use sour red "pie" cherries.

| | |
|---|---|
| Claret, or Burgundy, 2 pint bottles | St. Croix, Martinique, or |
| Any sour cherry juice, 1 cup | Haitian rum, 1 cup |
| Fine sugar, to taste; keep fairly | Pitted cherries, ½ cup |
|    acid | Charged water, 1 pint |
| Vanilla extract, 2 tsp or so | Garnish with violets |

Ice as above, and add a few bits of chopped violet petals to each cup as served.

THE *PFIRSCHBOWLE,* or PEACH PUNCH, for OUR REUNION in VIENNA, or ANYWHERE

This requires ripe peaches, *not* green ones a little coloured by standing in a shop. Scald, take off skins, slice, and dredge with plenty of confectioner's sugar, and let them marinate in their own sweet juices for two hours. First pour in a bottle of Rhine or Moselle wine, then a bottle of good Burgundy or claret. Put in the ice box, and just before serving uncork a bottle of iced champagne. Put an 8″ cube of ice in the bowl, and pour over. . . . To our way of thinking a couple of ounces of drier type apricot or peach brandy couldn't hurt this thought a mite.

## CHARLESTON'S ST. CECELIA SOCIETY PUNCH

Speaking of social niceties, for a good many generations no one in Tidewater South Carolina really mattered unless his name appeared on the annual ball list of St. Cecelia. Consequently it gradually became a fixed matter of family and the bluest of blood lines. Bank balances did not count as they did in New York's 400. Although the membership list has been expanded now and then along more sanely liberal lines, here is a Society started two hundred years ago, forty years before our Declaration of Independence was conceived, and whose prestige and power was so great that when the welkin rang in ancient Hibernian Hall, not one single newspaper ever mentioned a bit of what took place. . . . Gentlemen were gentlemen in those days, and the over-famed "freedom of the press" didn't pry into their social affairs, as they do nowadays with certain visible folk like, say, Ex-King Edward VIII. Furthermore the music plays behind a lace curtain, and ladies don't go to *la salle des dames* unchaperoned!

Peach or apricot brandy, 1 fifth; peach is traditional
Jamaica rum, 1 pint; and get good old rum
Dry champagne, 4 quarts
Cognac brandy, 1 bottle
Sugar, 3 cups

Fresh pineapple, 1 ripe one, sliced fine and cored
Lemons or limes, 6 lemons or 10 limes, sliced thin
Green tea, 1 quart
Club soda, or other good sparkling water, 2 quarts total

Slice lemon and pineapple and marinate, tightly covered, overnight with brandy. At noon of the evening when we plan to serve it add rum, tea, sugar and peach brandy. Blend well. Just before serving put in champagne first, then club soda. Chill cups for best results, and remember that good club soda, although costing a few cents more than 'the average local "charged water" or seltzer siphon, actually adds not a hint of antique brass to ruin the other worthy company of liquids! . . . Either Schweppes or Perrier are in order.

SIR FLEETWOOD'S *SHEPHERD'S SACK POSSET*, from the RECORDS of DR. WILLIAM KITCHINER, LONDON, 1817.

Centuries back it was quite the fashion to toss a bit of verse, blank, or blankety-blank, whether it were regarding a new or old sweetheart, a new horse, or a new drink. . . . Now this is a very old drink indeed, and Sir Fleetwood was a stout one with the wassail bowl. Of all the *Sacks* beloved by England, this was his favoured one. We quote it literally from the immortal Kitchiner.

> "From fam'd Barbadoes on the western Main
> Fetch Sugar, ounces four—fetch Sack from Spain,
> A pint,—and from the Eastern Indian Coast
> Nutmeg, the glory of our northern Toast;
> O'er flaming Coals let them together heat
> Till the all-conquering Sack dissolve the sweet;
> O'er such another Fire put Eggs, just ten,
> New-Born from Tread of Cock and Rump of Hen:
> Stir them with steady hand and conscience Pricking
> To see the untimely end of ten fine Chicken;
> From shining shelf take down the brazen skillet,—
> A quart of milk from gentle cow will fill it.
> When boiled and cold, put milk and Sack to Egg;
> Unite them firmly like the Triple League,
> And on the fire let them together dwell
> Till Miss sing twice—'You must not kiss and Tell,—'
> Each Lad and Lass take up a silver spoon,
> And fall on fiercely like a Starved Dragoon."

Don't judge the drink by the poetry, and just travel along cozily with this kitchen model Ogden Nash of a bygone century. . . . Sack, by the way, is any one of several light fairly strong wines imported into England from Spain and the Canary Islands. If you will substitute sherry, and perhaps a dash of good brandy there will be no complaints from the twice-singing Maid!

THE ANCIENT WASSAIL BOWL from an Ancient Elizabethan Formula, Circa 1602, & Truly Notable for Its Exceeding Mildness

In Saxon times this custom of the Wassail Bowl at feast days was an important ceremony, and later it became an accepted custom at Christmas Eve, when minstrels or choirs, or village singers went about singing carols where there was a candle lit in the window.

In the Feudal castles, and manor houses, the Wassail Bowl was borne into the banqueting Hall with songs and carols, and crowned with garlands.

| | |
|---|---|
| Nutmeg, ½ grated; or 2 tsp powdered | Sugar, 1 cup |
| | Eggs, yolks 6; whites 3 |
| Powdered or grated ginger, 1 tsp | Apples, 6 cored, but not pared |
| Cloves, 6 whole | Mace, ¼ tsp |
| Cinnamon, 1 inch of stick | Water |

Sherry or Madeira, 2 qts

Take spices and cover with a cup of cold water. Fetch to a boil; adding wine and sugar. Let heat up. . . . Meanwhile in the Wassail Bowl (Punchbowl) previously warmed:

Break in six yolks and three whites. Beat up. When wine is warm—not boiling—mix a teacupful with the egg. When a little warmer, add another cupful, and repeat until five cups have been used. . . . Now let the rest of the wine boil up well, and pour it into the bowl also, stirring well all the time, until it froths in attractive fashion. . . . Fill cored apples with sugar, sprinkle on a little of the spice and roast until nearly done. Time these to suit the end of the wine-pouring process. Throw them into the bowl, and serve the whole thing very hot. . . . Some stout hearts add a tumbler full of good cognac brandy to the whole—and we, after testing the business, heartily agree with them; since sherry of itself isn't potent enough to make any Saxon defend his native land, much less a 20th Century wassailer, with all we have been through during the one and a half decades that Saxons never even considered as drinkable fluid!

## TEN WEST INDIAN PLANTER'S PUNCHES, Swizzles, and like Ceremonies of a Pleasant Nature

Any set rules for these tropical institutions would last about as long as a set rule for a mint julep to please Louisville and Baltimore. There are as many Planter's Punches as there are—or were—planters; as many Swizzles as swizzlers.

After stays in Nassau, Cuba, Jamaica, Haiti, Curaçao, Venezuela, and both ends of the Canal Zone, we have found most of this drink family extremely good, especially those made of special aged Jamaica rum we've imbibed in the Myrtlebank Gardens, Kingston. Those listed here have, for one reason or another, stood out in our memories. . . . If there is any one thing which is hard and fast everywhere it is this: Get decent well-aged rum, and brandy or cognac, for all punches and West Indian drinks. Just because they are a bit disguised with tropical fruit juice is no sign that thirty seconds swizzling, shaking, or stirring will make up for eight years the raw spirit should have lain in wood casks.

The charm of all these exotics is their mellowness, their smoothness, and the gentleness with which they come, see and conquer.

One other thing: Don't try to use canned fruit juices of any kind and expect notability. In other words, fresh fruit lacking, call it a rum-canned-grapefruit-juice-ade, not a Planter's Punch.

Extreme chilliness is the brand of excellence, over and above these thoughts, and for this reason the soundest mixers *chill glasses, or in-*

*gredients, or both*—and in swizzles this includes the pitcher too; if we really want to show off, a good ⅛″ of white frost on the outside!

## ADMIRAL SCHLEY PUNCH
This is supposed to have been named after the American admiral, and we shouldn't mind such a pleasant piece of business being called after us.

St. Croix or Barbados rum, ½ jigger

Bourbon, ½ jigger
Sugar, 1 tsp
Lime, peel and juice, 1

Shake with fine ice, and turn into goblet—ice and all. Garnish with sprigs of mint, a stick of ripe pineapple, and so on.

## THE STANDARD ONE, TWO, THREE, FOUR, WEST INDIAN PLANTER's PUNCH, No. I
This is the original receipt from the very first discovery of the drink.

1 of Sour (lime juice); 2 of Sweet (sugar or *gomme* syrup); 3 of Strong (Jamaica rum); 4 of Weak (water and ice combined)—and use shaved or quite fine cracked ice, please. . . . Doctor this with the usual dash of Angostura, shake hard and serve—with ice left in the glass.

America, when not having time to dally with its drink as a correct West Indian planter is supposed to do, sometimes transposes the quantities of "strong" and "weak"—making the rum four parts and the water three, instead of as given above.

Barbados, Demerara, Martinique, Haitian, or Cuban Rum, can always replace Jamaica; and if using Bacardi mix *Carta de Oro,* for fuller flavour, not *Carta Blanca.*

## SANTIAGO de CUBA, *CARTA de ORO* BACARDI PLANTER's PUNCH
Bacardi Carta de Oro, 1½ jiggers
Sugar or grenadine, 1 tsp

Lime, strained juice, 1½
Mint and fresh fruit

Fill a large goblet with shaved ice well packed down, mix the liquids and pour over ice, then garnish with sliced orange, cherries, and a stick of fresh ripe pineapple, and plenty of fresh mint.

## SAVANNAH PLANTER'S PUNCH

Cotton, lumber and naval stores, rosin, turpentine spirits, that was —and still is, Savannah. The whole world sailed to Savannah's door up Tybee River, and many a West Indian Colonial found it—with Charleston—a first mainland step before reaching England. . . . This Planter's Punch varies quite a bit from those punches and swizzles we've inspected and brewed along the great circle of islands from Haiti to Trinidad and Curaçao. But it's a sound one; and as all sound potables should be—it's simple. Also it's tall. For one:

First chill the glasses—whether silver or crystal
Good Jamaica rum, wine glass; or 2 ponies, to taste
Cognac brandy, 2 jiggers
Lime, juice, 1; or juice ½ lemon
Fresh pineapple juice, ½ jigger

Pack the glasses tightly with *finely* shaved ice, pour in the liquids previously mixed, stir briskly for a moment with long spoon or swizzle stick. Garnish with a finger of ripe pineapple, a cherry, or a bit of orange. Serve when glass frosts. There's no dodging the fact that we must expect to use decent rum. This recently born swarm of new, strange rums can no more replace even a fair Jamaica, Barbados or Haitian rum, than Mr. Kreisler can play the *E Flat Nocturne* on a turnip crate. . . . The cognac lends the original touch here.

FIVE WEST INDIAN SWIZZLES of a COMFORTING DISPOSITION, & EMBRACING ONE of JAMAICA RUM, and FOUR of AUTHENTIC ORIGIN and other BASES, from the ROUGH LOG of FREDERICK ABILDGAARD FENGER

A JAMAICA RUM SWIZZLE from a PLANTATION OVERLOOKING the NORTHERN, or WINDWARD, PORT ANTONIO SECTION

> Jamaica rum, 1 full pint; or 2 measuring cups full
> Lime, juice 8 small; 6 large; or 6 average lemons
> *Gomme* syrup or sugar, 4 tsp
> Fresh mint, 1 doz sprigs

Mix liquids and sugar in pitcher with ice, frost with swizzle stick, pour out into commodious glasses, and garnish with sprig mint, and stick of fresh ripe pineapple, if some is handy.

WORDS to the LIQUID WISE No. XVII, NOTING that PRACTICALLY any PLANTER'S PUNCH, if MULTIPLIED SLIGHTLY into QUANTITY & SWIZZLED in a BOWL or PITCHER, BECOMES a "SWIZZLE"

> Don't be misled by the contradictory terms. A swizzle foundation could be any of the Planter's Punches given here—the usual technique for which parallels that of the Mint Julep, insofar as cooling goes.

THE FOUR so-CALLED "MALLINGHOLM SWIZZLES"—ALL of AUTHENTIC PROPORTION and CORRECT GEOGRAPHICAL ORIGIN, & furthermore MADE NOTABLE through the LOG of FREDERICK ABILDGAARD FENGER, OWNER & MASTER of the SCHOONER *DIABLESSE*

We seem to refer to Fritz Fenger quite a bit in this volume and if we do it is because he has covered the West Indies as thoroughly and intimately as anyone we know, and besides this is a gourmet and a compounder of spirituous liquids both potent and astonishing to the average landsman. Further than this he is a Danish-American yacht architect dwelling—to the public shock of the Board of Selectmen of whom he is a member—in the remote and pure town of Cohasset, in Massachusetts.

Back in the great sweep of Leeward and Windward Islands he is still known as "de mon on de boat," dating clean back twenty years or so when he sailed a canoe the size of an ample delicatessen dill pickle—as we have already mentioned—from Trinidad slap to the

Virgins. Now for the benefit of those who haven't sailed those waters we would like to remark that although this necklace of islands looks on the map to be within cruller toss of each other, they are actually separated by wide and rough cross-chop passages where the Caribbean and the Atlantic have a peas-porridge-hot game every six hours, pouring tides back and forth. The natives, who sail things out of sight of land we wouldn't use to cross an irrigation ditch, took one look at that canoe with its 4″ or so of freeboard and no rudder, and promptly began recollecting ancient prayers to sea gods. News of his progress went ahead of him via some sort of weird mackerel telegraph. And no matter where he would beach the YAKABOO, or at what hour, reverent dark men and women waited upon him, fearful of some sorcery, yet eager as children to touch him or any of his things. They fetched him food and drink, cured sea urchin festers, and stood and watched his tiny butterfly winged sails fade and vanish into a cockatoo-crest yellow dawn. At St. Thomas, capital of the Virgins, due to press of time, YAKABOO was hoisted aboard steamer and went thus to Boston.

Several years later DIABLESSE, a good husky down-east fisherman schooner retraced the course of the little YAKABOO, with greater leisure, plenty of seaworthiness, and with wife and young son as Mate and Bo'sun.

The first 4 swizzles garnered from Fenger are out of the files of a Dane he met in St. Thomas named Mallingholm, and who has since gone "where the angels (as Fenger says) live innocuously, so I've been instructed—dang it!"

He further informs us, with scant foundation of veracity—that these are mild and caponed affairs which "may be taken—in moderate abandon—without irremediable fraying out at either end."

These 4 excellent swizzles have been given in accurate scale drawings, so that the mixer may measure by eye by "placing a clean thumb nail at each level before pouring."

By adding 1 tumbler of ice water and ice enough, and 1/3 to ½ tsp of sugar, we get swizzles for 4 guests.

CALIBRATION CHART for FREDERICK ABILDGAARD FENGER'S *MALLINGHOLM* SWIZZLES, ABILDGAARD—CREDIT IT or not—BEING HIS GENUINE MIDDLE NAME & the ONE under which HE WROTE as *CAPTAIN ABILDGAARD* for SOME YEARS in *YACHTING* MAGAZINE

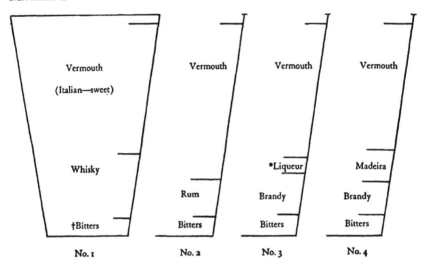

| No. 1 | No. 2 | No. 3 | No. 4 |

ADDENDA:

† Orange bitters lends a smooth change from Angostura in every case, when so desired.

\* Indicates benedictine or *Crème de Cacao*.

The bar glass shown is the conventional 5 to 6 oz size called a Star or Sour glass.

The amount of vermouth may be lessened in No. 2, and rum increased. In general, after a bit of practice, both vermouth and bitters should be regulated, to individual taste.

AFTER ICING WE SHAKE in a SHAKER or SWIZZLE with a SWIZZLE STICK, but DO NOT STRAIN. . . . THERE SHOULD BE a BEAD on EACH GLASS

THE WEST INDIAN SWIZZLE STICK, what IT IS

There is a wide cloud of misinformation on this subject. The authentic swizzle sticks are the peeled stem of a plant owning, at base, a fan-like branching of roots—the latter cut some 3″ long—and look-ing like small gnarled fingers. This branched end is sunk into the pitcher with ice and drink ingredients, the stem is held vertically be-tween palms, and rotated smartly by sliding the palms back and forth. They are procurable in all British West Indian possessions, for ob-vious reasons, and are a romantic touch; actually however a swizzle made out of this routine is no better than one chilled with a modern chromium plated metal swizzle stick. Like airplane propellers made of wood, and metal, the main question is do they stir up the air?

### THE WORLD FAMOUS QUARANTINE COCKTAIL, No. I
FAVOURITE in MANILA, where IT even OUTSTRIPS the PERENNIAL DRY MARTINI

This drink is quite rich, and one is enough before a dinner. The *anis del mono*—or *"anis* of the monkey head"—is the highly alcoholic type Spaniards use as a pre-breakfast eye opener all over the globe. If French anisette liqueur is used we had better increase the quantity to ½ tsp or so. . . . Take I jigger of Bacardi, I tsp each of gin and dry French vermouth, ½ jigger of orange juice, 2 tsp lemon juice, sugar to taste, and I tbsp of egg white. Add I or 2 drops of *anis,* shake with lots of cracked ice and turn into a Manhattan glass. Monk An-trim's receipt sent especially for this volume calls for I tbsp of com-bined gin and vermouth, and orange and lemon juice in equal amounts, about I tsp each. Egg white is more than the standard blend, being ½ a whole white.

### THE QUEEN CHARLOTTE COCKTAIL; NAMED, SO TELL
THEY the TALE, for QUEEN CHARLOTTE AMALIA—or AMALIE—now also the NAME for St. GEORGES in the AMERICAN VIRGIN ISLANDS

This is a lovely warm weather affair of a mildness which even a Quaker miss could not shy at! It was donated by the charming wife of a Pan-American Airways pilot on the big *Brazilian Clipper* for them as likes their likker weak.

Fill a tom collins glass half way up with finely cracked ice, turn in a scant pony of raspberry syrup, 2 to 3 jiggers of claret or Burgundy, the juice of 1 green lime or ½ lemon. Fill up with lemon soda and garnish with a sprig of mint.

NOW a REFRESHING COOLER from Barcelona Called "Red Snow," a Luscious & Pleasant Thing for Summer, & Mild Enough to Suit the Most Sedate of Men

The summer before several nations besides the Spanish undertook to alter the map of Spain to suit their own ideas, we had a very old and dependable friend who thought it a good idea at the time to cycle over Spain with a rucksack and paint box over her back. Spanish red wine is not vital, and we suggest Burgundy be substituted; or claret.

Strain the juice of ½ lemon or 1 small green lime, retain the spiral peel of the fruit, about 1 tsp sugar or grenadine syrup, 1 dash of orange flower water. Turn into this 1 cup of Burgundy, of Valdepeñas from Spanish La Mancha, or any good Spanish *vino tinto;* any good claret. Pack a big goblet with shaved ice and pour everything into it, or better still pour the blend into The Mixer with a cupful of finely cracked ice, and make it into a sherbet-like rosy tinted condition which, when it is poured into a goblet, speedily melts enough to drink but remains cold far longer than the usual claret lemonade that has merely been iced in the refrigerator. Finally dust a little nutmeg on top; the Spanish touch.

REMEMBER the MAINE, a Hazy Memory of a Night in Havana during the Unpleasantnesses of 1933, when Each Swallow Was Punctuated with Bombs Going off on the Prado, or the Sound of 3″ Shells Being Fired at the Hotel *NACIONAL,* then Haven for Certain Anti-Revolutionary Officers

Treat this one with the respect it deserves, gentlemen. Take a tall bar glass and toss in 3 lumps of ice. Onto this foundation donate the following in order given: 1 jigger of good rye whisky, ½ jigger Italian vermouth, 1 to 2 tsp of cherry brandy, ½ tsp absinthe or *Pernod Veritas.* Stir briskly in clock-wise fashion—this makes it sea-going, presumably!—turn into a big chilled saucer champagne glass, twisting a curl of green lime or lemon peel over the top.

## LEXINGTON, KENTUCKY, RIDING CLUB COCKTAIL

This is a fine whet to the negligent stomach, besides being an excellent cocktail seldom served in the north these Martini days. We are acquainted with a genuine Kentucky Colonel who serves this as his 1 concession to the cocktail era besides a Bourbon Old Fashioned. . . . Take of calisaya, 1 jigger, add a dash of Angostura and the same of acid phosphate. Stir with ice like a Martini and strain into a Manhattan glass. No garnish, please.

## THE YOKOHAMA ROMANCE COCKTAIL, Being a Yellow Peril Concocted by One Toyama, No. I Bar-Boy at a Yoko Night Spot Called "Romance" Cabaret

We don't include this merely in an effort to be "foreign" for truth was that the "Romance" Cabaret was a sorry place of blaring music and taxi-dancing small Japanese men with lovely fluid doll-like Japanese girls with bobbed hair and bangs. But upon being urged by Toyama to sample his masterpiece and we declined with thanks, he frosted one for us on the house, with his compliments. It is, to put it commonly, an accidental "natural" and in it went. That evening was painfully punctuated later when, after having chartered a fleet of bicycles from some coolies, we attempted to navigate cross lots toward the main godowns and docks where our ship was tied up, we ran blindly into a mass of earthquake rubble still unremoved after the disaster of 1923—fetching up all standing in an inverted position and semi-conscious, and from which we were finally extricated by the combined and random efforts of a gentleman from North Carolina who made cigarettes and a gentleman from Kalamazoo who made stoves and shipped them, for increment, direct to you. The cycle was reported a total loss.

The cocktail: 2 jiggers of old cognac, 1 jigger of cherry brandy, ¼ to ½ tsp of Rose's lime juice or lime syrup—the kind we see in soda fountains in the slender bumpy-surfaced bottle, and the juice of ½ a small green lime. Shake very hard with very fine ice and serve with some of this left in. Frozen in The Mixer, tropical style, is still better. Serve in a big saucer champagne glass. *Arigato* Toyama!

THE ROSY DAWN COCKTAIL, a Beloved Event from Our Last Visit to Hongkong, from which We Reappeared with a Bride without Knowing It, & We Should Have Told this One to Bob Ripley Who Was in Town at the Time—Secretary & All

For sentimental reasons this probably outranks all other cocktails in our past and present life, for it was through its rosy-inspired courage we got ourselves a wife, only we didn't know it until long afterward, and after we were married back here in the States.

We have the ingredients all noted on the calling card of F. P. Franklin, who then—and we hope now—is editor of the Hongkong *Telegraph*. It was first introduced to us by J. Handley Pegg, Esquire, Chief Engineer of His Majesty's Colonial Highway Department there. It involved a routine cocktail party aboard the *RESOLUTE* on one April evening, then dinner at a West End Chinese Club, and later on still—after many Rosy Dawns, Mrs. Franklin got so senti-mental about our recent fiancée that she said as long as she couldn't attend the wedding in person she would like to see us married some-how. So Handley Pegg went out of the room with her and came back with his collar and coat on backwards, and Franklin gave the bride away, and the gramophone played Mendelssohn, and there were flower girls and maids of honour, and God knows what else.

Then Mrs. Franklin started to cry and took off her own wedding ring, and said we had to use it. So we did, and Pegg married us out of the Anglican book of Common Prayer, and everything was very fine, and we capped the Rosy Dawns with vintage *Krug 1923*. Then just before sunrise Mrs. Franklin gave us a big cloisonné tub of freesia, and then we were sent down in Franklin's own chartered limousine, and our Bride started to cry in the motor launch as we got half way over to Kowloon-side, and said it was because she was so happy but

also because she had lost one of her pet jewel jade earrings she'd bar-
gained half a day to get up in Canton or somewhere. We never found
the earring, and had to make the other into a necklace pendant too—
and as for the tub of freesias, we toted the whole seventy pounds of
them along the Bund at Kowloon—and the sight of your humble
servant, thus burdened, was too much for the coolie roustabouts just
scratching themselves awake for the day's labour, and they howled
and giggled at the mad white man who would thus lose face aping
the porter's trade when he could hire it done. And as we came finally
up the spidery forward gangway the first fingers of a Rosy Dawn
searched up and over the stark mountains surrounding Hongkong's
superb harbour, and painted the hull of the *MARIPOSA* a maiden
blush tint where she lay just to the eastward of our own berth. Here
is the original receipt.

Take 1 liqueur glass *each* of the following: dry gin, orange curaçao,
and cherry brandy. Add 1 tsp Rose's lime juice, or soda fountain lime
syrup. Put in a big champagne glass filled with cracked ice, stir, and
fill with a touch of seltzer. . . . We later have found that by cutting
down the cherry brandy and curaçao to 1 liqueur glass total for both,
and tossing in 1 pony of cognac, we have a drier mix, and not quite
so sweet, yet still maintaining authority enough for any man.

THE SO-CALLED RUSSIAN COCKTAIL, a MEMORY of PEKING,
in 1926

In that year, which seems so very long ago now, Peking was a place
of sheer delight. Trade was better after the war, the memory of the
Revolution and massacre of White Russians was a vague and tragic
business to Russians who were young enough to forget what had
been. There was a lovely girl who maintained a shop selling jades
and Imperial tribute silks, carved ivories and kingfisher feather screens,
at the *Grande Hotel de Pekin*. And after a while we came to go about
to odd parts of the vast city together, and one evening at the small
jewel-like house on Pa-Pao Hutung where we had gone for some
decent *sukiyaki*—the only place in Peking where we could *see* what

made up the things we ate!—she commanded ingredients, and after a pause, had them brought to the small room with the sliding screens that gave out on a small garden close where the magnolias drifted the rose-snow of their petals against the high gray wall; and so she sat there in the bamboo print kimono they gave her to wear, and mixed a trio of these for old times' sake, to Russia as she had quit it ahead of bayonets in 1917, a pale gold haired child of 11 or 12.

Into a crystal goblet put 1 cup of finely cracked ice, and onto this pour 1½ jiggers of good cognac and the same of the best Gilka *kümmel,* stir for a moment and fill the goblet with chilled extra dry champagne. Garnish with a single flower petal, or bloom. It is not a drink to be taken lightly, but advisedly, reverently.

CAP HAITIEN RUM & HONEY, or *CLAIRENE au MIEL,* a WARY EXOTIC CONTRIBUTED by GLENN "STIFF" STEWART of EASTON, MARYLAND, & MIAMI BEACH, WHO SPENT MUCH TIME in HAITI as AMERICAN MINISTER

We have mentioned Glenn Stewart briefly in *Volume I,* and we can assure all readers that he is a gentleman of parts, who knows many dishes, many drinks, and probably more about pre-Columbian history than any layman alive. . . . *Clairene,* in Haiti, is merely raw white rum, but we have found that when ½ Bacardi and ½ Haitian or any good aged dark rum is substituted, the drink acquires character, discretion and merit. . . . Dissolve 1 tsp or 2 of strained honey with 1½ jiggers of this rum blend into an old fashioned cocktail glass. Stir well, turn into this fluid ½ the glass full of finely cracked ice and stir like a Martini to chill well. No bitters, no garnish.

THE SAIGON SPECIAL, another ODD DRINK from the CAPITAL CITY of FRENCH INDO-CHINA & DATING from the YEAR 1925

This dates back to 1925 when the good old *SS RESOLUTE* stopped in French Indo-China, and some of our friends undertook to fly upriver as near to the marvellous Cambodian ruins of Angkor, as might be sane, then to motor back via Pnom Penh—imagine a place called

Pnom Penh—to Bangkok to meet ship again at Pak Nam. . . . The plane reminded us of a celery crate decorated, respectively, with an electric fan and an evinrude motor. It sputtered and died finally coming to rest on the Saigon River, with no chance to walk home. . . . This addition to any anthology of dampness was one remembered aftermath when back in Saigon, and muttering about the contrariness of fate generally. On checking we find that it is a slightly sweeter Jerusalem Between-the-Sheets, plus a nip of egg white.

Cognac, 1 pony
Dry gin, ½ pony
Cointreau, ½ pony

Lemon juice, ½ tsp
Egg white, 2 tsp or so

Shake with cracked ice and serve in tall cocktail glass with stem. Garnish with cherry. Use no sugar, the cointreau lends sweetness.

SANTIAGO NIGHTCAP, from a STAY in SANTIAGO de CUBA, in the EARLY SPRING of 1930

This is another favour passed along to this field representative and wine tester by the late Señor Facuno Bacardi, it being his primary thought to donate something to woo sleep and restore the slightly frayed physical assembly. It is a simple drink, and would also make a fine picker-upper. . . . Take 1½ jiggers of Gold Seal Bacardi rum, add 1 pony of orange curaçao and the yolk of 1 egg. Shake hard with cracked ice and strain into a large saucer champagne glass.

THE SEPTEMBER MORN, FIRST DISCOVERED at the *INGLE-TERRE* BAR in HAVANA, CUBA, in the MONTH of JANUARY 1926

This is simply the famous Clover Club, as mixed originally at the Belleview Stratford in pre-prohibition times, only instead of being based on dry gin, it employs the rounder, less pungent foundation of Bacardi rum. At the Polo Club, in Manila, the September Morn has in addition, ½ pony of dry French vermouth. . . . Therefore: take 1½ jiggers of Gold Seal Bacardi, ½ tsp sugar, 2 tsp of egg white, ½ pony of raspberry syrup. Grenadine may substitute, but raspberry syrup is conventional. Now add the juice of 1 small green lime, or ½ a small lemon, carefully strained, of course. Shake well and serve in a flute cocktail glass with a stem. No garnish, and straws may be stuck to the lip of the glass—scarlet straws, please.

KELLY'S SHAMROCK SPECIAL, from the Bar at the Old Kelly's Ritz, which Was a Famous Cabaret at the Western, or Pacific Entrance of the Big Ditch, & which Used to Grow More & More Interesting with Every Floor Dating from Grade!

One of the eight or ten times we've prowled the Zone, it became prudent to spring two American friends from the local native city *Cuartel*—jail in Americano—where they were incarcerated for slight offenses not necessary to mention. The celebration, on St. Patrick's day, resulted in the following brain-child, in co-operation with the then head barkeep of Kelly's Ritz. . . . Barring this, shake with finely cracked ice.

Dry gin, 1 jigger
Lime, juice 1 small, ½ large
Green crème de menthe, 2 tsp

Bar sugar or syrup, ½ tsp
Egg, white 1

Mix with shaved ice, and frappe diligently—preferably with an electric machine like The Mixer; shake through a sieve into a tall cocktail glass with stem, garnish with a clover leaf or shamrock—we used a sprig of mint. This sieve business builds the drink into a conical mound.

THE FAMOUS SHANGHAI BUCK, a Classic in this Vast Port which Consumes—or Did Consume, at Least, before the Japanese Issue—More Bacardi Rum than any other City on Earth

The British Shanghai Club Bar, on the Bund at Shanghai, for years boasted the longest mahogany strip in the known world, but has of course long since been surpassed here, after America shrugged off the arid yoke of prohibition. The fact remains that it has more atmosphere right now to the square inch than most chromium plated night spots have per square acre. Years before the man on the street over here had ever heard of a Daiquiri, sane British colonials out in Shanghai's International Settlement knew and valued Bacardi rum for what it was—a *rum brandy,* mellowed and redistilled and aged. . . . Now at 11 A.M. those who can spare the time foregather for Shanghai Bucks or whisky pegs—a habit very disastrous to productive activity during the remainder of any business day, we learned. . . . Take a big 16 oz collins glass, put in 3 cubes of ice, 1 tsp or 2 of sugar, pour in 2 jiggers of Bacardi—White Seal or Gold Seal—and fill up with good ginger ale. The improved Shanghai Buck adds the juice of 1 green lime or ½ lemon, and uses grenadine instead of sugar, to get the handsome colour. Personally we prefer stone bottle ginger beer to ginger ale. It is a Jamaica Buck, or Barbados Buck, only using Bacardi instead of dark rum, or blended rums.

WORDS to the LIQUID WISE No. XVIII, on the UNDENIABLE EXCELLENCE of a FINE DRY SHERRY, or SHERRY & BITTERS, instead of the PERPETUAL BARRAGE of COCKTAILS

Here's 1 case where old Colonel E. Sifton Ponsonby-Fittich is perfectly right—for the English appreciated sherry long before our war of independence, recognizing it as one of the truly civilized drinks enjoyed by mankind. But a word of caution: don't get a jug of local, sweet, last-month's sherry and expect any cultured results. Sherry should be properly aged, of the dry or drier type. Bitters are optional. . . . We now offer a kernel of heresy which probably will cause many English to wish us harm: chill the sherry decanter if sherry and bitters are used. The sherry taste is just as fine, the whole thing more crisp and pungent. We even do it with sherry alone when using the drink for a pre-dinner appetizer, in warmer weather. . . . We feel, strictly, that sherry *and* bitters changes old sherry tradition.

THE WEST INDIAN SHRUB, from the BERMUDA FILES of ONE WILKINSON, ESQUIRE, UNFORTUNATELY DECEASED, but WHO OWNED CRYSTAL CAVE, & THINGS DOWN THERE in BERMUDA, & WHO WAS VERY COURTEOUS & KIND to US on OUR FIRST TRIP to that ENCHANTED SMALL ISLAND

This mild and cooling summer beverage may be made in the more northern climates out of wild cherries, tame cherries—all except the acid red pie cherry type—strawberries, blackberries, raspberries; almost any flavourful, fairly tart fruit will do. And the same goes for the tropics, of course. Mixed with ice and cool sweet water in a tall thin glass this Shrub recalls the days of bronze-faced planters seated on their galleries overlooking green seas of sugar cane; rice, indigo, or tobacco. It is an especial relief to the man who is wearied of the constant small hammer blows of more insistent, highly proofed, beverages. Incidentally we list a "Temperance" Shrub in some detail on Page 149.

We need a big double boiler, or better still, an earthenware pot big enough to hold all the fruit; and another pot big enough to hold pot Number I. . . . Extract the juice by putting the fruit in the upper container, which stands in the boiling water of the lower vessel. Dredge with sugar and add a stick or 2 of cinnamon. Simmer until juices are pretty well extracted from fruit, then strain through a jelly cloth. Add enough *gomme* syrup to suit taste, and make fairly sweet. Stand in a chilled place until sediment settles out, rack off through another filtering process and add 4 oz—½ cup—of cognac for each 1 qt bottle of the clear juice. Cork well, seal with rosin or paraffin, or wax—then store in a cool place of even temperature. Good to use at any time now. . . . This fruit juice may be clarified or "fined" by the ancient and proper Portuguese method on Page 159.

## THE SMILE

Antoine, in New Orleans, has through many years been a gathering place of people who possess good tastes of varying sorts. This specialty of his sometimes known as Antoine's Smile, is simple to make, the only requirement being that the apple brandy be not "Jersey lightning" six months in wood, but aged, and at least five years old—and the older the finer, of course.

| | |
|---|---|
| Aged apple brandy, or applejack, 1 pony | Lime, juice ½ small; or ¼ lemon Grenadine, 1 dash |

This is simply a drier and better version of the old Jack Rose, which allows half a pony grenadine to a jigger apple brandy and juice of a lemon, and is the precise shade of the famous jacqueminot rose.

WILSON'S SOUTH CAMP ROAD COCKTAIL, from JAMAICA, B.W.I. via TOM DAVIN
As usual with Davin, his words are worth a quote.
"If you include drinks with your eats here is my donation—which I captured in Jamaica enroute to Haiti, last winter. If you have no friend who drinks any good lawyer can prove it to be a fruit cocktail, even to the eyes of your very own Aunt Silica Fittich! Even your friend Hemingway, with his Anis del Mono-besotted tonsils will not be able to taste the ingredients. Try it yourself, but not more than two—and I mean that. . . . It was invented by a retired British army man—and how can England have any army when all her princely chaps are 'retired'—who lives in, or rather outside of, Kingston, named Wilson. His main vocation seems to be concocting odd beverages, and if this is any sample he's a wizard. Somehow this escaped his secret archives because he turned the formula over to the head barman at the South Camp Road Hostelry when dining some friends there. . . . As you-all say in Florida: 'Heah-tiz!'"

Dry gin, 2 jiggers
Grand marnier, ½ pony
Juice of large lime
Dash angostura, dash orange
   bitters
French vermouth, 2 jiggers

Absinthe, or Pernod Veritas, ½
   pony
Egg, white, 1, fresh as can be
Grenadine, to taste; about ½ tsp
Sugar or *gomme* syrup, about 2
   tsp, to taste

"Shake with lots of cracked ice and pour into a large saucer champagne glass capable of holding some six ounces of T.N.T.
"Now," continues Editor Davin, "report me this when ye can. Maybe I had a touch o' sun when I tried it last!"
P.S. Orange curaçao can substitute for grand marnier; *anis del*

*mono* could pinch hit for the absinthe, or *ojen*—the Spanish absinthe —would also work, lacking the real Swiss product.

THE RANGOON STAR RUBY, a Wonderful & Stimulating Cocktail from Lower-Burmah

In 1926 we disembarked in Burmah from a round-the-world ship, and spent several days there before hopping off to Calcutta in a little "Bibby" boat carrying a mess of Mohammedan pilgrims headed for Mecca as deck passengers, and who did all their own cooking right down there in plain sight. In Rangoon we joined up with several folk in the Strand bar of evenings to chin about the romantic Mandalay country far up the Irrawaddy River, and to talk over gems with Hamid and his brother from Colombo and Bombay, and to acquire a really fine zircon for someone else and a set of star sapphire dress studs for ourself. One American headed out on leave from certain ruby mining operations up-country told us he had invented himself a drink that everyone up at headquarters liked so well he was going to shout it to the world so that no man might be denied its virtues. He popped behind the bar before we could say "knife" and whipped up the following mixture which, due to its colour, he had christened the Star Ruby.

Take 1 jigger of good cognac, ½ pony of cherry brandy, ½ pony of French vermouth, 2 dashes each of orange bitters and lemon phosphate, then for added flavour 1 tsp of *kirsch,* or ½ tsp of maraschino. Shake with finely cracked ice, pour into a wine glass leaving a little ice floating, and let fall 6 drops of grenadine in the center of this chilly expanse for the ruby colour touch.

SUNDAY VESPERS, from the Repertoire of an American Official with Paramount Films Who Dwells near Queen Anne's Gate London

Here's a gentle thought for that long quiet, house-bound afternoon, just prior to evening services, when both the spiritual and bodily reservoirs need aiding and abetting. It should be served, in summer, very cold, frappéed briefly with not-too-fine ice. *Pax vobiscum,* my good fellow. We met this aid to mankind in 1932.

| | |
|---|---|
| Cognac, 1 jigger | Egg, 1 |
| Black coffee, 1 pony | Sugar, barspoon |
| Heavy cream, 2 jiggers | Clove and nutmeg, dash each, on |
| Port, 1 pony | top |

It should be served in some tall, stemmed glass.

NOTES on DRINKS with a TEQUILA BASE, & NATIVE to MEXICO

Tequila, along with Pulque and Mescal, make up the three national beverages. Pulque is the universal drink, mainly for the average person of average position. It is the fermented sap of the *Maguey* plant—which we call a century plant—and made by chopping out the central bud, or flower stalk so that the sap can collect in the scooped out heart of the plant itself. . . . Pulque is about as strong as beer, tastes like a combination of sour cider and whatever fermented fruit juice happens to be around, and smells—as has been told—faintly like a mildewed donkey. Needless to say it is not universally consumed by others than the hardy race in the land of its conception.

Mescal is the *distilled* fermented juice of the *Agave* or *Maguey* plant. The plant is dug up, leaves amputated and roasted. The juice is then extracted in a press, fermented and distilled. It is the same colour as our corn likker, has the same kick, plus an odd flavour which cannot be described.

Tequila is the finest of these three, being the distilled fermented juice of the *Zotol Maguey* plant, which grows almost entirely in the State of Jalisco. Properly aged it is a spirit of definite merit. It is very potent, colourless also, and has a strange exotic flavour which—like Holland gin—is an acquired taste.

The upstanding Mexican takes his tequila like our prohibition "Swiss Itch": First a suck of a quartered lemon, then the pinch of salt, then the tossed off jigger or pony of spirit. This process not only being a definite menace to the gullet and possible fire risk through lighted matches, we began going on a still hunt for some way to mix tequila. We were greeted with raised eyebrows, expressions of commiseration for waning sanity, open distrust. It was about the same situation which would parallel snooping about Paris for ways to dilute *champagne fine,* or aged brandy. It took several hundred miles of wandering about the surrounding towns and mountains before we struck our first evidence of cooperation—at the little corner place of one eminent lady known affectionately as Bertita, on the Cathedral Square of utterly lovely Taxco—pronounced "toss-ko."

What Bertita had done after long experimentation was to put in more lime juice and less sweet than we. As we said, tequila is an acquired taste, try it sometime. . . . Remember small ice makes the drink very cold, which improves the taste by taking some of the accent off tequila. Bertita's Special is listed 2d receipt below.

## OUR OWN TEQUILA COCKTAIL, *ARMILLITA CHICO*

Armillita is the idol of Mexico, their foremost, most finished, most graceful, most dramatic bullfighter. His work with the cape, banderillas, and sword rank him with the Spanish immortals of all time. He gets fifteen hundred dollars for a Sunday afternoon's performance, Hollywood please notice. Mexicans are beginning to rank him with Spain's Juan Belmonte whose life, by Allen Villiers, has just been published.

In dallying with tequila in the bosom of our own bar we finally set upon this formula as being worthwhile, and promptly dedicated it, a standing toast with Sydney Franklin by our side, to Armillita Chico.

| | |
|---|---|
| Tequila, 3 jiggers | Orange flower water, 2 dashes |
| Limes, strained juice, 2 | Grenadine, dash, for colour |

Fill electric shaker with all the finely shaved ice this amount will cover, frappe well, serve through a sieve, shaking to make the frappe stand up in a brief rosy, temporary cone. When this subsides drink to Armillita Chico, the idol of Mexico.

TEQUILA SPECIAL, à la BERTITA, Garnered, among other Things, in Lovely Taxco, in February of 1937

This is a shocker from the place of Bertita, across from the cathedral steps in Taxco, already mentioned. It is a cooler as well and Americans will find it very unusual. Take 2 ponies of good tequila, the juice of 1 lime, 1 tsp sugar and 2 dashes of orange bitters. Stir in a collins glass with lots of small ice, then fill with club soda. No garnish except crushed halves of the lime.

TEQUILA por MI AMANTE, or Tequila for My Beloved; Mexico City, 1937

This is a prepared beverage requiring patience and from three to four weeks.

Tequila, 1 pint          Ripe strawberries, 1 qt, cut in halves

Wash and stem the berries, put into an airtight jar or bottle, pour on enough tequila to cover. Shut tightly and stand for at least twenty-one days. Strain. . . . This berry process extracts some of the raw taste, adds a rosy dawn touch. Our Mexican drinks it straight always. We opine that handled in the same way as sloe gin, discoveries would be made. . . . Other fruit like wild cherries, blackberries, and so on could be tried.

TIGER'S MILK, what It Is, & Why; Dated from Peking, April 1931

We honestly consider this one of the most amazing and delicious building-up drinks we've ever known. That year we didn't go from Fusan to Seoul, Korea, to Mukden and then down to Peking, because the Japanese puppet makers had just started slamming the door, but we did get there on the crack blue train via Tientsin, from Chingwangtao. Yes, we coasted in through the break in the huge breath-taking battlements of the Tartar Wall, to the station by the Water Gate—so vital to the Allies during the Boxer Siege of the Legations in 1900.

We got that strange lift under the heart all men get when they step from the world we know straight back into the heart of a city dating for thousands of years. . . . Then, later, we met Gerber, manager of the Wagons-Lits on Legation Street, and next afternoon we went out and watched him exercise his "griffin" polo ponies—those short, stocky, hairy, half-wild little horses brought down from the northern plains by Larsen of Mongolia. Ponies, Gerber told us, were bought at auction, unclipped and untried, so that everyone—millionaire and lowly civilian alike—might play polo without needing a fortune to finance his string. Actually regulation polo ponies are banned from the sport in Peking. Then we found it quite chill after sunset, and we went back to Gerber's snug bar at the Wagons-Lits, and he ordered his Chino to mix a brace of Tiger's Milks—directly from the receipt left with him by a chap named Seaholm some time before, and who was related to the King of Sweden allegedly; and the receipt itself unchanged one iota. They called it Tiger's Milk, as Seaholm had, and it has since gone forth and become gradually recognized all over the world—either in original form or slightly changed to suit local preferences.

The main thing in No. I: Never use anything but really good aged brandy, *champagne fine,* not the usual cognac. The latter doesn't do the job properly.

TIGER'S MILK No. I, from the Gerber-Seaholm Formula, Peking, 1931

Command 2½ jiggers old liqueur brandy, or *champagne fine,* and put this in a shaker. Add 1 to 2 tsp of sugar or grenadine, to taste, ½ cup of heavy cream and ½ cup of milk—nothing else; no trimmings. Shake with several big pieces of ice and strain into a goblet. A dash of cinnamon or nutmeg is optional, but not originally authentic. We came, we saw, we drank. And later we imported a certain black eyed Russian peril, managed 1 for her; and we recall her first remark in syllables slightly husky, wholly charming, the slightly accented English slick as cream. "And do you now, mah frrrrahn, thees dreenk eet iss—how shall I say eet?—'food, dreenk, and lodging,' all at zee same tam!" . . . True, *ma soeur,* true!

TIGER'S MILK No. II, from the Bar Book of a Tiny Smiling Anna-mese Bar-Boy at the Phya-Thai Palace, Bangkok, Siam, in the Year 1932 . . . Tiger's Milk No. III is on Page 90

We had come in from a day around town—looking at a sleeping Buddha 90 feet or so long, at temples and *wats* searching upward to the sun; at *Wat Arun,* gleaming with porcelain insets, brilliant butter-fly-hued tiles, at the temple of the Emerald Buddha, the Wat Phra-Keo, with the sacred Gautama himself carved from a single emerald so runneth the tale—but green jasper to us—some 60 centimeters high, and with 3 changes of jewel and gold cloth clothing, to keep him comfortable during the rainy, the cold and the hot seasons. We were wearied of Buddha and Yagas, or guardian demons; we were tired of sightseeing altogether and wanted to rest and relax before going to the Royal Dancers in the—of all ideas!—*Roman* Garden of the Phya-Thai Palace that gala night. We wanted something to forget our weary insteps, or sun-toasted eyeballs, before freshening up and chang-ing for evening. We asked, through an interpreter of sorts, if the bar-boy might have anything possible to make a Tiger's Milk. The answer was that, evidently, the Gerber-Seaholm idea had penetrated there too, authorized by some hardy and careless soul like ourself with medical knowledge enough to realize that enough alcohol will strangle the microbes even in Siamese milk and cream—which is a chancey statement we might say. The Bacardi lends a typical British modification, a twist. . . . Old brandy 1½ jiggers, Bacardi Gold Seal the same; ½ cup each of thick cream and milk, then sweeten to taste. Shake vigorously for at least ½ minute with big lumps of ice and serve in a goblet. Dust with nutmeg, or ground mace, or cinnamon.

THE IMPROVED TURF COCKTAIL No. I, a Modification of Our Own from Dirty Dick's, Nassau, B.I., 1937

We first sampled this drink in Nassau quite some time back, hav-ing flown over Pan-American Airways, after the official tourist season was finished, with a 6-year bride and 4 friends, to do a bit of sailing and swimming and basking on undiscovered white sand beaches by vitriol blue coral water that is clearer than anywhere else in the whole universe. A gentleman of colour suggested this as a dry, appetizing taste-thrill at Dirty Dick's, and found it to be merely Holland gin and vermouth—nothing else except Angostura—in a 2 to 1 ratio. . . . After a bit of later experimentation on self and friends we discovered that addition of ½ a green lime—strained juice—and ½ tsp of grenadine or bar sugar works miracles with this drink.

TURF COCKTAIL No. II, from the Taj Mahal Hotel, on Apollo Bundar, in Bombay, Saturday, February 14th, 1931, to Be Exact; Served after the Running of the Maharajah of Rajpipla Gold Cup at the Western India Turf Club, Ltd.

We had won all of sixty-seven rupees on this gold-cup, 23,000-rupees race, and were feeling very horsy and turfy, and tired of the eternal *chotapegs*—just plain Scotch and not-too-cold soda, without ice, of the last few days—and were open for suggestions. G. J. Mack, local Manager for General Motors Export, suggested a Turf Cocktail, of a recognized mix, and after a barrage of Hindustani this resulted, much to everyone's amazement: 1 jigger of dry gin, 1 pony of French vermouth, 1 tsp of absinthe, or *Pernod Veritas;* donate 1 tsp of maraschino and a dash of orange or Abbots bitters. Stir in a bar glass like a Martini and serve in a Manhattan glass, ungarnished.

TURF COCKTAIL No. III, from the Havana Country Club, Winter of 1930

This is virtually the same as No. II, only using old Tom gin for a base, orange bitters, and everything else the same.

THE VIRGIN'S PRAYER, a Memory from Versailles, in the Summer of 1926

That summer when we were living in Paris, we met many people across the street from our own domicile, in Harry's American Bar—already a happy memory to countless Americans. And one night we

were there with a person not apt to mention, listening to Tommy Ly-
man sing *Montmartre Rose,* and wondering what we were going to
do next day, when a stalwart young chap barged up and invited himself to our table—a practice which we are not likely to view with any
great amount of enthusiasm in Paris, Paraguay or Patagonia.

But this time it was all right. His name was O'Malley and he had a
Cadillac 8, and after the war he had married him a French wife who
got lonesome when he took her to Union City, New Jersey—and we
don't have to be French to be that!—and so he had brought her back
to France, Cadillac and all. And why the hell did I spend 12 dollars
a day to Franco-Belgique tours for a motor car when I could hire his
for 9 or less. Certainly, why? . . . Well, O'Malley not only had a
Cadillac 8 and a French wife, but he knew all 16 of the current crop
of Tiller girls living in their dormitory with a matron and chaperones
and all, over in Montmartre. But unless they had been misbehaving
and were under censure, they were all allowed nights out until 12
midnight, so we started at the end of the line and went along, count-
ing off from right to left; and what dancing partners; what grand
fun they were! Well, one afternoon we and O'Malley and our current
assignment of Tiller were out at Versailles absorbing French history,
then toward evening we stopped at a big sort of a chateau turned into
a restaurant-hotel not too far from the great Palace, for a little liquid
nourishment. And while we were waiting they brought us a bowl of
big red ripe cherries in cracked ice, and O'Malley had an idea. "I
know," he said, holding up a cherry pit, "I'll *invent* a drink."

Now a gentleman from Union City, New Jersey, who had a French
wife and a Cadillac 8, in Paris, and who hired out to Franco-Belgique
tours yet also hired out for less to us, was shock enough for any one
stay in Paris; but one who further invented drinks, made us slightly
dizzy. "Of course. Sure. *Invent* one," we added with all the conviction
we feel when we see cinemas of Senators kissing babies.

"Celeste's old man works at the Florida. Her old man invents drinks
too. We invent drinks together," he explained. Celeste was O'Malley's
wife, of course. "We invent swell drinks."

So O'Malley asked for a nutcracker in his Union City, New Jersey, French, and bottles of things, and a shaker and a bowl of ice, and the maitre-d'hotel had it fetched with a suspicious but he'll-pay-beaucoup-for-his-fun gleam in his agate eyes, and O'Malley mixed. He first cracked 4 cherry pits with that darned nutcracker and dropped them in a cocktail glass. Then he put 1½ jiggers of *kirsch,* 1 pony of cherry brandy, 1 tsp of maraschino, into the shaker, and shook it with the ice. Then he poured it onto the broken pits, stirred it for a second to let the aromatic bitter odour and taste penetrate the drink, then handed it to me. And it was good.

"That, Pal,"—O'Malley was the soul of companionship for a chauffeur-companion, we might state—"is a swell drink, see? That drink has what it takes—imagination, see? That's it, imagination. No drink is worth a damn without imagination. It doesn't take any imagination to just say 'Scotchansoda,' now does it? It's good enough to give Celeste's old man, and if it's good enough for that it's plenty good enough for a name. It must be garnished with 2 red cherries, Eh? 2; sure! . . . Let's name it the Virgin's Prayer. Eh? What do you think, Esle?" Esle was our Miss Tiller *du jour.* Esle was just eighteen, with curly brown hair and brown eyes, and breakfast ankles. She was very English, very sane, very passionate. She looked at him calmly. She sipped the drink.

"I don't trust the Irish, O'Malley," she said evenly; "or their names." . . . "*Garçon,* scotchansoda," she said to the hovering waiter.

Now of course we don't expect that when our most dutiful readers are faced with a bowl of cherries they will all have nutcrackers within ordering distance. Or Tiller girls. But if they have, and the spirit of adventure is not dead, they may try this pungent drink. Try an O'Malley Virgin's Prayer. It really is a sound cocktail, and worthy to be known among all men.

VANILLA PUNCH, another Receipt from the Plantation Files of One Clymer Brooke, Mentioned Elsewhere in this Work

Brooke was the one who fell in love with Tahiti, and left the round-the-world cruise of the schooner *CHANCE,* along with Dodd and the rest of their Yale outfit, and whose adventures are neatly told in *From Great Dipper to Southern Cross.* Well, Brooke ended up hobnobbing with princesses on Moorea, owning some sort of a vanilla plantation. We met him out of Yoko, bound for Hawaii in 1931 when he was bound back to the states like a sea-going Lochinvar to marry him a bride. . . . *Salut* Clymer.

Take a bar glass and fill it with shaved or very finely cracked ice, add 2 tsp of fresh strained lime juice, the same of yellow curaçao, and 1 tbsp of grenadine. Now turn in 2 jiggers of cognac, and either a scant ½ pony of vanilla extract, or 1 full pony of *Crème de Vanille.* Stir, turn ice and all into a tall thin glass or goblet, garnish with sticks of fresh ripe pineapple, a cherry or 2, and a sprig of something to brighten up attractively. This is fairly sweet, so be sure and step up the lime juice if a drier drink is wanted.


THE HARVARD *VERITAS,* CONTRIBUTED by FREDERICK A. R. THOMPSON, at the TIME MANAGING EDITOR of *COMMONWEAL,* a CATHOLIC INTERNATIONAL WEEKLY

This drink is famous enough along the Charles River, and especially at the Harvard Club in New York, and good enough in its own right to be listed here. It is a sort of emancipated Between the Sheets, only with currant flavouring. Take 1 pony each of dry gin, cointreau and strained lemon—or lime, better—juice. Shake well with finely cracked ice, strain into a flute cocktail glass with a stem, and pour in 2 tbsp of *crème de cassis* for trimming.


COCKTAIL *au VICOMTE de MAUDUIT,* BEING a LOVELY THING MADE of ROSE BRANDY

Vicomte de Mauduit is one of Europe's most exacting gourmets and his volume *The Vicomte in the Kitchen* is one of the most charming volumes on food and wine ever printed in the English language. His knowledge of wines is thoroughgoing, but even though tartly French, his mental processes are still agile and cosmopolitan enough to grant brief space to decent cocktails. We have taken pains to test out this, his own especial origination, and can attest it to be one of the most delicate and palate tickling amateur originations we have ever met. In this one case we have taken the liberty of reprinting another's own formula, in the spirit of pleasant drinking and gentle living; and with a bow of thanks to Monsieur le Vicomte.

Take 1 pony each of dry gin, French dry vermouth and rose brandy—another original formula of the Vicomte's and which we also note with grateful acknowledgment on Page 155—and put in a bar glass. Stir with several fairly large lumps of ice and strain into a Manhattan glass. Garnish with a candied pink rose petal carefully floated on top. A delicate, original cocktail indeed.

THE OLD WALDORF'S LAST, Invented—so Runneth the Tale —as the Last Original Cocktail to Come from the Mellow Old Waldorf Bar at Fifth Avenue & 34th Street

This is not, strictly, an exotic. It is a good ladies' drink under any condition, and any spirituous combination to put the period to those grand old days when titanic, two-fisted Wall Streeters and important folk from all over the world used to stand 6 or 8 deep before mahogany during the 5 to 8 P.M. cocktail "hour," is well worthy of inclusion on any list of international receipts. . . . Take 1 pony each of dry gin, orange curaçao and heavy cream. Shake and strain into a Manhattan glass. That is all.

THE WAXMAN SPECIAL COCKTAIL, which We Assume to Be after the Original Specification of Percy Waxman, Associate Editor of COSMOPOLITAN Magazine

We discovered this one last spring when this volume first began emerging into final, concise form. Oddly enough we stumbled over it at the lovely pavilion-bar at the Palm Beach Colony, which proved that the true grapevine telegraph must be at work telling the news of

its worth, from New York to there. . . . Take 1 pony each of old Tom gin, Italian vermouth and decent applejack. Shake briskly with finely cracked ice, strain into a Manhattan glass, and with a few lumps left floating contribute ½ pony of yellow chartreuse at the last. This final touch is what sets it apart from its fellows; and, of course, the applejack flavour too.

Le *RAT BLANC,* or WHITE RAT, a Left Bank Touch, Sampled in Paris at the Urging of a Friend

This is a stout and pungent thing, so be wary of absorbing it in too ambitious quantity or we cannot be responsible for any subsequent inclination or action! . . . To 1 jigger of absinthe add ½ pony of *anis del mono,* or lacking this, anisette. Shake with very fine ice like a frappe, and serve in a Manhattan glass, leaving a trifle of the ice still in the finished drink. No garnish, please.

THE IMMORTAL ZAZARAC COCKTAIL, which Takes us Back Many Years to the Old Days before the Drouth, & to New Orleans

This is the famous original from the Zazarac Bar. Since France outlawed absinthe much of the world's best was made by French Creole New Orleans. The other main essential is to use decent bourbon whisky. There still is a great deal of young blended whisky masquerading as bourbon, here in these United States. . . . Put 1 jigger of bourbon into a shaker, toss in ½ tsp of sugar, add 1 tsp of Italian vermouth and the same of absinthe, or lacking this, *Pernod Veritas.* Contribute 2 or 3 good dashes of Peychaud's bitters—now obtainable in all big towns—shake with cracked ice and serve in an Old Fashioned cocktail glass topped with a little soda, and end up with a twist of lemon or orange peel on top. . . . It is also made by mixing in the glass itself, just like an Old Fashioned, using ½ lump of sugar, saturating this with bitters, and muddling well before adding ice and spirits.

THE ZAMBOANGA "ZEINIE" COCKTAIL, another PALATE-TWISTER from the LAND where the MONKEYS HAVE NO TAILS

This drink found its way down through the Islands to Mindanao from Manila, and we found it in the little Overseas Club standing high above the milk-warm waters of the Sulu Sea, on the suggestion of a new friend, just met; and while perusing the first edition of that Norm Anthony-George Delacorte opus *Ballyhoo,* which after having passed from hand to hand through most of the U.S. Army in the Islands from Colonels down was slightly tattered, but still placed in a rack of honour.

Cognac, 1 jigger

Maraschino, 1 tsp

Lime, juice, ½

Fresh pineapple syrup, 3 dashes

Angostura, 3 dashes

Twist lime peel

Shake well with shaved ice, letting some of ice go into glass; twist some of the peel on top to extract oil, and add one olive. Use a Manhattan glass. . . . Pineapple syrup same as used at soda fountains.

AN EXOTIC COCONUT-COGNAC COCKTAIL from *CAP HAITIEN, REPUBLIC de HAITI,* and which Is CALLED the *ZOMBIE*

Any one who knows his Haiti and his *Vaudou* knows what a *Zombie* is; and for those who don't, a Zombie is merely a departed brother who, for reasons not generally attractive, has been called back from the Spirit World, labours without pay, without food, without complaint, in a weird sort of spirit bondage. . . . We have just helped "spring" an artist friend, Christopher Clark, from a five months' stay in Cap Haitien, where he had been soaking up material and madly painting the unbelievable scenery and even more unbelievable people of Haiti, as a follow-up to the wave of acclaim which greeted his *The Crapshooters,* in last year's American Art Exhibit at Rockefeller Center, and we fetched him via Pan American to do a mural for us.

Chris brought back a long list of amazing cookery receipts, too late for this volume, but we are squeezing in this *Zombie* Cocktail, he

claiming that it will put the spirits to work for you, but whether they or ourselves, are in bondage, is something for each man to decide according to occasion and the needs thereof.

Enriched coconut milk, see below, 1 cup or so
Cognac, 3 jiggers

Maraschino, 2 ponies
Angostura, 2 or 3 dashes
Very finely cracked or shaved ice

Put in shaker with lots of very finely cracked ice, shake hard and turn ice and all—*à la Daiquiri*—into small, chilled goblets. . . . Another variation, and a much better flavoured one we find, is found by using only two jiggers cognac, and one jigger old Haitian—or other medium dark—rum.

Enriched coconut milk: Get a ripe coconut anywhere. Bore two holes in eyes and drain out water into saucepan—being careful to strain out fibres or bits of shell. . . . Crack open nut, peel off brown outer skin from kernel, and either grate, grind, or cut up fine and add to water. . . . Fetch to a simmer for five minutes. Put through a fine cloth, squeezing out the final rich cream by hand. Ripe fresh coconuts can be had in most good grocery stores these days. . . . Those possessing The Mixer will save an incredible amount of time by cutting up kernel, with brown part unremoved, into the top container of The Mixer; turn in the coconut juice. Reduce to a pulp at high speed for 1 minute, then rub through a very fine sieve, or strain through several thicknesses of cloth.

AN EVEN ONE DOZEN TEMPERANCE DELIGHTS, which after ALL Is nearly TWO WEEKS' SUPPLY

NOT ALL intelligent folk approve or militantly disapprove of spirituous beverage. There simply happen to be quite a few rational souls who don't care for anything containing alcohol. Being half of Quaker stock we have noted such phenomena right in our own family. Also there are beverages for the extremely young.

This being the case, and refreshments are indicated, what to serve besides tea, coffee, milk or water? To our own rough and unpredictable mind there is nothing under heaven more discouraging than weak lemonade, once past the age of 10—except pink, and at circuses. How often in our own history have we seen guests gaze skyward and pray for a sign so that dear old Aunt Trilby Fittich wouldn't serve them cookies and lemonade! Therefore, sharply aware of this problem from our own case, we have gone to considerable effort in snupping these selected Temperance Delights. We now feel that we can face a P.T.A. meeting unafraid, look a strawberry social in the teeth without bowing our head in abject and citric shame.

Beside our own palm-shrouded cornerstone there is nothing under heaven's sweet canopy so baffling as suddenly being confronted with test of producing some non-alcoholic beverage claiming credit for anything but the usual bellywash of lemon, orange, sugar and ice. This is no laughing matter, either. This sort of zero hour may pop up to haunt us at any unexpected moment; and usually when brains are bled white, scraping an all-time low, and showing all the originality of stuffing for a kapok windowseat pad. Yes, it may easily be a neighbouring daughter's 6th birthday, or Aunt Deleria Fittich descending from Clebbett City in the worst hot spell since '83. And to our way of thinking there still never has been an excusable lemonade except pink, and at circuses!

These mild-mannered coolers come from here and there around the world, and the bare fact of presenting them in a drinking volume of our own conception makes us feel very fine, and remote and pure and worth while, for a change.

THE ANGOSTURA FIZZ, sometimes CALLED the TRINIDAD FIZZ, BEING a RECEIPT GLEANED from ONE of OUR FRIENDS PILOTING the BIG BRAZILIAN CLIPPER from HERE to TRINIDAD & RIO & on SOUTH to "B. A."

This mild fizz is again like initial olive sampling; either it suits or it doesn't, and subsequent trials often show sudden shift to appreciation. It is a well-known stomachic along the humid shores of Trinidad, in British Guiana; wherever the climate is hot and the humidity high,

and stomachs stage sit-down strikes and view all thought of food—present or future—with entire lack of enthusiasm. Further than this, the cinchona bark elixir in the Angostura, the other herbs and valuable simples, are a definite first line defense against malaria and other amoebic fevers—especially in warding off their after effect in later months when all actual peril is past.

Take 1 pony of Angostura bitters, add 1 tsp of sugar or grenadine, the juice of ½ lemon or 1 lime, the white of 1 egg and 1 tbsp of thick cream—or slightly less. Shake with cracked ice like a cocktail, turn into a goblet and fill to suit individual taste with club soda, seltzer, vichy, or whatever lures the mind. Vary the sweet also, to suit taste. It is a very original, cooling drink as well as a valuable tonic to those dwelling in hot countries. Garnish with sticks of ripe fresh pineapple, always.

CASSIS & SODA, the OLD CLASSIC from anyWHERE in FRANCE

This is well known to all traveling Americans nowadays but is important enough to list for those who are merely contemplating a trip abroad. As we have already explained, cassis is the syrup and juice made from black French currants. . . . Take from 1 to 2 jiggers of cassis, chill as above, turn into a tumbler or goblet with ice, and fill to taste with soda; or merely mix like an ordinary highball, directly in the glass without shaking first. Angostura is optional. It is very refreshing in hot weather, also.

THE PANAMA "MOCK DAISY" CRUSTA, from CRISTOBAL at the ATLANTIC END of the PANAMA CANAL ZONE, which ODDLY ENOUGH Is ACTUALLY WEST of the PACIFIC END at BALBOA

Take the juice of 2 limes and put into a tumbler or goblet with fine ice, the crystal having been rubbed first with the lime shells and the lip dipped in powdered sugar, allowing all possible to cling for about ½″ down the side. Now add 1 pony of raspberry syrup, fill glass with enough club soda to suit taste, and float on ½ to 1 tsp of grenadine. Garnish with stick of ripe pineapple, 2 or 3 ripe raspberries frozen in ice cubes; a sprig of green mint.

EXPLODED old ALEWIVES' TALES No. II, PLEADING that
JUST BECAUSE PAST TEMPERANCE DRINKS HAVE usu-
ally BEEN UNATTRACTIVE & UNGARNISHED, this SIN
SHOULD NOT PREVAIL in MODERN TIMES

Again we urge readers to consider that any drink that intrigues the
eye has already half conquered. Ice cubes may be tinted in a second
to afford any desired shade; sprigs of green mint, cherries, strawberries, raspberries, and other fresh or candied fruits; rose and violet
petals—*au naturelle* or candied, anything pretty the heart desires may
quickly be frozen into each cube. The variety is limited solely by the
imagination. . . . To suspend fruits in center of cube—freeze first
with tray half full; then center up fruits, add water to fill tray full,
and freeze again. If garnish is desired on top of cubes, fill tray almost
full, freeze; tee up fruit and freeze again after adding a tiny bit of
water.

To our mind a sweet temperance drink has to look mighty, mighty
pretty to be intriguing. This may also apply to other citizens confronted with spirituous aridity at any current function!

GENERAL J. K. L. HARKRIDER'S FAMOUS STONE BOTTLE GINGER
BEER No. I, a FINE TIME-TESTED RECEIPT for this AROMATIC BEVERAGE
so ESSENTIAL in JAMAICA & SHANGHAI BUCKS, in SINGAPORE RAFFLES
GIN SLINGS, as WELL as a TASTY COOLER in ITS OWN TEMPERATE
RIGHT, FOUND in LONDON SUMMER of 1932

This is one of the oldest temperance beverage receipts we own, and
dates well back into Georgian days in rural England, *Circa* 1766. To
our way of thinking a rich ginger beer is to average ginger ale as
Napoleon brandy is to Nawth Ca'lina white mule. Stone bottles may
be ordered in for us by the country grocer, on a few days' notice, and
in big towns we may find "empties" in any good delicatessen or provision store. Of course this ginger beer may be bottled in glass, but
that too is like modernizing any mellowed and ancient custom, or
like a charming girl in sport slacks who wears high heels; for then
certain of the charm flies out the window, through needless incon-
sistency.

Brief comparison of these two formulae shows that No. II, that of
the famous Dr. Pereira, employs honey and no yeast since . . . *"The*

*Honey gives the Beverage a Peculiar Softness, and from not being Fermented with Yeast, it is Less Violent when Opened, but requires to be kept a Somewhat Longer Time before Use."*
General Harkrider's receipt calls for:

| | |
|---|---|
| 2½ lbs of sugar | 2 oz of ginger root |
| ½ oz cream of tartar | 2½ gallons of boiling water |
| 4 lemons, juice and rind | 2 tbsp fresh brewer's yeast |

Peel the lemons thin and put the cut up rind and strained juice in an earthenware crock, together with the bruised ginger root, the sugar and cream of tartar. Add the boiling water and when lukewarm stir in the brewer's yeast. Cover with a cloth and let ferment until next day. Now skim the yeast foam from the top, pour carefully through several thicknesses of cheesecloth, being careful also not to agitate the sediment in the crock. Put in stone bottles, thoroughly sterilized in boiling water. Ready to use in 2 weeks or so. If no ginger root is available add 1 tbsp of ground ginger to the hot water brew, or better still 2 tbsp of tincture of Jamaica ginger; stir well, and taste. Then add more ginger—ground or essence—1 tsp at a time until it suits the taste.

The lemon juice and rind are what point up this receipt. Sugar also may be stepped up slightly, to taste. This brew is enough to fill 3 doz average stone bottles.

STONE BOTTLE GINGER BEER No. II, without Yeast, from the Famous Receipt of Dr. Pereira on Discussing Diet, and Dating Back Well over Half a Century; & Discovered by Us in London, Summer of 1932
To our knowledge this receipt dates back more than 60 years in England, and has always been a favourite with home-brewers of their own stone bottle ginger beer. It is very simple, and once again we suggest using Jamaica ginger tincture or essence, if no ginger root is available; and ground ginger if no liquid essence—gradually increas-

ing the dose and stirring into the boiling hot water until it is pungent enough to suit us.

| | |
|---|---|
| 5 lbs of sugar | ½ cup of strained lemon juice |
| ¼ lb, about ½ cup, of strained honey | 5 oz of bruised ginger root |
| | ¼ white of 1 egg |
| 4½ gallons of water | Cut up peel of the lemons |
| 1 scant tsp of lemon extract | |

Boil the bruised ginger root in 3 qts of water for ½ hr; now add the sugar, lemon juice, honey and peel. Turn in the rest of the water—15 qts to be exact, or 3¾ gals, and briskly boiling at the time, too. Let cool gradually and when cold strain through several thicknesses of cloth, then stir in the egg white to clarify; also the lemon extract. . . . Let stand in a crock for 4 days, then bottle in sterilized stone bottles. This receipt will keep for many months, and is enough for slightly over 8 doz bottles.

Personally we prefer receipt No. I, as it has more sparkle and life—something essential to the drinks mentioned in this volume. We also suggest adding 3 cups of honey to No. II, deducting that much sugar.

CARDINAL PUNCH, from the FILES of the LATE C. H. B. QUEN-NELL, MENTIONED ELSEWHERE in these VOLUMES, and GRACIOUSLY CONTRIBUTED as a TYPICAL OLD-TIME ENGLISH RECEIPT from the COUNTRY in & around BERKHAMSTEAD, HERTFORDSHIRE

Take 2 qts of uncooked cranberries, and simmer them in just enough water to cover until soft, together with the yellow peel of 2 lemons. When berries are very tender crush them up and strain through a jelly cloth. Let cool and then add the juice of the 2 lemons, 4 cups of sugar, 1 pint of orange juice and about 2 qts of cold water. Chill now, turn into a bowl containing a big single lump of ice, and point up with 4 bottles of really good ginger ale or ginger beer. It is an aromatic, pungent and tart drink, with a lovely colour. . . . It may also be poured into glasses or goblets half filled with cracked ice, and drunk through brightly coloured straws.

MANDARIN PUNCH, a Receipt Garnered away Back in 1931, from Lady Bredon, for a Whole Generation Social Dictator of Peking's Legation Quarter Set

There are rare occasions when a Peking host or hostess has to produce a temperance punch, and this species makes a welcome relief for the usual. Actually this punch is more or less of an essence with fruit juices, and is usually served exactly like raspberry vinegar—poured to taste over cracked fine ice which almost fills the glass, with water added to suit final ideas of strength and flavour.

Melt out 2 cups of sugar with 2 doz whole cloves, 2 sticks of cinnamon bark, add ½ cup of water and cook for 10 minutes; draw from the fire and let cool. At that point stir in 2 cups of orange juice, and about ½ cup of lemon or lime juice. Strain through cheesecloth, let stand for ½ hr and mix in the following: 3 drops of spearmint oil, buyable at any pharmacy, 1 tbsp finely chopped candied ginger root, 1 bunch of green mint tips snipped fine with scissors. Mix to taste with cracked ice in tumblers or goblets; stirring with each spoonful so as not to miss the solids in this syrup. Fill up with plain water or soda.

A DELICIOUS & PRETTY BEVERAGE MADE from Fresh Grenadines, or Pomegranates, which Will Be Good News to Dwellers in all Subtropical or Tropical Climates; One from City of Jaipur, in India

The lovely roseate tint of pomegranate juice is what makes grenadine syrup so attractive in mixed drinks, and here is a secret from Rajputana, and the city ruled by the Maharajah of Jaipur, mentioned elsewhere in this volume. For centuries the pomegranate's coral-coloured blossom and low-hanging, blushing fruit have been immortalized by poet and tale teller throughout the fantastic courts of Persia, Arabia, Egypt, and further East. Here from our window we can see some ½ doz bushes bending low under their burden of fruits—yet no one we have ever known in America—except ourself—ever does anything about them, even though they seem to grow in every other southern back yard! . . . Simply break open the fruit, over a big bowl as the ruby coloured, pulp-bound seeds tend to fly this way and that as the main rind breaks. Discard every bit of rind as it is bitter as gall, and turn seeds into a fruit press or a potato ricer.

Press out the magenta tinted juice, and mix with *gomme* syrup in ratio of about 2 tbsp of the syrup to every cup of juice. Now pack glasses with fine ice, pour in enough of this luscious fresh juice to fill, stir in the juice of ½ a green lime. Garnish brightly with red cherries, sticks of fresh pineapple, and serve with brightly tinted cellophane straws. Again, sugar syrup as to taste; also the lime juice—depending upon size of the latter fruits.

BLACK TEA PUNCH, from KANDY, in CEYLON, which REFRESHED Us after a MOTOR DRIVE up through the MOUNTAINS from COLOMBO, by WAY of the VASTLY INTERESTING TROPICAL GARDENS at PERADEYNIA, in the YEAR 1931

Sir Tommy Lipton's chief bailiwick was out there in the incredibly rich mountain soils of Ceylon, which many believe to have been the Garden of Eden—even to an imprint of Adam's foot in gigantic size on a table-topped mountain we have seen, winding up through the steep hills. It is only natural, then, that being both British and near some of the finest tea gardens in all the world, that this punch should have been served for benefit of those who did not believe in alcoholic liquids for inner decoration.

Take 3 cups of quite strong, freshly brewed, black tea. Add 1 qt of strained orange juice, 1 cup of strained lime or lemon juice, 2 cups of raspberry syrup and 1 cup of crushed—fresh if possible—pineapple pounded to a pulp in a mortar, or better still, in The Mixer. Add sugar, now, to taste; pour over a single large lump of ice in a bowl, and add 2 qts of good sparkling water.

RASPBERRY VINEGAR, MADE from the FRESH FRUIT ITSELF; from a VERY, VERY OLD ENGLISH RECEIPT WE FOUND in ST. ALBANS, HERTFORDSHIRE, in the SUMMER of 1932

One of our earliest and most delightful memories during summer vacations from school was our spring visits every other year to the home of our favourite Aunt Josephine Leaming, either in Philadelphia, or at her country place out on the Main Line in Wayne, Pennsylvania.

Not only was she one of the most beautiful ladies ever born in America or Europe, but one of the most elegant, the most up-to-date even in her seventies; one of the most understanding of cryptic small-boy likes and dislikes; one of the most considerate of all those about her court—for that, actually, was what it really was. . . . And so amid a swarm of Leamings, and Heckschers, and Carsons and Storks, she would entertain in her lovely garden—and for the youngsters would be ginger beer, or more unusual still, great tumblers of thinnest crystal, filled to the brim with pale rose raspberry vinegar, with a bouquet of mint raising its fragrant emerald head in the center. . . . Raspberry vinegar!—How far we drifted apart during the hectic days of the Late Attempted Drouth! . . . How we missed you. How glad we are now and then to go sensible once more, and sip one of you, instead of a Tom Collins, or similar grownup acceptances. . . . Of course good raspberry vinegar may be bought in any fine delicacy shop, but try making your own. It's lots more fun, and saves purse strain.

| | |
|---|---|
| Raspberries, dead ripe, 1 lb | Raspberries, 1 lb (again) |
| White *wine* vinegar, 1 qt | Raspberries, 1 lb (again) |
| (Or failing this, diluted white | Sugar, just over 1 lb per pint of |
|     vinegar) |     resultant juice |

Put the 1st lb of raspberries in a bowl, and bruise well. Pour white wine vinegar over them—wine vinegar has a much more delicate flavour than either cider or malt vinegars, and can be bought from Italian shops, or made by exposing any good sweet domestic wine to the air by simply pulling the cork, adding 1 tbsp of vinegar, and letting it stand for a short time in that state.

Next day strain liquor through a cloth onto another pound of well-crushed raspberries. Stand overnight, strain, and pour onto the third batch of crushed berries. . . . *Do not squeeze the fruit* overmuch as this will cause it to ferment, which is not desired. . . . Wet a canvas bag with a little of the raspberry vinegar, and strain the whole business into a stoneware or glass container onto one pound of white sugar—lump sugar is recommended—per each pint of juice. Stir until dissolved. Put jar in pot of water, bringing latter to a simmer. Skim now and again until it grows clear and no further scum rises. Let it cool and bottle. . . . When cold it will have a consistency like heavy syrup, and a teaspoon or so diluted in water with cracked ice makes one of the most delicately flavoured summer thirst-quenchers in the world. . . . Fine for children, invalids; non-alcoholic, and one of the few non-alcoholic drinks worth touching besides water, milk, tea and coffee.

REPULSE BAY "RHUBARB HIGHBALL," from the SUMMER RESORT of HONGKONG, in CHINA, SPRING 1926
The drive up over the mountains, with its view of the Harbour and a maze of little islands dotting steel blue water amazingly like Puget Sound in certain aspects, from Hongkong to Repulse Bay, is one of the most inspiring anywhere. Repulse Bay is a beautiful setting, and small beach bungalows dot the horseshoe curve on either side of the big hotel there. One of the most amazing things we saw, surprising, at least, was a Chinese town on the way where our car exploded a flock of chickens dyed brilliant crimson, rose, cobalt blue and chrome yellow—just why, God only knew.

The Chinese have used rhubarb for countless centuries, both to eat and in specifics for varying ailments not apt to mention in this work. It was not strange, then, that the No. I Boy of our host of the day had converted the temperance members of his household to this drink. . . . Dice 6 cups of pink-stemmed rhubarb. Mix 4 cups of sugar with 2 of water, heat in a double boiler, and add rhubarb before it boils. Simmer until tender, then rub through a sieve and mix in the ratio of 1 cup of rhubarb syrup to the same of orange juice. . . . Pack glasses with fine ice, fill 2/3 full or so, with this business, and top off with club soda. A sprig of fresh green mint adds zest, and bright straws also. As before, the amount of fruit syrups and juices, to ice and sparkling water, is to individual taste; there is no safe, set, formula for every race and climate!

THE NASSAU TEA SHAKE, from a TRIP to NASSAU RECENTLY, and SERVED to THOSE WHO PREFERRED NOT to GAZE upon the CUP when IT WAS red with WINE

This is an invigorating drink and we wonder why it has not been more generally known and appreciated in the States. Simply take ½ cup of strong black tea, sugar to taste, and a whole—very fresh—egg. Pop in a shaker with lots of fairly large cracked ice; shake, then strain into a sour glass, or small tumbler—with or without ice, and with or without a topping of chilled club soda.

WEST INDIAN "TEMPERANCE" SHRUB, which MAY BE MADE from VARYING SPECIES of FRESH FRUITS, BERRIES, or what NOT —to SEASON & to TASTE; NOTED during a STAY in BERMUDA NOT too LONG AGO

This cooling summer thirst-quencher may be made out of wild or tame cherries, raspberries, strawberries or blackberries—any such northern fodder; and likewise of sun-ripened sea grapes, pineapple, mangoes, Surinam cherries, carissas, and a host of other tropical fruits and berries such as the *Eugenia Jambolina*. . . . Mixed with finely cracked ice and sweet water, it recalls the days of bronze-faced planters —well, sipping their real Shrubs or Planter's punches, while the women-folk, the children, sipped their "Temperance" Shrubs!

All we need is a crockery pot large enough to hold the fruit; a metal pot large enough to hold the crockery affair. Extract the juice by dredging fruit well with sugar, adding a stick or so of cinnamon, placing in crock, and this in turn in metal pot. Fill latter, now, with water—making a glorified sort of double boiler. Simmer until juices

are pretty well drawn from the fruit, covered. Strain through a jelly
bag, and strain again if any amount of sediment is still in sight. Add
more sugar, to taste, to make a fairly sweet syrup; stir in the juice of
1 lime for each cup of syrup. . . . Fill tumblers with fine ice, then
pour in as much of this fruit syrup as they will take, garnishing with
bright red or green cherries, and sipping through brightly tinted
straws. . . . The true West Indian Shrub has already been given on
Page 123.

CERTAIN PROVEN FORMULAE for the HOME CONSTRUCTION
of SUCH FLUID NEEDS as BITTERS, BOUNCES, & BRANDIES; WINES, MEADS,
& CORDIALS; to SAY NOTHING of a ROSE LIQUEUR BRANDY by a VI-
COMTE, & the SIMPLE INSTRUCTION for MAKING GUM—or *GOMME,*
or BAR—SYRUP

FIRST a BRIEF DISCOURSE on the HEALTH-GIVING TRIBE of
BITTERS, INCLUDING THREE RECEIPTS for THEIR COMPOUNDITION—
BEING an ALLEGED FORMULA for ANGOSTURA, ONE for ORANGE, & ONE
for HELL-FIRE BITTERS—sometimes CALLED "CAYENNE WINE."

Let us wave our white bar towel in a good-natured plea for truce
right at the outset, and affirm that this receipt for Angostura bitters
makes no claim to be the one hundred per cent, unchangeable, priceless and violently kept secret formula. By the same token, if we
breathed our last in tonight's sleep, the heirs and assigns of Dr. Johann
Gottlieb Benjamin Siegert—one-time surgeon in Bleucher's army (we
trust the Angostura receipt booklet means the Blücher who, aged and
infirm, made that incredibly severe forced march to aid Wellington,
and even though he was "late," nevertheless added the vital crushing
effect against Napoleon at Waterloo)—should lower all house flags
at half mast for the vats of their liquid we have consumed, or caused
to be consumed in our warped and intermittent career.

Let it never be said that so starry-eyed a devotee at the Angostura
shrine would ever claim that their "world's best kept secret" had ever

crept out into light of day, in spite of the 7 people—all members of the Siegert family—who have courted insomnia and shattered nervous tone guarding it from profane eyes of a mercenary and covetous world all those 115 years since 1824! According to the book of Angostura, 3 of these are still alive and active, and we hope our favourite male actor Frank Morgan is one of them—as the rumour goes.

Angostura was originated as a tonic, a simple to ward off fevers, miasmas, tropical swamp mists, and the general assortment of mauve willies that beset Nordics under the equator—and the content of quinine or cinchona definitely had virtue along this line. However, as is so often the case with truly worth-while ventures, fate stuck her tongue in cheek, and decreed that the bitters invented for health should prove not only to be one of the best titillaters of the jaded appetite, but by far the best priceless ingredient in all sorts of cocktails and mixed drinks; as well as in many of the tastiest exotic food receipts we have sampled around the world.

Actually there are 6 main kinds of bitters sold on the open market: Angostura, orange, Peychaud's, Calisaya, Amer Picon, and Boker's. Hell-Fire Bitters or Cayenne Wine, are local semi-amateur tropical creations. Peach bitters, Boonekamp's and others may be found in first flight provision houses catering in hard-to-find, and usually imported oddments of drink and good food. Of all these Angostura is by far the most important. We now append a formula for Trinidad bitters we had given us by a friend who lived in Port of Spain, and which dated many years back into an old publication he had discovered among some family accumulations in settling an estate. The old text claimed this to be the leaked-out secret formula for Angostura, but of course we cannot confirm this as being true without verification from the Siegert clan—which is about as likely as we would tee up our right eyeball for a shot over the water hole at Del Monte! We will say this though: our own pharmacy supplied us with all the ingredients over 2 years ago. Those that weren't ground or pounded fine we reduced to that state in a small kitchen mortar we own. The rest, the blending with spirits, was easy; the result was an inconceivably more economical form of bitters with the same flavour, action and virtue.

Cinchona bark, 8 drachms

Lemon peel, 2 drachms

Orange peel, 2 drachms

Cardamon seeds, shelled and
crushed, ½ drachm

Camomile flowers, 2 drachms

Bark cinnamon, ½ drachm

Raisins, ¼ lb

Best grain alcohol, 2 qts

All ingredients must be ground or pounded fine except the raisins, and these are first chopped fine, then mixed thoroughly with everything else. Seal tightly in a 2 qt jar and pour in enough of the finest grain alcohol obtainable, to fill—which will be a scant 2 qts. Let stand at an even, fairly warm temperature for 6 weeks, stirring or shaking vigorously twice every day. Strain, then strain through a cloth; pressing at the last to extract essentials from the sediment. Stir and strain once more, and bottle for use. *Bon chance, Messieurs.*

NOW A FORMULA for the Home Composition of Orange Bitters by the Amateur

Here's another relatively expensive item as now priced in small bottles for the American market; and easily made at home. In view of the incredible gallons of Dry Martini Cocktails consumed every hour throughout the world—each one requiring a dash or so of Orange Bitters—this thought appears to possess valence. Dried orange peel, ½ lb, chopped fine. Burnt sugar, about 4 tbsp. Good grain alcohol, 4 cups; cologne spirits is best if possible. Cardamon, caraway and coriander seeds, ½ drachm each. These last come from the corner drug store.

First chop the orange peel very fine, add herb seeds and pour on alcohol, then stand in a sealed jar for 15 days, agitating every day. Pour off spirits through a cloth, and seal again. Take the seeds and peel, put them in a saucepan, crushing with a wooden muddler. Cover them with boiling water, simmer 5 minutes; put in covered jar for

2 days, then strain this off and add to the spirits. Put in burnt sugar for colour. Filter again, let stand until it settles perfectly clear, then bottle for use—being careful not to agitate the slight precipitation or sediment during this final operation.

HELL-FIRE BITTERS or CAYENNE WINE, another Receipt from the Island of Trinidad, in the British West Indies, and Now and Again Used in Gin-and-Bitters, & Other Similar Sharp Drinks instead of routine Bitters by Stout Englishmen with Boiler Plate Gastric Linings

This is an old, old receipt dating to 1817 in print right here before us—and likely long before that, because the British knew Port of Spain a century and a half before. In fact we have just been diving up coins, cannons, shot, crystal goblets and other miscellaneous relics from *HMS WINCHESTER,* 60 guns, 933 tons, commanded by one John Soule, and while bound from Jamaica to England, sank in a gale on a certain coral barrier reef, 24th September 1695—and have the loot to prove it! And photographs; and cinema film.

This Hell-Fire Bitters is an excellent cooking and seasoning sauce for fish, salads, soups and meats, when mixed half and half with strained lime juice and stood for 2 wks, in an uncovered bottle, before using—a fact which has been disclosed in *Volume I.*

Pound up 2 cups of scarlet round bird peppers, or small chilis or cayenne peppers. Put in a saucepan with 1 cup of tart white wine; simmer up once and turn everything into a pint jar, add 1 cup of cognac brandy and seal jar tight. Let steep for 14 days, strain through several thicknesses of cloth and bottle for use. *When used solely for seasoning food,* put everything through a fine sieve. These peppers have a vast amount of flavour in their scarlet skin and flesh, entirely aside from the intense heat of their oils. Seeds for their home growth in ordinary window boxes, flower pots, or rusty tin cans!, may be bought at any half-way seed store.

If no fresh peppers are possible simply stir ¼ oz of ground cayenne pepper into the wine-brandy mix. Claret and brandy, claret alone, sherry and brandy, sherry alone, and brandy alone, are also authentic steeping fluids. Actually it is not a "bitters" at all unless a little cinchona bark is added—and ½ drachm or so is plenty, strained out at the last along with the pepper pods.

## BAR SYRUP, KNOWN as GUM, or *GOMME* SYRUP, & which SHOULD BE on EVERY BAR

There is a reason for bar syrup to the practical eye of the professional, for in many iced drinks—especially those wanted in a hurry, ordinary sugar seems to take an age to dissolve. Remember all the Tom Collinses that were double sweet in the last sip? Well, *gomme* syrup dissolves evenly and quickly. It isn't quite so romantic, perhaps, but is far saner.

Many receipts call merely for sugar and water, but we supply the true old formula with egg white to clarify the syrup to the desired crystal limpid texture so necessary. . . . Dissolve 2 lbs of sugar—about 4 cups—in 1 cup of water. Stir in the well beaten white of 1 egg. Boil up briskly, and when scum rises take the skimming spoon and skim diligently. When the syrup is clear the job is done. Let it cool and bottle for future use. It may be coloured or not, according to the whim of the host. We must confess that a little light green colouring matter in Tom Collins syrup is mighty pretty!

## FIRST ONE BOUNCE, then the BRANDIES

This Cherry Bounce receipt is to all intents and purposes a form of cherry brandy, or liquor, made more frequently than not from wild, or other small, dark, highly flavoured cherries not suitable for the table market. It would make a valuable agent for flavouring many cocktails, or served as a cordial to be taken with coffee. . . . Simply take a sizeable jar, having an absolutely tight cover. Half fill it with cherries that have been washed, and if possible with stems snipped half way off so stems will bleed, and bruise the fruit with a muddler. Dust with a little sugar, then fill up with brandy. Put on cover loosely and let stand for 4 weeks, then mash up fruit thoroughly but in this case don't break any seeds. . . . Strain through a thick jelly cloth, or folded cloth. Sweeten with *gomme* syrup to taste. Bottle tightly and stand another 4 weeks before sampling.


AN OLD ENGLISH CHERRY BRANDY RECEIPT, that AFFORDS a SPICED & DELICIOUS LIQUEUR as FINELY FLAVOURED as any of the BEST IMPORTED AFFAIRS, & FAR KINDER to the CHEQUEBOOK; from BOXMOOR, HERTFORDSHIRE, in 1932

Take 6 lbs of wild, or other small black cherries—but never the red "pie cherry" variety, please, and after washing them with clipped stems on add to 2 lbs of ripe fresh strawberries. Add 2 to 3 lbs of sugar, 1 doz whole cloves, 1 tsp cinnamon—or 2 whole sticks—2 tsp of nutmeg, a bunch of fresh green mint tips. Put fruit and spices in a small wood cask and bruise slightly with a wooden stick. Add 6 qts of brandy and let stand with bung very slightly open for 10 days—or until fermentation has stopped. Now siphon off the liquid, filter into a clean container. Empty out keg and scald—then refill with the fluid, driving in the bung. It is cricket to start sampling in 60 days. . . . A few cracked cherry pits are also suggested to add their characteristic bitter taste, and which were not suggested in the Cherry Bounce just noted. A fairly good average of sugar is to allow a scant ½ cup of sugar to each pound of fruit. Smaller amounts require their relative proportions.


VICOMTE de MAUDUIT'S ROSE LIQUEUR BRANDY

If there is a more charming, instructive and altogether delightful book on food and drink than Vicomte de Mauduit's *The Vicomte in the Kitchen,* it does not stand on our shelves. Possessing, as we do, every book in English and many translations, dealing with foods, and many dealing with spirits and wines, the issue we take with amateurs usually is their opinionatedness on the one hand, and their lack of travel—except in Western Europe—on the other. Their volumes are works of art when it comes to what they actually know, have cooked and eaten; but when it comes to many exotic foods and drinks, they are hoist by the petard of their credence for what others—travelers—have written on those unfamiliar subjects. The result is often a slight cloud of ridiculous misinformation blighting an otherwise sound book.

Vicomte de Mauduit, however, sticks to what he personally knows, or has himself originated, or has known to have been originated by gourmet friends. He is charmingly frank about his own information on wines, claiming "a brilliant training and a consummate experience," on the subject. Above all, however, it is the bright clean blade of his originality which pleases us most. He is not content to stick to eternally traditional variations of this or that, but with the wit of an angel or an amiable devil, figures out trimming all his own! This rose brandy receipt we quote from his volume, rendering a respectful homage and credit for its loveliness. We have tried it ourself and find that the fastidious guest who silently judges his host by the not-too-complicated excellence of his food and drink, obtains a fanatical and delighted gleam in the eye when it passes his lips. We cannot say why, but Monsieur le Vicomte's further thoroughness in listing the names of the red roses best suited for this liqueur, also satisfies us wholly. Just why we cannot say, but we are vastly uplifted, packed with a toast-warm and intimate titillation at the thought that the fragrant rose-brandy cocktail we sip was yielded up by the willing death of Lady Helen Maglona. This plane of reasoning is somewhat baffled however, should we become fragrantly swacked on a quartet brewed from the rufous petals of a General McArthur, or a George Dickson!

## TO MAKE THE ROSE LIQUEUR BRANDY

Take 8 big red roses—and don't go around under the fond misconception that because no one is checking up, that yellow, white, or pink roses will do. The Vicomte says red roses are *en regle,* and *au fait*—and that means red roses! These furthermore must be picked *after a rainless night and before the morning sun strikes them,* for, like tender herbs to be dried, much of the fragrant volatile oil dissipates itself on the morning air as soon as the sun beats down on blooms or leaf tips.

Separate the petals, discard dewdrops, and inferior petal specimens, and snip off yellow or white areas around the stamen region. Now put petals in a jar with 1 qt of really decent cognac poured over them. Be sure it is covered tightly, and agitate it with a gentle and considerate hand every week. After a month of this scented bath add a *gomme* syrup generated from the wedding of 3 cups of sugar with 2 cups of *distilled water,* and handled as follows. . . . Boil briskly for 20 minutes, skimming off scum, then put in the selected petals of 1 doz more red roses, dusted and tossed first with powdered sugar. Let the saucepan boil up again, then simmer gently for 1 hr tightly covered.

Now filter the 1st rose petal-brandy infusion from the jar, and rack it into a large sterile bottle. A filter paper is of course best here. Then add the rose petal syrup, likewise filtered through a tammy or several thicknesses of cloth, working it through with a spoon. Stir the final mixture, then let stand uncorked except for a bit of cloth over bottle neck for 12 hrs, then cork and seal with wax. . . . Our experience has been that there is a very slight sediment which settles out of this blend, and if the bottles are once more filtered after a couple of weeks standing undisturbed, the result is all the heart could desire. . . . Receipt for the *Vicomte's Cocktail,* made of this rose brandy, may be found on Page 135.

## NOW to CREATE a WORTHY CIDER—which Is CERTAINLY as IMPORTANT an EVENT as FABRICATING a PROFITABLE MOUSE TRAP, or HOT WATER BAG, or HAIR TONIC

The Normandy chateau country is famous for its apples, for its Calvados apple brandy, for its cider; for its cider champagne which, if properly made and aged, is as fine in its own manner as champagne made from Rheims grapes, for instance. This is an old French receipt we picked up in Paris 12 years back, and although cider making differs in its finer trimmings between France and—let's say—the Yakima

Valley, which, incidentally, is in Washington, and is pronounced *Yack*-a-maw and not ya-*Key*-ma, the basic fermentation principles are forever the same. Cider has been made for thousands of years and due to the fearful, muddy hogwash our rural folk insist on inflicting upon their customers, it is widely neglected by those who should know better.

As a matter of fact, and with all due credit to our Pacific Northwest stalwarts, the tart, more flavourful Eastern apples really are better for fine cider—apples like the favourite winesap, for instance. The rules are really quite simple.

1. Use apples not quite ripe, if we want sparkle, snap and finest flavour in cider.
2. Don't be both lazy and stingy by gathering up a bin of wormy windfalls, unless we really admire that sad bruised-apple taste. Cider is an important business and deserves first grade fruit, not something we wouldn't dare feed to swine. Science has not yet been able to announce any virtue in crushed worms, entirely aside from their distinct lack of *distingué*. Inferior fruit is what ruins most ciders.
3. Mellow these apples for 10 days to 2 wks, depending on briskness of weather—the colder the longer—by spreading them out on dry straw in a dry barn. This permits mucilage to break down, and perhaps the starch, for all of us!—and starts development of carbonic acid which insures that delightful sparkle so lacking in almost all professional, and most amateur, ciders.
4. The apples are now ground to a pulp and juice pressed out through coarse strong cotton bags. A small hand cider press is used in small amounts, filtering the juice well.
5. Put juice in open tub or vat at a constant temperature of around 60° Fahrenheit, covered with a cloth to prevent entry of dust, entomological specimens, and general rural addenda. . . . Allow 2 days for weak cider; 8 to 10 days for strong; or in latter event, when sediment has subsided. Beyond this point the vinegar trend develops apace—abortive and acid beverage, at best, and not one to be admired.
6. Rack off into clean wooden kegs and store in cellar where fairly cool, even temperature is assured.
7. Drink now if we cannot wait, but remember it will really be a divine nectar by the coming spring!

NOW a CAREFULLY CHOSEN LIST of Pleasant Wines, First of which Is a Simple Norman Type of Champagne, which Requires No Yeast

Take cider that still has a very slight sparkle—about 5 or 6 days old, on the above scale. Rack it off through a filtering cloth, or paper, into a sterile keg that has been rinsed with scalding water. To a 10 gallon keg allow 3 cups of the finest grain alcohol, or about 2 bottles of brandy, whisky, or gin—if nothing else, and 3 lbs of sugar. Stir and let stand for 10 to 12 days with bung in loose. Now "fine," or settle, the wine by the routine given just below, and let settle 4 days longer —about 14 days in all. Rack carefully into champagne bottles, filtering again if at all cloudy. Cork with sound corks, and if we don't wish the risk of bombardment from inner bottle pressure, wire them or tie them on very tightly.

Under no condition use ordinary wine or other bottles. They are not made to stand high pressure, and the cellar will be filled with flying glass, and very untidy explosions. We know!

HOW to "FINE," or Clarify Wine the Portuguese Way, a Receipt Dated 1736, and Found in Gibraltar Starting a Voyage Through the Mediterranean, via Mallorca, Villefranche, Naples, & Athens, to Haifa, which Is in Palestine, in the Early Spring of 1931

Allow 5 egg whites and 1 tbsp of salt to each 10 gals of wine. Beat these together into a froth; draw off 1 pint or so of the wine and add to the eggs. Stir well and add this to the container of wine to be clarified. In a few days it will be "fine"—from 3 to 5 usually does the trick. The egg mixture settles out, carrying finely suspended bits of lees and sediment with it.

ENGLISH BLACKBERRY WINE, No. I, from Near Whipsnade, Hertfordshire, 1932

This receipt is a time-tested one and has been in use to our knowledge since 1832. Contrary to the *U. S. A.* country style, fermentation is started *before* adding any sugar.

Blackberries, any amount
Boiling water, enough to cover
Granulated sugar, 1 lb for every gallon juice
Brandy or gin (brandy preferred), ½ cup per gallon mash

Blackberries should be fresh and "gathered on a fine dry day." There is no mention of washing, and we presume that the dust and various impedimenta of the region (as in the Spey-side Scotch whisky distilleries) are left intact to aid in fermentation and to donate special flavour. . . . Cover with briskly boiling water and stand all night to draw out juices. Strain through sieve into crock or cask, and let ferment for fifteen days in a place not too warm, nor yet with any chill. Here you add your pound of sugar and pint of spirits to every gallon juice. This presumably halts all further thought of fermentation, and the potion is bottled for future uses. Or practically immediate use.

ENGLISH BLACKBERRY WINE No. II, a Receipt from Bicester, through which We Journeyed on the Way to Banbury, to See an Old Lady about a White Horse, Summer of 1932—and which is Exactly 101 Years Old: the Receipt, not the Lady—& to Get Some Banbury Cakes

Gather fruit dead ripe on a dry day. Have a crock, or wood keg without head, and a tap or faucet a couple of inches above bottom. Mash berries well, pour on boiling water enough to cover. Let them stand with a cloth cover, for 3 or 4 days, where temperature is fairly steady and not too chill. Pulp will then rise to surface in a crust. Open tap and draw off wine into another container, and add one pound of sugar per gallon. Mix well and put into a scalded keg, let stand with bung out until it stops working. Have keg almost full. When wine stops working drive in the bung. Rack off in six months and bottle, or scald out keg again, return wine and let stand tightly bunged for another six months. The latter is much better, but virtually impossible to the average amateur, lacking patience.

## OLD ENGLISH DANDELION WINE, Being a Formula Fetched across the Atlantic in the 17th Century, by Sailing Ship, and Dated from Saybrook, Connecticut, *CIRCA* 1677

Water, 2½ gallons
Dandelion blooms, 6 qts (dry
    measure)
Ginger, 1 tbsp, ground
Raisins, 3 cups, chopped
Lemons, 6, juice and grated peel,
    yellow part only

Oranges, 6, juice and grated peel,
    as above
Yeast, ¼ cake fresh; ½ cake
    compressed, or 1 tbsp brew-
    er's type
Two and a half gallon keg, 1,
    scalded out

We remember one of the high spots in our *"Advanced"* Biology V Course in college covered the enzymatic action of fruits and so on—and in case that word sounds puzzling it simply means what ferments such items usefully—and otherwise. . . . And at one point we were sent out to gather dandelions, which were fixed in a big glass laboratory crock of glass, and bottled as wine, and tested as early as commencement. So much for the liberal arts courses. . . . This ancient receipt is much better and more elaborate, although every bit as easy to brew.

Mix dandelions with water and boil for thirty minutes, timed after boiling starts. Strain, and mix in ginger, sugar, and grated peel of lemon and orange, simmering for another half hour. Pour into stoneware crock, and then add lemon and orange juice. When lukewarm, spread yeast on toast and float on, or stir in compressed or brewer's yeast. . . . When fermentation has stopped, siphon and strain off into keg into which raisins have already been put. . . . Rack off after four months or so, and bottle.

## OLD ENGLISH ELDERBERRY WINE, also an Old English Specification

We lived that summer of 1932 in Hayward House, Box Lane, Boxmoor, Herts.,—all of that, and in cruising the hedgerows in one of those animated chafing dishes with right handed drives that true

Britons laughingly call "motors" we collected many interesting things
—including this one extra fine elder wine. The spicing is what makes
it so good.

Two and a half gallon wooden
   keg, 1, scalded out
Elderberries, 5 qts (dry measure)
Pale brown raw sugar, 2 cups
   per qt of juice
Ginger, ½ tsp

Allspice, 1 tsp
Cloves, 1 tsp
Brandy, 1 pint
Yeast, ¼ cake fresh; 1 cake com-
   pressed; 1½ tbsp brewer's

Crush fruit and pour on water. Put through a sieve. Measure juice
and add 2 pounds of raw sugar (brown will do but not so well) to
each liquid quart. Add spices and simmer for 15 minutes. Pour as-is
into your stoneware crock, spread yeast on toast (if fresh) and float
on, or moisten compressed with a little sugar, and stir in. . . . Elder-
berry wine must be in a warm place as it fails to ferment as promptly
as other fruit juices. . . . When it stops working, strain into our keg,
adding 1 pint of good cognac, and drive in bung tight. Rack off and
bottle in 4 months—longer if we can wait.

ANCIENT BRITISH WINE OF MULBERRIES, CIRCA 1757,
from the COTTSWOLD

Here is another classic wine which is not only simple to make but
cheap as may be for anyone with even a single mulberry tree.

Mulberries, 10 qts, dry measure
Spring or rain water, 4 qts
Sugar, 6½ cups (pale brown raw
   is best)

Two and a half gallon keg, 1,
   scalded out
Spring or rain water, 2½ gallons
Sugar, 8 lbs or trifle less
A little isinglass to clarify

If isinglass is used make as follows: crush mulberries in a granite
basin, add water and stand all night in a warm place. Strain through
a sieve, and add sugar. When thoroughly dissolved, barrel. Break up
isinglass in small bits, dissolve in juice, stir into barrel, adding the
second batch of sugar and water. When it has stopped working, bung

up tight—and leave a little air space in the keg. . . . Rack off in four to six months, and bottle.

CORDIALS, or LIQUEURS, to Grace any Cellar & Compounded by the Amateur Himself
Please let us explain on this page that there are many, many superb liqueurs which cannot under any stretch of imagination be assembled in the home by amateur mixers, no matter how sincere and diligent. In the first place the very best of these fragrant potions are firstfruits of varying secrets, guarded for generations—hundreds of years, even—which presumes knowledge of certain herbs or ingredients which guarantee their celebrated flavour. Also age is a definite factor, both in the character of ingredients, and subsequent mellowing of the cordials themselves. This factor too is a discouragement in our impatient era!

In other words, we do not claim to be able to make benedictine, chartreuse, and like immortals for all of these reasons. But we very definitely do claim knowledge of certain secrets gathered in Europe, mainly, whereby several delightful liqueurs may be made by the amateur—some of which are *not* at all available in the open market today; and furthermore their accomplishment insures tariff impossible under our existing ad valorem import duties which our lawmakers impose on foreign spirits whether or not they compete at all with American industries they rush to "protect" long after the industries themselves are out of their swaddling clothes.

We therefore offer this dozen or so of receipts, formulae, for making cordials that won't require infinite patience, aging of product, or ingredients too expensive or foreign for practical employment.

A BRANDY of ROSES, which We Have Called "Rose Liqueur Brandy, *au VICOMTE de MAUDUIT*"
This fragrant and delicate bit of genius has already been entered on these pages, being a Brandy as well as a liqueur, and we suggest turning to Page 155, for the formula.

GREEN *CRÈME de MENTHE,* an Excellent Receipt We Collected for this Volume in Paris Some Years Ago

This is delightfully simple, and as all *Crème de Menthes* are essentially synthetic mixes—in other words assembled and not the result of special distillations all their own, the amateur can do as well as the professional.

Oil of peppermint, in any pharmacy, 1 drachm
Good spring or well water, bottled or otherwise, 2 qts
Best grain spirits; or cologne spirits, better still, about 2½ cups
*Gomme* syrup, to taste
Green colouring, to emerald shade

Blend peppermint oil and spirits, then stir into the sweetened water. The amount of sugar in this last should be determined by tasting good *crème de menthe,* and matching it. Now add colouring, stand covered tightly in a wide-mouthed jar for 5 days, then take a new white blotting paper and carefully skim off all excess peppermint oil. The 2½ cups suggested for spirits content is 20 oz, or roughly 33 1/3% alcoholic strength, by volume.

OTHER CORDIALS of Similar Essential Oil Construction May Be Made Easily

Liqueurs of anis, caraway (which parallels kümmel), clove, and other liqueurs may be made in exactly the same way, and in the same approximate ratio. Essential oils are available, and much simpler to use than by infusing seeds or peels in spirits.

THE CELEBRATED RECEIPTS of Dr. William Kitchiner, & Dated 1817, for Orange Curaçaos No. I, & No. II

| | |
|---|---|
| Dried Seville Orange peel, pounded fine, 5 oz | Best rectified, or cologne, spirits, 1 qt |
| (Or the fresh peel of a Shaddock, Grapefruit, ditto) | *Gomme* Syrup, See Page 154, 1 qt |

Pour 180 proof spirits on peel; cork and stand for a fourtn't; strain through cheesecloth first, add syrup, and filter once through a chemical filter paper (obtainable at good drug stores).

NOTE: About the only decent curaçao on the American market now has to be imported from Holland—where most of it is made, despite the Island of Curaçao, off the Venezuelan coast, being nearer to America. Our import duties on such delectables are so ridiculously high that one would think them a roundabout way of collecting the much-publicized War Debt.

## ORANGE CURAÇAO No. II

The easier of the two, in modern times.

> Sweet oil of Orange Peel, 2 drachms (¼ oz)
> Best rectified, or cologne, spirits, 1 pint
> *Gomme* Syrup, See Page 154, 1 pint

Simply add orange oil to spirits. Add the sugar syrup, shake well, and stand overnight. Line a funnel with muslin, strain, then put through filter paper three times until it is quite "bright," as Dr. Kitchiner calls it. . . . The Doctor states: "This Liqueur is an admirable cordial, (with coffee), and a tea-spoonful in a tumbler of water is a very refreshing Summer Drink, and a great improvement to punch."

## MARIGOLD LIQUEUR, from the *COTE d'AZUR,* which Is in FRANCE; 1932

Here is a delicious adventure for those in the country with plenty of marigold blossoms coming along faster than we know what to do with them.

| | |
|---|---|
| Marigold petals, ½ peck | Water, 6 qts |
| Strained honey, 1 lb | Sugar, 3½ lbs, brown |
| Raisins, chopped a little, scant lb | |

Petals may be gathered, with dew off, over a few days' period. Mix sugar, honey, raisins, and water, let boil up for fifteen minutes, then after clearing with white and shell of an egg, strain well, heat up to boil again and pour over petals. Stand in tightly covered crock or enamel kettle around 70 degrees Fahrenheit for twenty-four hours. Stir, and cover once more, and repeat for three days. Strain, put in wood keg; add grated rind of three oranges and another pound of sugar. Add a yeast cake and cover bung with cloth and when fermentation stops add a pint of brandy, stir in half an ounce of dissolved isinglass, or other clearing agent, and bung tightly. After four months rack off carefully into bottles; cork tightly. Ready for use in six months.

## ORGEAT or ALMOND SYRUP, from a Receipt Dating back to 1817

This syrup is used in flavouring certain delicate and oddly conceived cocktails. The receipt may be compounded as follows:

Jordan almonds, blanched, 1 lb
Bitter almonds, blanched, 1 lb
Rose-water, 2 cups
Orange-flower water, 1 tbsp (½ gill or so)
Spring or rain water, 2 cups

Pound almonds very fine in a mortar or bowl, first adding the orange-flower water to keep from oiling. Then add rose water and spring water and rub through a fine sieve until the almonds are dry.

## ROCK and RYE

All of us have seen this eye-titillating array of goodies imprisoned in spiritual bliss in a large squarish bottle. How many of us have thought to assemble a bit for ourselves. It's very simple indeed.

Rye whisky, 1/5 gallon, not a full quart
Jamaica rum, jigger
Rock candy, ½ cup, leave in large lumps
Whole cloves, 1 doz
Quartered small California orange, peel left on
Quartered seedless lemon, peel left on
Stick of cinnamon, or two

Put ingredients in jar, cover with rye, and stand for a fortnight. Strain out spices through fine cloth or filter paper. Put back on fruit until needed.

To serve: Cut spiral orange rind, also one spiral lemon rind, put in whisky glass, and pour liquor over. . . . Can be served hot with excellent effect to fight off colds, influenzas, miasmas, megrims, swamp mists, and blackwater fevers. In fact any sort of excuse seems to work.

## ENGLISH MEAD, from THREE VERY OLD RECEIPTS

Far back in the dim past when thick-armed giant Saxon kings dined in raftered halls, with flaxen-haired ladies below the salt, at the lower tables, mead has been drunk in England. Huge horns washed down haunches of venison, and the bones were tossed over shoulder to the stag-hounds clamouring on the rush-strewn floors. Then more flagons were brought, the minstrels sang, the cooking fires were poked up so that sparks flew upward through the murky rafters, and another haunch of deer meat was skewered on the black iron spit. The Saxons were mighty men, mighty in battle, mighty with food trencher and wassail bowl.

## OLD ENGLISH MEAD No. I, the COTTAGER'S DELIGHT

From a receipt dated 1677

Strained honey, 2 cups
Water, 4 quarts; rain water or spring water is best
Sugar, brown or white, ½ cup
Lemon, peel, 1 chopped fine; and juice 1

Yeast, ½ cake spread on bit of toast, floating; or 1 tsp of brewer's
(Or 1 oz compressed baker's yeast)
Egg, whites 2, beaten well

Mix honey, water and sugar; add eggs, simmering slowly. When scum stops forming, add lemon peel, juice; and yeast when it has become just lukewarm. Stand in a crock in a warm spot until it stops working, then bottle as we would beer—either with caps or corks, tied down for luck.

SAXON MEAD No. II, Approved Method of Brewing, & Older than Eld

Eggs, whites 6, beaten well
Water, 12 gallons; rain or spring
   water best
Honey, 20 lbs
Ginger, nutmeg, cinnamon, pow-
   dered clove, 1 tbsp each

Rosemary, 1 sprig if you can
   find it; or 3 tbsp dried
   needles
Yeast, 1 cake, worked into a
   cream with warm water; or
   2 tbsp of brewer's

Mix egg white with water, and add the honey. Boil for an hour, skimming now and then; and add our spices and herbs. When cool, add yeast, and put into cask not closed, so it may work; keeping in a warm place at even temperature. When fermentation ceases, seal the bung, and let stand six months in a cool place of even temperature. At the end of that time it should be racked off and bottled.

STRONG OLD ENGLISH MEAD No. III, Dated A.D. 1736

Back in the year 1736 one E. Smith, in his *Compleat Housewife*— of London imprint—saw fit to list various noble dishes and potations of the time, among which was one for Mead, which appears to be among the accepted best of that time.

Spring water, 10 gallons
Honey, about 20 lbs
Mace, 8 blades to 10 gallons
Whole cloves, 24 to 10 gallons
   (We should say 48)
Ginger root, 2 roots to 10 gal-
   lons; or 1½ to 2 tbsp, ground
Cayenne pepper, ¼ ounce to 10
   gallons

Cinnamon, 4 sticks
Nutmegs, 3, quartered or grated;
   or 3 tbsp, ground
Lemons, 4, sliced thin with
   rind on
Rosemary, 2 sprigs
Yeast, 1 modern cake spread on
   toast, or 1½ to 2 tbsp brewer's yeast

Heat spring water until nicely warm to the hand, then add enough honey to float a small *Fresh!* egg. Boil it gently for an hour, skimming as necessary. Then add the other ingredients—and after simmering for half an hour, discard the rosemary—turning the whole business spices and all into a large earthenware crock. . . . Float a piece of toast spread with a cake of yeast. Strain it into a clean scalded cask. After three months take out the spice bag, rack off and bottle it. In six weeks, then, our Englishman recommends to start sampling.

PERRY, BEING CONCEIVED from the JUICE of PEARS, and ONE of the MOST ANCIENT & DELICATE of THEM ALL, an ENGLISH RECEIPT of 1817

Perry is pear cider, and one of the early European drinks. It makes a delicate and delicious beverage, especially in summer when refreshing tastes are a help to fight humidity and other complaints following hot weather.

Pears should be sweet, and just under-ripe when picked for perry. If too sweet and ripe, and not astringent at the start, they will develop too much vinegar taste when juice is matured into full age.

Grind up pears exactly like apples, and press out juice. The fermentation is the same as cider, except there is no great amount of scum, and for this reason it is hard to tell just when fermentation ceases—a point coincidental with the stronger variety of this drink. . . . Just before fermentation stops in perry, draw it off from the main part of the lees, or dregs. Scald out the lees. Put it back into the tub or crock again until the fermentation is done—about the same as cider. Put it in kegs, and bottle it next spring—if there is any left at that late date!

A FEW TIMELY KERNELS of ADVICE for THOSE THREATENED with IMMINENT DEPARTURE for the BARS; or HAVING ARRIVED, HAVE, through this CRISIS or that, BECOME FACED with ANY of DIVERS EMERGENCIES

We have already lightly mentioned that plenary intoxication is contrary to lasting solvency, happiness—either during the final stages of becoming swacked, or on the morn after. The dividing line, however, between quitting a brightly pleasant stimulation and this sad estate is actually finer than we know; and until we find a proven way of regulating our liquid absorption as this condition approaches, any pleasant drinker may be betrayed by his own enthusiasms, or in proving his balance or his manhood as a 2-fisted bottle-man!

Particularly is this true on large and involved congregations, such as country weekends, trips on yachts, and other divers sequences—especially if liquors are visible in large supply and amateur mixers among the guests are given carte blanche to explore and blend to their heart's content. Therefore, should the barometer tend to forecast such alarming possibility, and we—through real or false pride, weak mind, fallible stomach, to cash a bet, revenge a rival, or impress a lady—feel certain of liability ourself, there is always one tried and true way of minimizing subsequent toxic effect, which is vastly gratifying to the party of the 1st part, mystifying to rival, and impressive to the girl. It is a drugless way, and incidentally in actual practice we find that the farther an inebriate keeps away from stiff drugs, the better for all concerned.

So, therefore, before the 1st stirrup cup take a scant 2 tsp of olive oil —gingerly, and repeat at 15 minute intervals, to a total of 6 tsp in all. Take these gingerly, and in no event try to take all 6 at once without having proved it harmless in the past. We once, in vasty youth, tried taking 2 oz of the oil in one gulp. To our collective sorrow the effect upon our timid and shrinking gastric unit proved far more violent than any man-made emetic.

TO ALLAY a MILD, or EVEN SEVERE, SYNCOPE, sometimes CALLED FAINTING, from POTATION

Should any guest, male or female, through any form of miscalculation fall upon this evil estate they should—in mild cases—be speedily placed upon a seat with knees spread. Then with the hands clasped behind the nape of the neck, urge the patient to draw his head down in that position as far toward the floor as physically possible. This forces some of the blood back into the brain, and the seizure may pass. . . . If not, and after 5 minutes, the condition still obtains—get him into a recumbent position; loosen clothing, especially at the throat.

Be sure there is an open window close by, present an uncovered bottle of smelling salts intermittently beneath the patient's proboscis, and bathe his, or her, temples with eau de cologne or rubbing alcohol. Lacking this, bathe temples with a lump of ice, ice water, ice water and vinegar.

In extreme cases remove the shoes from feet, and apply a very hot hot water bag thereto; watch the pulse and if it really becomes weak or gives any tendency toward flutter, do not hesitate to arouse the nearest physician. Above all, especially if hysterics are a by-product, forcefully refuse aid from any inebriate or amateur hands, no matter how willing. Bustle, hustle and hysterics are contagious; calm and good-natured sympathy works wonders. Where the patient can swallow, 30 to 40 drops of *sal volatile* in strong black unsweetened coffee is a vast help.

TO ALLEVIATE APPARENT DEATH from Toxic Poisonings, & Especially Should, in any Happenstance, the Quality of the Liquor Be Suspect

Happily enough, while there are a good many comparatively youthful distillations of American gins and whiskys, their production, the reputation of their manufacturer, and a rigid government ruling and inspection make adulteration at the source impossible. However, there are in rare cases certain people who do illegal adulteration to make an unholy profit at the risk of others. And in such case the symptoms are usually sudden and violent enough to publish the emergency. In any case where a violent illness is felt, or apparent, administer an emetic at once. It is better to tax a patient-guest unnecessarily than to chance severe conclusion, and anyway, since the patient quickly regains a feeling of exhausted well-being no one will ever be the wiser.

There are 3 species of emetics that are usually possible in any household at a moment's notice:

1. *Mustard*. . . . Mix 1 fairly heaping tsp with 1 glass of warm water, or warm milk. Drink it all.
2. *Salt*. . . . The same, or slightly stronger mixture; also in warm water.

3. *Ipecacuanha.* . . . This simple is an emetic, a diaphoretic, and an expectorant. Mix from 10 to 20 grains of the drug with ¼ cup of water—depending on patient's ruggedness of physique. Repeat every ½ hr until gastric evacuation is accomplished. After 3 doses stop, and call a physician. Ipecacuanha is poisonous in overdose.

TO SALVAGE A GUEST from the EFFECTS of HANGING—by ROPE, not the MORNING AFTER

This is, we are happy to say, a most unlikely emergency; but we surmise, on occasion, that an amateur mixer—either through remorse at the horror of his concoctions, through self-induced intoxication and a weariness of life and life's problems, may seek to take his own life by knotting one end of a bar towel, or cocktail apron, over the nearest chandelier and noose it about his own neck. . . . In any such case we quote an ancient English routine which should kill or cure.

1. Don't dawdle or joke. Hanging is no fun and must be handled quickly or not at all.
2. Cut him, or her, down.
3. Carry the patient to the nearest open space on the floor, and strip off clothing; or if still breathing, take to the bedroom for this process. Wrap him in hot blankets with hot water bottles. Apply hot water bottles, hot bricks, hot bags of sand, or hot glass bottles—Ah those Britishers are a hardy race!—to the armpits, to the soles of the feet, between the thighs; and especially along the spine.
4. Rub the surface of the body with hands enclosed in wool gloves, Aunt Aphasia Fittich's red flannel shorts, or dad's golf stockings. . . . Under no condition use alcohol, either rubbing or drinking, on the body's surface.
5. Where respiration has ceased, don't go in for all this routine but place patient face down fully clothed on the living room rug, head on one side, tongue pulled free—and proceed with drowning 1st aid, see any Boy Scout Manual. . . . Or, briefly: kneel astride patient's hips, facing his head. . . . Place both palms on either side of spine, over the lower ribs; then gradually throw our weight forward on them until virtually supporting the whole weight of our upper body. Release pressure at once, but release it slowly. This whole pressure and release routine should take 4 seconds. Only 1 person is needed to save life by this so-called Schäffer Method. It really supplies almost as much air as normal respiration.

## CONCUSSIONS & VIOLENT SHOCKS

This is a civilized and free country, but now and again men, being nothing but great big boys at heart, lay themselves open to this form of violence or that—either from barging into ½ open doors in the twilight, or through audible or secret notice of the lovely blonde creature at the next table. Now whether this sad eventuality come through a water carafe bent across the victim's head by a disciplining wife or sweetheart, or the lady's male escort at next table executes a purge, we advise prompt first aid as follows: remove to seclusion and quiet; expel all curiosity seekers, candid camera fiends, reporters, ex-wives or sweethearts, enemies, friends or partisans.

In severe shock and concussion, the face is pale, the body surfaces cold; the forehead often clammy, the pulse weak, the breathing slow and very gentle, the pupils contracted to pinpoints. . . . 1st try to arouse by shouting at patient. Give a jigger of brandy and water, if able to swallow, and either before or after this thoughtful act, subimpose an open bottle of smelling salts at nostrils. Loosen clothing, remove shoes, and chafe the feet—applying hot water bottle or other heating agency to the soles. Chafe the surface of the body generally. Keep in a prone position until revival. Then stop ears to all postmortems.

## TO ALLEVIATE the EMBARRASSING EVENTUALITY of a RUDDY & BLOODSHOT EYE

There are many very fine and new-fangled collyriums for this silent confession to one thing or another, but nothing is much better than the old yeoman's simple: simmer 3 sprigs of snipped parsley in enough water to cover for 5 or 6 minutes. Strain, let cool, and apply with cup or eye dropper. In 15 minutes the danger signal has vanished!

## TO ACCOMPLISH DEFEAT of the HICCOUGH, HICCUP, or HIQUET*

This, dear friends, is a spasm of the diaphragm caused by acidity,

* As these unpleasant spasms almost always result from a too-acid condition, half a teaspoonful of bicarbonate of soda (of Arm & Hammer Brand) in a glass of water will positively effect a cure. The Publisher.

indigestion, a pungent liquid or solid having been in recent contact with the inner lining of throat and stomach; from spleen and vapours of both general and special nature. . . . There are probably more old wives tales about such cure as there are spinsters on earth. Sipping water while standing on the head is allegedly effective; so is sipping water through a napkin—especially when the patient holds his, or her, own nose, while another sympathetic friend stops the ears. . . . Vinegar, to the amount of 2 tsp, taken undiluted, has salvaged many. The same faith is also placed in a lump of sugar with 4 drops of oil of peppermint on it. . . . In the days of our grandfather, a pinch of snuff was offered. Personally we always munch a cube of ice, continue the campaign along original lines if it takes all summer, and don't worry.

In other words any shock of sorts may, or may not, solve the riddle. We recall hiccoughs being promptly cured once in Seattle, by a resourceful husband who became mildly intolerant of all the 1 doz or so friendly suggestions to his thus-afflicted wife, all of which had failed, and who emptied a siphon of well-chilled seltzer water down the front of his wife's newest evening frock. The hiccoughs were promptly cured, but we regret to report the lady almost immediately departed for a brief residence in a certain well known city in Nevada.

THE BENGAL HOT DROPS, sometimes KNOWN in SINGAPORE as "RAFFLES' QUIET RELIEF"

Even though we may be careful and lucky enough to avoid the curse of amoebic alimentary disorders in India, or anywhere in the Near or Far East, or in the Tropics generally, we sometimes become a prey—through nourishment on too-ripe fruits, or from other cause— to what the old British medicos loved to call "coliks, grypinges, spleenes, vapours, and other flatulencies, or scours." It is a sorry plight indeed, and no remedy handy, so we append this proven simple as one of the most valuable we have ever known, and administered as it is a sort of drink, it is far more pleasant to take internally than the maze of usual hot drops, blackberry cordials—so called—and other remedies.

Take 1 jigger of cognac, the same of blackberry brandy, turn into an Old Fashioned glass. Add 1 dash oil of peppermint and 3 dashes Jamaica ginger. Stir, dust nutmeg on top, waft up a prayer to any patron saint, and hope for the best. Not only is the uncertainty, the restless tendency done, but the mental and physical system is pleasantly toned into a new and more solid foundation of cheerfulness.

FOR *MAL de TÊTE,* a Proven Remedy which Will Probably Call Down the Anathema of All Graduate Physicians yet which Has on More than One Occasion, Saved Our Own Life

Take 2 Tom Collins glasses. Into 1 put 1 cup of water, 3 dashes of aromatic spirits of ammonia, 2 dashes of phosphate. Into the empty glass put 1½ heaping teaspoons of bromo seltzer. Mix back and forth, and when ½ subsided, drink.

WORDS to the LIQUID WISE No. XIX, on a TRIED and TRUE METHOD of PICKING UP the SAD REMAINS of OUR BEST CRYSTAL WINE GLASSES, SHATTERED by the ACCIDENTAL or CARELESS HAND, & without INDUCED HEMORRHAGE through SURFACE CUTS on the HANDS

Moisten a wad of common cotton very slightly, and after picking up the larger pieces, employ a blotting motion to the areas infested with tiny sharp bits. They will come away on the cotton.

MISCELLANEOUS BAR EQUIPMENT without which the Mixer is Pointedly a Lame Duck

1 paring knife costing not less than seventy-five cents, and a small cutting board.
1 lemon squeezer
1 pair of lime tweezers
1 medium coarse strainer about 1 pint size
1 long-handled bar spoon
1 corkscrew—a decent one with a comfortable handle
1 bottle cap opener
5 quill or squirter tops, for bitters and grenadine bottles
1 ice shaver or very fine crusher for juleps, and so on. This can either be electric, or manual. . . . A heavy canvas bag and wood mallet is as

good as any. . . . If getting one of those gadgets which grind up ice cubes finely, don't try to beat the game by getting one for seventy cents; go to a decent place and get one big enough to hold more than one cube at a time, and conserve sanity.

At least 2 doz cherry picks for Manhattans, and so on.

1 big bar glass with strainer and a pouring type of top, and very long-handled spoon for stirring. This for Martinis, and allied, stirred drinks.

1 hand or mechanical shaker of around two quarts capacity.

1 small hand shaker holding two large or four average cocktails, for the *occasion à deux*.

1 pair mittens with jingle-bells on them, for feminine shaking to protect the hands from chill—and saving squeals and complaints.

1 apron. The field is as wide as the Pacific on this—varying from the white professional "sarong" type, to fancies like we get given now and then, of pied-piper colours, and printed thoroughly all over with various cocktail receipts.

Containers needed:

1 each for lump, granulated, brown, and powdered sugars.

1 bottle, cruet, or what not for *gomme* syrup.

3 attractive and not too large glass containers for red and green maraschino cherries, small pearl onions, or other garnishes.

1 glass or glazed pottery honey pot.

1 smart cream pitcher, and silver is handsomest.

These are all needed for any half way complete bar, so don't procrastinate about getting them.

Spice jars needed:

1 each for whole cloves, grated nutmeg, powdered cinnamon, and the covers should fit well to keep aromatics from dissipating in the air.

Small bars need only cloves and nutmeg; very small bars, cloves only.

1 swizzle stick, either the wooden West Indian type, or the smart modern metal kind all good household supply stores stock. This for frosting West Indian Swizzles and similar colonial thirst-quenchers.

1 egg beater for egg noggs and similar fancies.

1 package of *short* straws for juleps, and that society of sweet, creamy affairs, which for known reasons are called "ladies" drinks. These come in bright colours of cellophane, and so on.

At least 2 doz small bar napkins, of paper, linen, or what not.

As many of the following list of glasses as the traffic will bear.

A PLEA for LARGER GLASSES, and a Lower High-Tide Level of Pouring

Use a larger glass rather than a smaller one. Much as we admire some of the liquids in Sloppy Joe's and in other places attracting trade through pouring drinks so full they slop over, a sound cocktail should *never be poured more than three-quarters full*. . . . Skimpy cocktails are an insult—hence graduate to oversize glasses.

STEMMED COCKTAIL GLASSES ARE BEST

Except for the Old Fashioned, all cocktail glasses should have stems. Heat of hand takes chill from drink if no stem; something certainly not to be desired. Now that the mad ignorance of the recent drouth is happily past, let's get back to some of the historic niceties of our national drinks, we urge.

EIGHT, or so, SHAPES of GLASSES NEEDED for Proper Mixed Drink Equipment

Many people hold that all cocktails can be served in the usual two ounce Manhattan type glass; and just as rightly we contend that anyone can wear a crimson bow tie with tails.

1. The standard 2 oz Manhattan type glass, with stem. Must be on all bars.
2. Tall, slender type with stem, holding around 3 oz; for Daiquiris, Alexanders, and so on. . . . Should be on large and average bars. Omit for small bars.
3. The squatty, thick bottomed old fashioned glass, holding about 4 oz. . . . Should be on all bars, regardless of size.
4. The tumbler-shaped sour or "star" glass, holding about six ounces. Needed for large bars, mainly. Not needed for small ones.
5. Tall goblets for New Orleans and allied fizzes. They should be around 10 to 14 oz to our way of thinking. . . . Only needed for elaborate and fairly complete bars.
6. Highball glasses, thin, tumbler shape, and holding 8 oz minimum, 10 is better, and 12 will save a lot of pouring labour. . . . Some of these are needed even on the smallest bars, which can find use for Tom Collins work as well.
7. Tall taper-sided goblets for champagne, and other really important

items like the Peking Tiger's Milk on Page 130. . . . These should not be less than 10 ounces we hold, and can go all the way up to 16, depending on glass source and host's generosity. . . . Only needed on pretty elaborate bars. Big rounded goblets will also do, but the taper side is what the world expects.
8. 16 oz straight-sided Tom Collins glasses, which are also used for mint juleps when hosts do not have silver cups. . . . These must not be less than 12 oz under any circumstances, 14 better, and 16 just about indicated. . . . The 16-oz Collins handles 1 pint of club soda or sparkling water.

## SHAKERS in GENERAL

We've had all sorts of shakers from the aluminum ones they give away at Gosling Brothers in Bermuda and Soccony & Speed, Gibraltar, to case customers—through gigantic lighthouses, nickel silver jobs we took over one year for outside lacquering in Kyoto, Japan, and picked up the next, to sterling ones made up for us on Silver Street, Peking.

We have always felt that other metal than sterling reacts badly to liquor and acids, and aluminum especially lends a "brassy" taste. However, the newer chromium jobs appear unaffected. . . . In other words, if we cannot afford silver, get one chromium-plated inside and out, or glass with chrome top. . . . Certain cocktails like dry Martinis, should always be stirred in a bar glass, never shaken—and this routine is always given under the drink receipt. . . . The new electric cocktail shaker—known as The Mixer—is treated on Page 6.

## THE MEASUREMENTS ARE SIMPLE, & APPLY to ALL MIXED DRINKS MENTIONED in this VOLUME

1 DASH . . . This means what comes from a bottle with a quill or "squirter" top, with an average hard movement of the hand. . . . *Approximately 3 drops.*
1 PONY . . . 1 oz, level full.
1 JIGGER . . . 1½ oz, level full.
1 BARSPOON . . . This is a long handled spoon used for measuring or stirring. . . . *Approximately 1 tsp.*
1 PINCH . . . What we can pick up between thumb and forefinger—

such as grated nutmeg, cinnamon, and the like. . . . *Approximately* ⅛ *tsp, or a trifle less,* depending on how well we pinch.

PLEASE MEASURE EXACTLY, not CARELESSLY, LAVISHLY, or STINGILY!

Just as in cookery, the amateur often fails because he approximates measurements. *All amounts given here are level full, unless otherwise noted.* . . . No matter what certain skeptics may say good cocktail and other fancy drink mixing is an exacting chemical art—just as modern music is an art. If we are lemonade squeezers at heart better not bother to mix at all, or else be graceful enough to approach the subject in a professional manner.

A FINAL NOTE, *en PASSANT,* on the QUANTITY USE of ANGOSTURA BITTERS, as well as SOME SLIGHT ADVICE on ITS GENERAL EMPLOYMENT

Most amateur mixers, including ourself, squirt in bitters more or less by the touch system. We know too that whereas 1 dash does for a single cocktail, what to do for a gallon? Standing before a large container making 60 dashes would be rather silly, and slow, and would send the usual mind to psychopathic wards before the night was pinned back. The answer is, allow 1 tsp of Angostura per 1 qt of mixed cocktails or drinks.

LIQUIDS NECESSARY to BRIGHT BARRING, either on a SMALLER or a LARGER SCALE

There are two sides to this business. If we go and list what an elaborate outfit can afford, those with a 3 by 6 alcove equipped to brew 8 or 10 of the simple standbys, and with neither inclination nor gold to play with more, will shout bloody murder. . . . Those readers with increment enough to stock a fair to unusual bar also have their say. And if we *can* buy things why not get money into circulation and really make an elaborate cocktail book something to use, not merely to read and skip between Old Fashioned, Martini, and Manhattan? The first-chop bar should have every single thing on this list; the cost should run in the neighbourhood of two hundred dollars, depending on geography.

The average bar amateur should run through the list and pick out those in most general use throughout the receipts.

Small bars should stick to the following. Dry, sloe, and old Tom gin; bourbon, rye, Scotch; orange and angostura bitters; French and Italian vermouth; grenadine and plain bar syrup; and a little each of the following:

Absinthe, benedictine, apricot brandy, cognac brandy, crème de menthe, cointreau, curaçao, maraschino, port, dry sherry, Rose's lime syrup, raspberry syrup, honey, orange-flower water, and a Sparklets siphon.

Even this small-bar list looks lengthy, and totals around fifty dollars without the Sparklets. But let's look at it this way:

Any mixing spot will serve a given number of potations per annum. If we only have gin, bourbon, and rye, with grenadine and angostura, that doesn't mean we'll consume any less cubic centimeters of alcohol than with the above assortment—which actually is capable of an amazing number of permutations and combinations. . . . The first investment is larger, but the yearly outgo in dollars will remain the same. . . . In one case we may gain name for pecunious and uninteresting assortments to offer a guest—in the latter we straightway become mighty clever and interesting fellows indeed. Good reputation is so rare, it would seem a canny gesture to cotton on to what little is going around through this simple expedient of stocking two dozen active ingredients in plain sight.

Of course many exotics and oddities are lacking, but if we include those given here nothing will be found wanting, believe us.

## NOW for the LIQUIDS THEMSELVES

ABSINTHE . . . Needed both for frappés, drips; but mainly in tiny quantities to fetch out the other tastes in cocktails—importantly, pickeruppers.

Now made principally in Switzerland, being banned in France. It is a highly toxic beverage based on wormwood elixirs, with a very odd and intriguing taste. It is an absolute essential for every well-stocked bar—mainly as a flavouring agent.

ANIS . . . A potent Spanish liqueur made of aniseed and other simples. *Anis del Mono* is the old favourite. Needed oftener than the average mixer believes. A fine morning eye-opener indeed.

ANISETTE . . . A French aniseed cordial. Not only good as a liqueur, for the various tummy aches which beset humanity, but often commanded in cocktails. Sweeter and milder than Spanish.

APPLE BRANDY, or APPLEJACK . . . Needed these days for several excellent cocktails and taller drinks, but not necessary for the small bar except on special occasions. . . . Don't get Jersey Lightning that some friend has put down in the wood since last fall, get it at least four or five years old. It is a very deceiving fluid, and when not watched will induce a happy state from the waist down, closely approaching voluntary paralysis. We speak feelingly.

APRICOT BRANDY . . . Invaluable both as a cordial and for certain cocktails such as the Grande Bretagne. . . . The best imported dry type is indicated, as overly-sweet attempts spoil the drink entirely, unless used as a straight cordial. Eschew American brands.

AQUAVIT . . . A clear potent spirit from the Scandinavian countries, and drunk in tiny thimblefuls, with a toss of the head. Aside from being a kind gesture to visiting Danes, and so on, it is practically uncalled-for in mixing. The general flavour is reminiscent of caraway. Say *sköl*.

AROMATIC SPIRITS of AMMONIA . . . No bar should be without this morning after saviour, as well as such itinerant feminine emergencies such as faintings, swoonings—either real or assumed. . . . Chemically it is $NH_3$, distilled from a pungent gas, which in its former state is of scant interest to mixers.

ARRACK or RACK . . . A distilled, variable, and erratic spirit found throughout the Far East; without enough flavour to attract western palates. It may be made from fermented palm toddy, from *muohwa* flowers, fermented sugar cane refuse, rice mash. Some cocktails indicate it, and like tequila, if aged it has merit. . . . Only for large bars; and only decent brands are recommended.

BENEDICTINE . . . One of the most important liqueurs, and made for centuries out of sugar, herbs, spirits, and divers secret elixirs by the French Benedictine monks at Fecamp. . . . French copyists among the laymen state that it is compounded by blending the essences of angelica root, arnica blooms, lemon peels, thyme, cardamons, peppermint, cassia, hyssop, and cloves, blended and aged with pure water, sweetening, and the finest cologne spirits. . . . Everyone knows the squatty bottle with the D.O.M. label, and the big seal of scarlet wax. . . . Not too good as a mixing agent, as it lacks character, and loses its delicate flavours. . . . Best for cordials with coffee or without. . . . Not often indicated for cocktails, in spite of unjustified activity along this line by the manufacturers and importers, we've found it unremarkable except in pousse cafés. It is too sweet for most cocktails, and isn't vigorous enough in flavour to overcome the strong spirits and bitters.

THE SIX MAIN BITTERS . . . Angostura and orange bitters must be on every bar shelf, be it ever so humble. Next in importance are Calisaya —made on a quinine base and sometimes used in considerable quantity in cocktails—or quinine bitters; New Orleans Peychaud, Boker's and Amer Picon. . . . They are lots of fun to toy with, and in many things like gin, sherry, vermouth, make a simple cocktail of great service, which some people claim are the only really good ones anyway!

BRANDY, COGNAC, and *CHAMPAGNE FINE,* sometimes CALLED *"FINE"* . . . Brandy is simply distilled grape wine, aged in wood casks. Cognac is brandy from the finest possible region for its excellent construction—the Cognac region of France. No brandy not from Cognac is permitted to use the word on labels. . . . *Champagne fine is* merely very old, very fine, and very excellent brandy. *Fine* is only used in one cocktail to our knowledge, being entirely too precious and delightful in itself to be outraged by admixture with less aristocratic spirits. . . . Napoleon brandy is probably the best-known *Fine.* It runs about thirty dollars per fifth, and the finest is dated around 1832 or slightly later. Its price advances with age and rarity of vintage. Brandy was discovered through the keenness of a Dutch apothecary who, when seeing that the Cognac grape region, through a huge bumper crop, was producing more wine than could be shipped, thought up the idea of reducing the freight by extracting water by heat,—the same to be put back later at the consumers' end. . . . Although this didn't prove sound as to wine handling, the distilled wine turned into a new and mellow fluid of bouquet and potency which the original could never hope to equal— and thus brandy was given to the world, of which the well-known Hennessy cognac is a typical example founded in 1765. . . . Beside all the fancy tests tasters apply to brandy, the main one for laymen like ourselves is as follows: Poor brandy when sipped neat burns harshly on the tongue, and flavour vanishes quickly. Sound brandy, on the contrary, does not burn sharply and leaves a flavour and bouquet which lingers pleasantly. . . . Sip it slowly, roll it on the tongue—and the result should be like ripe grapes under warm harvest-time sun. . . . The bouquet of good brandy lingers in the glass long after the liquid itself is gone.

Brandy is taken in three principal ways: Mixed with other things, and alone, either in a small brandy glass, or in the large globe glasses. In the latter case the globe should be warmed between palms. This bodily warmth startles the perfumes into wakefulness, and they arise to greet nose as well as lip—and the brandy is then sipped slowly, a very tiny bit at a time.

Almost beyond all other spirits brandy requires enough aging, as only in this way can the delicate qualities be properly brought out, and rawness mellowed. Brandies from certain years are blended with other years, so that an even quality may be maintained. The colourless, raw distilled wine becomes mellowed and darkened from the wooden casks. Actually 1 bottle of aged brandy requires the distillation of about 10 bottles of wine.

Brandy out of wood never ages, and 1 bottled in 1900 after 10 years in wood is still 10 years old in 1939. Remember to check on this when buying rare brandy.

CRÈME de CACAO . . . Needed in at least one important cocktail, and a favourite with the ladies as a cordial with coffee. Naturally has a potent chocolate flavour from cacao beans from which cocoa and chocolate come.

CRÈME de CASSIS . . . French black currant syrup, useful with vermouth as an appetizing cooler. Also used at rare intervals in special cocktails. Good with soda for non-alcoholic summer beverages.

CERTOSA . . . No one who has ever been outside Florence to the lovely little monastery with its old gardens and the one privileged Padre who is allowed to speak that day, will ever forget Certosa. . . . We have half a dozen of their brightly painted and glazed bottles, shaped like globes in eagles claws, Della Robbia bambinos and Virgins in flat bottles. . . . And within yellow and green liqueurs much like Chartreuse, only Italian. Their strawberry Certosa is especially, and oddly delicious. . . . Never used for cocktails, just as liqueurs, and with coffee. Pronounced Chair-*toes'*-a.

CHARTREUSE . . . One of the cordial immortals of all time. Like Benedictine and Certosa, Chartreuse is the product of monks—this time of the Carthusian Order, and formerly only at their establishment in the French Alps called Grande Chartreuse. . . . Unfortunately this order was banished from France to Spain just after the turn of the century and, at Tarragona, they again set up with their secret formula compounded of elixirs from odd and rare herbs, water, sugar, and fine spirits. . . . Naturally all of France sprouted imitations. Clever chemical folk pronounce it made up of the following essences: Sweet flag, orange peel, peppermint oil, dried tops of hyssop, balm, leaves of balm, angelica seeds and root, wormwood, tonka bean, cardamons, as well as well known spices such as mace, cloves and cinnamon. Nice, simple little formula, this!

Green is most pungent, expensive, and a bottle will run as high as forty dollars alleged gold per quart, in the older supplies. . . . Yellow is just as good, and more aromatic; and is not only invaluable as a liqueur with coffee, in *pousses cafés,* but is the final decoration for a Gin Daisy, and other delicate drinks. . . . White is sweetest.

CHERRY BRANDY . . . Danish *Kirseboer* is best, and may be one hundred years of age! In more recent vintages it is widely used in many cocktails, as well as a liqueur and *pousse café.*

COINTREAU . . . Can't do without. Not only is it one of the six favourite liqueurs of the world, but is indicated in several very important cocktails like Between the Sheets.

CORDIAL MÉDOC . . . Not used often in cocktails, but with coffee, and alone. It is one of the most delicate liqueurs extant, giving a rich after-taste hinting at peach pits, and bitter almonds—very, very far away, but pleasantly there.

CURAÇAO . . . Made from special undisclosed spices, and from the peel of oranges grown in the rather barren little island of that name belonging to Holland off the Venezuelan coast. The best is made in Holland, although we've had some interesting green Curaçao on the island itself, in Willemstad, the tiny Capital. . . . Yellow is most used, and has the most helpful flavour, both as a liqueur, *pousse café,* or in cocktails.

*DAMIANA* . . . One of those indeterminable French liqueurs made for scant reliable purpose, and indicated in a few *pousse cafés,* and those cocktails intended for profitable feminine absorption. As mentioned elsewhere, the label is worth the price of admission. . . . Should be on elaborate bars, mainly; otherwise it is strictly a bedside table liquid.

DANTZIGER GOLDWASSER . . . Purely a matter of swank, but always effective when with a handsome lady. It is also called *Eau de Vie de Dantzig,* and is a cordial with a pleasant but unimportant taste, in which flecks of real gold leaf flutter and swim about when it is only slightly shaken. The gold does no harm and no good.

DUBONNET . . . A French creation based on wine fortified with herbs, and this and that. Universally accepted in France for years, it is just becoming appreciated again in America. There are a few cocktails calling for it. Only needed in the more elaborate establishments.

FIORI ALIPINI . . . The tall attractive bottle of delicious liqueur in which a rock candy tree rears its realistic trunk and branches. A fine liqueur, but never indicated for cocktails.

## FOUR GINS MUST BE IN EVERY BAR

DRY GIN . . . A white spirit flavoured with juniper oils, and too well known to describe here. All we can plead for is to get a decent grade, and stick to it. No bar can be without dry gin, and be called a bar.

HOLLAND GIN, or HOLLANDS, and sometimes *SCHNAPPS* . . . This is a vigorously flavoured gin which must appear on all sizeable bars. It has a very potent juniper taste, aids digestion, promotes appetite, and is needed in several important cocktails like Death in the Gulf Stream.

OLD TOM GIN . . . Old Tom has an oilier texture and a slight orange taste. Indispensable.

SLOE GIN . . . Totally unlike other gins, being flavoured with the astringent blackthorn fruit, or sloe berry. It is ruby red, sweetish, and makes delightful and mild fizzes, rickeys, and so on. . . . Should be on hand in all well-appointed bars of average type and above.

GRAND MARNIER . . . A delicious French liqueur and useful as a *pousse café*, but never specified for cocktails. Tastes faintly like a combination of curaçao, cordial médoc and Benedictine—with orange basis predominant.

GRENADINE . . . This, as the name indicates, is a syrup flavoured with the juice of pomegranates. No bar, regardless of its modesty can be without this need. . . . Don't be deceived by inferior American imitations of the real thing. Be sure and get the imported.

HONEY . . . This man-stolen product of bee's industry is, in its strained state, useful now and then in special cocktails. A small, cup-size, covered porcelain or china container should be on every thoroughgoing bar.

*KIRSCHWASSER,* or KIRSCH . . . This odd liqueur is made principally in the Black Forest sector of Germany, in France and Switzerland from small black wild cherries. These are fermented in wooden containers, stirred at intervals, and probably a few of the cherry pits are crushed with the cherries—which imparts the faint hint of bitter almonds. . . . Taken as a liqueur it is somewhat of an acquired taste, but in punches or in cocktails the flavour intrigues everyone who tries them. Kirsch is, of course, the same as *Kirschwasser.* No bar can be without a bottle.

KÜMMEL . . . A white, pungent liqueur made from cumin and caraway seeds, with the latter taste dominant. A great favourite with the Russians of royal days as most of it was made in Riga, pre-Soviet. Now

Germany produces most of it. . . . Like *anis* and anisette, kümmel is a great stomachic, relieves pains, collywobbles, aids digestion, and is specified in enough cocktails that it should be on the shelf of every average bar. . . . Swans, bears, and what-not, determine the shape of the bottles, and those with sugar precipitated on the bottom are held to be best—one brand having a sugar-frosted sprig of edelweiss in the swan's neck.

ROSE'S LIME SYRUP, and LIME CORDIAL . . . The former is a pungent oil-of-lime syrup coming in tall, slender, decorative bottles so often seen behind good soda fountains. It is indicated in the Gimlet Cocktail, Page 37, and bears a lot of experimentation. . . . Lime Cordial can be made by mixing this about half and half with *gomme* syrup, see Page 154. . . . Lime syrup of soda fountain type also approximates the result. These should be used more by American mixers!

MADEIRA . . . A bottle indicated for the well-stocked outfit. It is called for in one special cocktail, and used as flavouring in others.

MARASCHINO . . . Another delicious cherry derivative, fermented and distilled, then flavoured by the bruised cherry stones themselves. Maraschino is so essential that no fairly equipped bar can afford to be without it.

CRÈME de MENTHE . . . Two kinds of peppermint flavoured liqueurs; green and white. The former for flavouring special cocktails, for frappés; the latter for Stingers; both for cordials. . . . Must be on every complete amateur bar shelf.

CRÈME de NOYAU . . . A very sweet but potent apricot liqueur. Wise men take it with coffee, and only one or two. In peach and apricot pits there is a cyanide influence which most people don't know about, and over dosing will definitely become injurious. In small amounts it is perfectly safe. . . . In France they also frappé it in a glass of fine ice, livened up with a little seltzer or soda.

OJEN . . . The so-called Spanish Absinthe. Needed by larger bars, and used like ordinary Absinthe. For many years this was made in New Orleans.

ORANGE-FLOWER WATER . . . A delightful flavouring agent for many delicious drinks like New Orleans Fizzes. Not used in every day practice, but necessary for the average complete mixer.

ORGEAT SYRUP . . . One of the needed bar flavours, compounded from almonds, orange-flower water, and sugar, see Page 166. Every well-stocked bar must have it; small bars ignore it.

*PARFAIT AMOUR* . . . Another of those highly coloured cordials hatched in the fertile and agile brain of France. It is also erroneously conceded improbably persuasive powers, but is very pretty in *pousse cafés,* and many ladies prefer it with coffee.

PEACH BRANDY . . . Mainly domestic. It makes a nice, although very sweet, business to take with coffee. . . . Used in Georgia Mint Julep, as on Page 66.

PORT WINE . . . Needed in enough unusual cocktails to make it necessary on any fairly well stocked shelf. Also an essential after coffee in any civilized community.

ROSE WATER . . . Used very rarely; only for the most elaborate bars.

RUM of THREE BASIC TYPES . . . Bacardi, *Carta de Oro,* and *Carta Blanca;* which are light brandy-type rums. . . . Barbados, St. Croix, Haitian, or Demerara rum, which are the darker, medium type. . . . Jamaica, the dark, richly flavoured type. . . . All three are needed. . . . All rums are distilled from fermented sugar cane products. . . . Watch Demerara rum! We've run into some nice gentle types from there that run 160 proof—or 80% alcohol! The strongest bourbon is only 50%.

SAKI . . . Japanese rice wine, and much like Chinese rice wine. It is mild, useless for cocktails, but heated quite hot makes the proper accompaniment for *Suki-yaki,* the Japanese classical dish. Saki service sets with thimble cups and porcelain bottle are obtainable in larger cities or from Japanese or Chinese restaurant folk.

SHERRY . . . The dry type makes the finest cocktail known, served as-is with a dash of bitters. All bars must have a bottle, for there are still essentially sane people who prefer it to any chilled, mixed drink.

SWEDISH or CALORIC PUNCH . . . A much overrated affair, and which always stands neglected on our shelves for long. Drunk mainly by folk who expect a stout blow, and get a pat instead. Hints palely at rum and no one knows what else.

THE SIX CHIEF SYRUPS . . . Plain *gomme* sugar, or bar syrup—as on Page 154; grenadine as on Page 186; lime, pineapple, raspberry and strawberry—the latter quartet being those used at better soda fountains. Average to big bars need all five; small bars, plain syrup and grenadine.

TEQUILA . . . An exotic from Mexico which impressed us enough to run in three or five mixed drinks and cocktails. It is buyable in most average American towns, on slight notice—and everywhere in the Southwest. . . . Distilled from the *Maguey* plant, see Page 127.

VANILLA . . . *Crème de Vanille* is usually specified for cocktails but there are a very few exotics which indicate the extract, and in this case a raid on the kitchen shelf will probably bear fruit.

CRÈME *de VANILLE* . . . Indicated in a few cocktails, but rarely. Only for large bars.

VERMOUTH . . . There are two basic types: The dark, more richly flavoured Italian variety imperative in many cocktails, as well as alone, with soda, and with cassis, as an aperitif; the light, or "dry" French vermouth, without which a Dry Martini would be a wet, old-fashioned Martini. . . . Both are wines fortified, and stepped up with various secret herbs. They aid digestion, promote appetite. . . . No bar can be without both, and better have two bottles of each. They go fast!

CRÈME *de VIOLETTE,* and CRÈME *YVETTE* . . . Made with violette flower essence and of a rich violet hue used to colour certain few cocktails; much preferred by girls who think they are being sophisticated in ordering something out of such a funny shaped bottle, and by gentlemen who erroneously think it possesses congressional powers little short of miraculous.

VODKA . . . This, although for a time banned by the Soviet, is still easily to be had. Theoretically it should never be sipped, but tossed off

JIGGER, BEAKER, & GLASS

with a flip of the head, like Aquavit, which in many ways it resembles. It is a potent white liquor which should be on every complete bar shelf, but unnecessary to medium or small bars. Formerly made from rye and barley malt it is now made from corn and potatoes. The proof runs as high as 120, which means 60% alcohol, so take care.

THE COMPANY of WHISKIES, which ARE BOURBON, IRISH, RYE, and SCOTCH . . . Bourbon and rye are needed for very many important cocktails, besides a host of mixed drinks. . . . Irish is indicated for a few cocktails, hot toddies, and highballs. . . . Scotch is not a happy cocktail mixer, unfortunately, and its main value is in a highball called "whiskysoda" around the civilized and uncivilized world.

The smallest bars need bourbon *or* rye, and Scotch. Medium require bourbon, rye and Scotch. . . . Large require Irish as well.

Bourbon, Irish, and rye run close to 100 proof or 50% alcohol. Scotch a trifle milder, around 40%. . . . All are distilled from malted or fermented grain: corn, barley, rye, and so on, and flavoured by the waters, minerals, dusts, pollens and what-not native to their place of origin.

Due to the same mysterious natural factors which make the Spey River Valley good for Scotch—just so the water, climate, and so on of Maryland prove toward good rye, and Kentucky toward sound bourbons. . . . This is no argument against the location of the immense modern distilleries everywhere—but a simple statement of proven history. . . . There are peanut-fed smoked hams outside Virginia—but Virginia is known to the world; there are crabs and crabs, but the Florida and West Indies stone or Morro Crab is something else; there are soups and soups, but a New Orleans gumbo is super—just like brandy from France's Cognac region, scuppernong wine from our own North Carolina, Angostura bitters from Trinidad. . . . Bear this in mind when American whisky stocks get decently aged and within range of a sane man's bank balance again. . . . As they will!

Taken sanely and in moderation whisky is beneficial, aids digestion, helps throw off colds, megrims, and influenzas. Used improperly the effect is just as bad as stuffing on too many starchy foods, taking no exercise, or disliking our neighbour.

WHITE MULE, CAWN LIKKER, SHINE, MOON, et al. . . . Regardless of alias this sequence simply means the raw, new, colourless, distilled product of fermented corn mash, sugar and water. . . . If well made, of decent materials, in a proper still, with the fusel oil rectified out, and aged in wood it starts to be bourbon whisky after not less than four years in the wood of charred oak casks. . . .

None of the manufacturers of bourbons should have any right to call any corn whisky "bourbon" until it has aged at least four or five years, but the demand so exceeded supply that all rules were off.

As far as corn likker goes we have drunk it from a fellow quail and turkey shooter's still in the Big Swamp country of Central Florida—made in a copper wash boiler, run through an old shotgun barrel, and a length of iron pipe into a galvanized washtub covered with a cotton blanket; drunk it in the "dry" mountain sections of Nawth C'hlina last summer. We have drunk it straight, with water, with juices, and disguises. We have drunk it scalding hot on chill October evenings, with cloves, brown sugar, and lemon peel. We've drunk it cold.

In spite of hades and elevated water that old cawn bouquet comes shearing through like a rusty can opener to smite us between the eyes. . . . Hot with cloves, and so on is best; drowned in grapefruit juice is about the only cold method possible. . . . No matter what, that cawn has a scent of decaying vegetation blended with the fluid men used to put in old ship lanterns; and taken neat it burns with all the restless fires of hell.

As you may gather we don't recommend cawn—mentally, morally; or for general wear and tear and declined insurance risk, physically. We certainly don't—until after at least five years in charred oak casks.


A FEW NOTES on the CARE & SERVICE of Our Best Usual Wines, as They Affect the Amateur

We always have believed that one reason most Americans know nothing about wines except champagne, claret, port, and sherry, is due to a practical non-existence of a truly leisured class within our shores. Everyone who doesn't leap out of warm sheets at command of an alarmclock daily, rush through a shave, a hurried breakfast and a dash to an office is—for reasons no sane soul has ever been able to explain to us—viewed as not quite Worth While, and lacking the proper attitude toward life. Any young person under fifty who stops work when he has enough worldly wealth to eliminate the daily grind, is a butt for whispers, raised eyebrows; he is considered not quite Worth While.

What we mean is that nothing about wine can be hurried. It takes an allotted length of time for grapes to grow and ripen, more time to ferment, still more to age properly in barrels and later in bottles. It takes a man time to learn about wines, time to drink them, a lifetime of appreciation to value them. The chap who is Worth While, and who spends half his life sprinting to offices, naturally hasn't time in all that milling about to slow down enough to notice wines. He wants quick action from his spirits, not leisurely sipping and pauses for appreciation. Few Americans have ever learned to play. There is nothing sadder than most American Big Business out of the office. We have seen a lot of it lately in that predicament, and a more restless, half-lost bunch of sagging muscles, golf alibis, and short breaths we've never seen.

Abroad, in all the wine lands, men have learned to play—at least after a fashion—leisurely, calmly; not fiercely, as though it were a matter of grim life and death. Our Britisher starts his week-end Friday noon, often as not. A whole French family will lie under trees throughout a Sunday, doing nothing in particular—a form of relaxation which would have the American Man Who Matters in a padded cell from sheer triple-distilled boredom.

Our great outdoors inheritance in conquering the great west has left us with story and song about two-fisted, two-gun, five-fingered drinkers of raw likker—who tossed off a tumbler full of red eye without a blink. All this sort of thing has got us to thinking we are a stout race of monstrous manly fellows, and the thought of dallying with a cobwebby wine cork, and sipping such meek and mild fluids out of a tiny and delicately stemmed glass, appears just the slightest bit effeminate; something grown men left to the companions of older women and visiting alleged foreign titles.

In other words America has always consumed hard liquor. She always will, but we are delighted to see the recent renaissance of interest in proper wines, along with that renaissance in good cookery we mention through *Volume I*—and most encouraging of all, interest in our truly fine American wines, of the type made by our friend Paul Garrett's family for well over 100 years.

Actually our first experience with wine service is utterly simple, easy, and without any more problem than a little chilling if, and where, indicated.

## THE FIRST A B C of WINE SERVICE

*White Wines:* go with seafood, light-meat poultry; with fruits, sweets, and desserts. . . . Champagne, although white, is traditional with game or throughout any meal, if and when desired.

*Red Wines:* go with meats generally, and dark meats in particular; with entrée, game, and roast. . . . Port goes with cheese.

Not with Salad: as a general rule wine is skipped during the salad course, the acid dressing interferes with the true wine taste.

## WINE TEMPERATURES

White wines must be chilled, except of course the tawny fortified types like sherry, Madeira, Marsala and so on.

Red wines should never be chilled, except what we buy as Sparkling Burgundy. . . . Bordeaux red wine should be served a trifle higher in temperature than the dining room. . . . Burgundy red should be slightly cooler, or as it comes from cellar.

The easiest way to handle a red claret wine is to decant it and let stand in the dining room for three or four hours before pouring, see Pages 195 & 196.

Serving a red wine really chilled would hamper its taste and flavour severely. For further thoughts on red wines in the Tropics, turn to Pages 197 & 198, and not too distant, below.

## SIP WINE, DON'T DRINK IT

Somewhere the fiction got about that wine was made solely to quench thirst. So it may be, beside the hearth of our worthy and horny handed son of toil, perhaps, but no amateur worthy of the name ever gulps decent wine. Water is for satisfying thirst, wine is to be sipped and enjoyed.

First twirl a half filled glass, and watch the lovely jewel-like colour fan up on the empty inner side; then sniff it in leisurely fashion to catch the bouquet.

Sip, twirl the tongue, and enjoy each succeeding nuance of taste as it strikes the taste buds, palate, and rebounds through a renewed sense of smell from the posterior section of the nasal cavity. Then swallow, and catch the final after-taste.

Americans can't get used to having restaurants put bottles away for clients to call on later. Some wines, of course, do not keep for more than a few hours after being opened, but most regular patrons of any given spot have their bottles labelled, corked tightly, and properly cared for until their next visit. For this reason, and possible Scotch instincts through not wishing a waiter to get an unused half bottle, Americans gulp all their wine to the last drop—thereby not only drinking too fast but surfeiting themselves with so much vinous fluid that true appreciation, after the first brief introduction, is impossible.

WORDS to the DRINKING WISE No. XX, on the OPENING of GLASS STOPPERS of DECANTERS if and when STUCK
Dr. Kitchiner, 1823

"With a feather rub a drop or two of salad oil around the stopper, close to the mouth of the Decanter, which must then be placed before the fire . . . not too close . . . the heat will cause the oil to insinuate itself between stopper and Neck.

"When Bottle or Decanter has grown warm, *gently* strike the Stopper on one side, and then the other, with any light wooden instrument; then try it with the Hand; if it will not yet move, place again before the fire, adding another drop of oil. After a while strike again as before. . . . However tightly it may be fastened in, you will at length succeed in loosening it."

This is a sound bit of advice, for we remember the sad experience of breaking a specially fine cut crystal decanter stopper in a brandy decanter we'd just picked up in London. The sweetness of the spirit had sealed the stopper in tight as glue, and we were impatient. . . . The quickest modern way is to put the outer neck of the decanter under quite hot water from the spiggot; tap stopper lightly with something made of wood—anything not metal, and a twist of the wrist will usually loosen it—the heat having expanded the neck to a size larger than the still chilled glass stopper.

## THE CEREMONY of STORING and UNCORKING any WINE WORTH the EFFORT

Immediately below we give routine for opening and decanting fine claret, which is a ceremony in itself, and here we will list briefly the strict rules. Neglect of any indicates the same lack of courtesy toward a discriminating guest as would be consequent to appearing in a soiled linen collar.

1. Store in cellar on racks with necks slightly up. This eliminates the risk of sediment on the cork.
2. A truly fine wine should be gently lifted from rack, wiped off and put carefully in buffet or wine-basket three or four days before serving, so that any disturbed sediment can settle once more. . . . Wine bottles worth opening are always dusty. Take them up gently so as not to stir up; carry them like new born babes, put down gently.
3. Carefully wipe off the neck, then remove foil, sealing wax, and such. . . . But *don't overdo* and wipe all the signs of age from the bottle—it is a happy picture to the epicure.
4. Use corkscrew precisely, don't shake bottle; drawing cork with a gently slow action, if the self-drawing corkscrew isn't on hand—don't yank it out for the dramatic effect of the pop.
5. It is good form to hold bottle in white napkin or cloth, and when cork is out, to wipe out neck carefully—being very careful that no old cork falls into the wine. A speck of cork in a glass is almost like a fly in soup, *Messieurs*. The final gesture is to offer cork to guest of honour for his inspection, who shall murmur audibly his appreciation.
6. If wine is to be decanted at this point, do the job against any sort of strong light, pouring steadily, gently, and stop precisely when the first film of sediment rises to a point where the next cubic centimeter will cause it to flow out into the decanter. . . . Better waste an ounce of wine than chance spoiling what we have decanted.
7. If not to be decanted, have a little poured first into the host or hostess's glass. When we see this done on foreign ships or restaurants it isn't just an idle gesture. . . . From the Borgia regime it indicated the host's willingness to prove to guest that the usual dram of poison was omitted as a special favour! . . . In more kindly times it indicates that the host pours the first few drops for a preliminary sniff and taste. Poor bouquet, or "corked" flavour is then detected before subjugating the guest to this embarrassment, and the bottle can be replaced. It is merely a courteous gesture worth keeping alive.

A PROPER CARE & HANDLING ROUTINE for the Most
Tweaky Wine of All—Claret

1. Claret must always be handled like a new born babe.
2. Remove claret from the cellar at least 1 day ahead of time.
3. Stand *uncorked* in a slightly warmer than dining room temperature, but *do not heat.*
4. If fairly young wine stand uncorked for one hour, if older, for up to eight hours. This process is called *"chambre,"* or fetching it to "room" condition.
5. Draw corks ourself, carefully. Sediment kills claret, and ninety American bottles out of a hundred are killed, my friends. . . .
6. Have decanter a couple of degrees warmer than dining room, and put wine into it slowly but continuously from bottle to decanter—*against the light.*
7. When we see sediment flowing toward bottle neck, stop pouring. That lost glass of wine may pain us, but will ruin the rest.
8. Put decanter on dining room sideboard with the *stopper out.*
9. Drink claret out of large, *thin,* plain glasses.

A new or young claret will show a purplish bubble as it first strikes the glass, and is unrecommended for internal consumption. If the bubble is a rich red, it is matured, ripe and sound. If bubbles are rich tawny brown it is over twenty years old, perhaps more. We may then sit back and brood upon the delicacies of a truly worthwhile wine.

This simple routine actually takes only a few moments of our time. The reason we never do it properly is that it requires the mental effort of thought about a fine point of good living, which many otherwise important and influential people think foppish, fussy, European, and highly unnecessary. . . . These above 9 rules must be observed if our claret is worth the bringing home from the shop. Think it over. How many of us have ever had decent claret, either in a restaurant, or at home.

The average American restaurant's technique on wine is crude and brutally simple. It is snatched off the rack when ordered, and either served cellar (or rack) temperature for most red wines, or chilled more or less. It is handled roughly, carelessly. The cork pops, curious, envious, heads raise at neighbouring tables at this wide display of lavishness, lower again. The wine is hastily poured out—and there we are gentlemen—we are drinking wine, and God help us!

EXPLODED OLD ALEWIVES' TALE No. III, IMPROPRIETY
of HEATING CLARETS
No matter what nice old Aunt Peola Fittich remembers about claret in London's famous old inn *The Cheshire Cheese,* never heat claret artificially. Place it in the room where it is to be served, in the forenoon, properly decanted, with the stopper out. Pour at night without further treatment.

A WORD on the CORRECT SERVICE of WINES with MEALS, GIVING FOUR EXAMPLES, or so, of WINE SEQUENCES & SIMILAR ADDENDA
THIS CHAPTER on wines makes no pretense to go into types, qualities, traditional vintages, and the like. This information, often the life work of gentlemen far more qualified than ourself to speak of such matters, is readily available from hundreds of sources—one of the most charming being a small pocket-size volume by a gentleman and a gourmet in his own right, Julian Street, entitled *Where Paris Dines;* and no amateur should be without it on his shelves.

But many of these books by experts fail to remember that the average American amateur, not conceived in a wine-drinking land, may need a helping hand to guide him over the first barriers. Not being primarily able to concern ourself with extravagant vintages, Americans generally prefer peace and mixed drinks rather than wars and rumours of wars, and infinite wine knowledge. What we note below are just about all the needful service essentials.

Let us explain 2 points which have always struck us as not usually made clear to the amateur. In the first place Game can be a relatively unimportant course, technically an Entrée, or it may be the whole focal point of a meal—like a vast platter of wild duck, or wild turkey, and there may be no conventional Roast course included in such a meal. The other is: where we live in the tropics and dining room temperature may, on infrequent summer days, be close to 80 or 85 degrees Fahrenheit, we consider it proper to chill all still red wines gently to around 60 degrees—and we don't give a worm-eaten fig what long haired Gallic gentleman may tear his bangs out by the roots when he hears of this heresy.

We haven't drunk as much wine as a Frenchman but we have drunk about as much—probably a great deal more—red wine in the tropics, the Oriental hot countries, than the average Frenchman. Therefore, bearing in mind there are no cellars in such *pays chauds* that maintain a temperature around 65 degrees, even at 70! anywhere, we cry that too-warm red wine is just as bad in its way as too-warm white wine; and we earnestly recommend that readers think over this point in summer. We feel that red wine should be cool—not warm, not chilled. This goes for sherry too, which we find tastes infinitely better here in Florida when slightly cooled. It is a simple matter of reason, and not letting ourself be bound and swept away by what we've read about red wines, what some lame-wit, conceited ass has screamed at us after his first and only 5 day stay in Paris; all the fuss and fume that people kick up about a subject which is far worse than any mild mishandling of wine could ever be!

A SIMPLE FRENCH WINE SEQUENCE with MEALS, No. I

WITH OYSTERS or SEAFOOD COCKTAIL, and SOUP . . . White wine; Chablis, or Pouilly; chilled.

WITH the ROAST . . . Red wine; still Burgundy at cellar temperature; claret at room temperature.

WITH DESSERT . . . Chablis or Pouilly, as at the start; but better still would be a somewhat sweeter wine of the average Sauterne type.

NOW a SIMPLE EUROPEAN SEQUENCE of WINE with MEALS, No. II

WITH OYSTERS or SEAFOOD COCKTAIL, and SOUP . . . Dry white wine; Rhine or Moselle; chilled.

WITH the ROAST . . . A sound glass of any good red wine, not sweet;

room temperature if claret; cellar temperature if Burgundy; Spanish dry red wine, or Chianti.

WITH DESSERT or FRUIT . . . A good glass of cool Sauterne, well-chilled champagne; or the same white wine as at the start.

## A SIMPLE YET PLEASANTLY EFFECTIVE EUROPEAN SEQUENCE No. III, to GRATIFY a PARTICULAR AMATEUR GOURMET

WITH HORS d'OEUVRE . . . Pale dry sherry and bitters. Vermouth or Dubonnet, or Amer Picon; room temperature.

WITH OYSTERS or SEAFOOD COCKTAIL . . . A good Chablis, vintage Rhine, or Chilean White *Undurraga,* chilled.

WITH SOUP . . . Old dry sherry, room temperature.

WITH FISH . . . Still white *Montrachet* Burgundy, chilled.

WITH ENTRÉE . . . Light Bordeaux claret, room temperature.

WITH GAME . . . Champagne of good vintage year, chilled well.

WITH ROAST . . . Red Burgundy, or Château bottled claret; former cellar temperature, latter room temperature.

WITH DESSERT or PASTRY . . . A sound Madeira, room temperature.

WITH CHEESE . . . Port of a good year, room temperature.

FRUIT . . . Tokay, or Malaga, room temperature.

COFFEE . . . *Champagne fine,* green Chartreuse, Drambuie, room temperature.

In this latter list the service of white Burgundy, of a good year, instead of the usual white Bordeaux, brands any host as being gentleman and scholar, and deucedly stout fellow as well. . . . It is a touch which some true amateur is bound to remark, and one quiet word of praise on our *Montrachet* is worth all the parrot-like praise of casual champagne, from a multitude. . . . Chilean Rhine type *Undurraga* we discovered four years ago on a Grace Line boat on a Panama trip. It is as fine as most Rhines, and greatly approved by connoisseurs, we now find. Comes in a cute squatty bottle.

## A SPECIAL OCCASION SEQUENCE No. IV, & GOOD ENOUGH for ROYALTY

WITH HORS d'OEUVRE GENERALLY . . . Be sure and don't

serve too rich hors d'oeuvre before a fine dinner; skip mayonnaise types.
. . . Serve a fine dry sherry, with or without bitters, or a Daiquiri, not
too sweet, see Pages 30 & 31.

WITH CAVIAR . . . Vodka or *kümmel* in liqueur glasses, or a really
good Dry Martini.

WITH OYSTERS . . . Chablis, *La Moutonne* or *Grenouilles,* of good
year. *Schloss Johannisberger* Rhine, or *Berncasteler Doktor* Moselle, of
excellent years, chilled.

WITH SOUP . . . Fine old dry sherry.

WITH FISH . . . Still white Burgundy like *Meursault Perrières,* a white
*Côtes-du-Rhône Hermitage,* or dry white Bordeaux *Château Haut-
Brion Blanc,* or *Château Margaux Pavillon Blanc*—choosing a good
year; chilled.

WITH ENTRÉE . . . A fine light claret like *Château Carbonnieux
Rouge* of good year, or *Château Haut-Brion Rouge* might be better still,
to tie up with its white sister accompanying the piscatorial friend above;
room temperature.

WITH GAME . . . Vary the procedure with a white still champagne, instead of the usual sparkling champagne which would do well with
game—all this provided the game be fairly light like pheasant, and not
dark like hare, wild duck, or venison. . . . In former case a good white
still champagne would be a *Verzenay* of *Sillery;* for darker game try a
red still champagne like *Château Montflaubert* or *Ay.* In the case of still
white champagne, chill; in serving red still champagne it can be chilled
slightly, or served like Burgundy from a cool cellar.

WITH ROAST . . . *Grand Vin Romanée Conti,* or *Grand Vin Clos de
Vougeot,* choosing a vintage year for red Burgundies, and serving cellar
temperature not over 65 degrees Fahrenheit.

WITH VERY SPECIAL VEGETABLES . . . A good Tokay is in
order. Room temperature.

WITH DESSERT or SWEET . . . Choose a fine Sauterne, of which
*Château Yquem* is finest of all, or *Château Guiraud,* or *Château Rieus-
sec;* or a glass of fine Tokay or Madeira—all should be of good years.
Sauterne may be cooled; the others room temperature, of course.

WITH CHEESE . . . A fine old ruby or tawny port, of good vintage,
but if the cheese is of a strong type omit wine altogether.

WITH COFFEE . . . A fine liqueur Brandy, or *champagne fine;* Cordial Médoc, or Green Chartreuse.

WORDS to the DRINKING WISE No. XXI, on the EXCEL-
LENCE of SERVING THE CHEESE BEFORE the DESSERT
   The French they are a canny race. Knowing that only a sip of red
wine can possibly harmonize with cheese, then change our order, and
serve it before the sweet—thus enabling a guest to use his final few
sips of Burgundy in proper fashion. Otherwise it means an extra wine
course like a good port. Try it some time. No one will notice until
the thing is done, then they will see the logic.

WORDS to the DRINKING WISE No. XXII, on the BEST MO-
MENT for SERVING CHAMPAGNE at a MEAL
   Just note the sequence above. If other wines precede it, always serve
the champagne with the *first hot meat course,* in this case the game.
If sparkling wine is served after too many hot courses, gases are re-
leased more potently, causing a tendency toward heartburn, for those
who tend. A great many tend.

A THOUGHT on SERVING ONE WINE THROUGHOUT
the MEAL
   Many gourmets often and connoisseurs who know whereof they
speak, claim that all this business of having four or five varieties of
wine with a meal is sheer boasting, and that if a wine is sound enough
to deserve to serve at all, it is good enough for the whole meal. . . .
Usually this means some white wine—Rhine, Moselle, Bordeaux, still
Burgundy white, or something similar. A white wine will go with
the meat whereas red wine simply doesn't seem to suit caviar, oysters,
delicate boiled fishes, and seafood like shrimps and lobsters—and
with sweets or dessert a white wine fetches out the flavours better.
. . . In fact there is one school which calls for a dry champagne of
decent vintage now and then for a complete meal, claiming that with
fruits and desserts of all sorts the harmony is particularly gratifying.
   Sometime when we elect to serve champagne right through a meal
make the added gesture of serving a dry type with the meal up to the
dessert, then changing to a slightly sweeter kind—as dry wine does
not march quite so well with sweets, and sweet pastries.

WINE at TEA TIME

The smartest people in America used to serve sweet wine—Catawba, or Virginia Dare scuppernong, with cake or tiny small cakes, just as in France a sweet Bordeaux or champagne was often served with cakes in the late afternoon. . . . Ports, sherries, Malagas, Madeiras and Marsalas were also offered. . . . The old custom has merit. Why not offer favoured callers a nip of decent wine and handsome small cakes, to relieve the eternal tea and macaroons, or cocktails? We've tried it and the combination tastes so good it's well worth consideration.

EXPLODED OLD ALEWIVES' TALE No. IV, OVERRULING the COMMON BELIEF here in AMERICA, that a TRULY MAGNIFICENT RED VINTAGE WINE—such as an ANCIENT PORT, a PRICELESS *HOSPICE de BEAUNE* BURGUNDY, or a *CHÂTEAU LAFITE* CLARET—CAN BE OPENED by DRAWING the CORK

Let us hasten to explain this does not apply to average wines, but to the priceless citizens in bottles; to those grand seigneurs whose name and dating should be mentioned only in bated breath. . . . In such ancient affairs it is just as ruinous to spoil the excellence through agitation—even with the greatest care—in cork pulling. An agitated great red wine becomes an average red wine, immediately. There is no more sanity in such spoilage than there is in checking a Raphael madonna, uncrated, in a baggage van.

Go to the nearest good hotel or club and get a pair of bottle tongs. Heat them quite hot and fasten about the bottle neck just below the lower cork end. Count 10, take tongs away, and touch the spot with a pad of cloth soaked in cold water. The neck cracks all around in a clean break—no fuss, no splinters. . . . Even during this slight activity a fine old red wine should be lifted gently as a babe, and carried so; no sudden jolts, no agitation whatsoever. Only in this way can the ancient sediments remain in their undisturbed position, and be kept from clouding, injuring the whole bottle.

"Gloomy or depressed people should never be given good food, or any sort of wines or alcoholic beverages, as neither will go down well. The first quality a gourmet must possess is *joie de vivre* which implies a sparkling, natural satisfaction with life, a genuine appreciation of all good things in life, a disregard for the bad things, and the creation of happiness all around him.

". . . *Bons vivants* do not overeat or overdrink; they leave the table with room for further gastronomic enchantments. . . . Indigestion and intoxication are the two worst punishments a gourmet could receive. . . .

". . . Speaking of intoxication, it is curious to note that it embraces five stages: jocose, bellicose, lachrymose, comotose, and morotose. The first two are not only respectable, but very, very nice; the third not quite so respectable and not quite so nice; the fourth not respectable at all, and not a bit nice. As for the fifth, well, it finishes one."

*The Vicomte in the Kitchen,*
By Vicomte de Mauduit,
1933

# INDEX OF DRINKS

*END*